GW01019449

SEVEN MILE LAKE

Scenes from a Minnesota Life

Jean Gandesbery

MINERVA PRESS
LONDON
MIAMI DELHI SYDNEY

SEVEN MILE LAKE: *Scenes from a Minnesota Life*

ISBN 0 75410 844 9

First Published 1999 by
MINERVA PRESS
315–317 Regent Street
London W1R 7YB

Printed in Great Britain for Minerva Press

SEVEN MILE LAKE
Scenes from a Minnesota Life

For Diane Johnson: mentor, inspiration, friend;
and for Robert Gandesbery, lifetime mate and partner.

Acknowledgments

Gratitude and affection to those colleagues and friends who read the manuscript and offered their insights, suggestions and encouragement: Joan Carr; Dorothy Gilbert; Terri Joseph; Judy Kirscht; David and Rosalie Lynn.

Prologue

The Lake (1954)

Unlike any of the other towns in the area, New Bonn possessed a lake. Although the townspeople merely referred to it as 'the lake' ('I'm going down by the lake' was a constant refrain), it did have a name. It was called Seven Mile Lake, not because it was seven miles across, nor seven miles deep, but because it had seven miles of shoreline. It was a dinky, muddy lake, and by the time Joan and her parents had moved to New Bonn the lake had dried up so much that Joan had no difficulty walking across it without getting her hair wet.

The bottom had at least six inches of soft clay, so that whenever Joan took a step she felt the slimy, cold muck between her toes. This sensation was not altogether unpleasant, but it did force her to frequently check for bloodsuckers. She never did find any of those loathsome creatures between her toes at that lake; instead they were found mostly in northern Minnesota, where most of Minnesota's renowned ten thousand really were located. There, most lakes were named according to simple variations of the arbor theme: Birch Lake, Big Birch Lake; Pine Lake, Lower Pine Lake. There, at those wonderful blue lakes where the shorelines were so long that they were not thought of in miles, resided the fat, elusive walleyed pike, and there were the Whispering Pines Resorts, the Breezy Inns, and the Indian Harbors. There, among the fat pike and the reeds and water lilies, dwelled the bloodsuckers which indiscriminately attached themselves to legs, navels or boats.

Seven Mile Lake had no fish either, unless the ugly bullheads that skulked around the shoreline can be considered fish. People in New Bonn put them in the same league with grasshoppers and frogs – pests – but harmless unless they got out of hand. There was only one person who persisted in fishing the lake, and he really didn't count either, since he was one of the town defectives, a forty-year-old man who wore the castoff clothes of the family that had taken him in years ago. He slept in the back of a shoe repair store and spent his days fishing, summer and winter. Having no proper home, and a wardrobe that was little better than rags, combined with a constant smell of lake water and the occasional bullhead that he charmed and caught, he stank both powerfully and uniquely. Yet he bore no flavor of legend as orphans frequently do in other times or in other places; he was simply one of the town's subspecies that no one cared about. Not menacing, but not very interesting either.

Everyone used the lake. In the summer the kids swam in it and dove off its diving platform, trying their swan dives and jackknives, while the younger ones perfected their cannonballs. Joan and her friends learned to swim from shore to dock – a distance of no more than forty feet – without getting their cigarettes wet. Once on the dock they would lie in the sun and smoke, occasionally dropping off the boards to dunk themselves. There on the dock they considered themselves safe from the watchful eyes of the community, at least safer than sitting in a car. In cars someone was always catching them, and it was never very long – usually no more than a day or so – when someone's mother was told by a well-meaning person that her daughter had been seen in the company of those smoking cigarettes. Mrs. Nelson, Joan's mother, had been approached so frequently at club meetings and grocery stores that she had lost track of the accusations. Invariably the questioner would begin by saying, 'Joan doesn't smoke, does she? The reason I ask is because I saw her down by the lake the other day with Maryann and Franny, who were smoking.' Mrs. Nelson finally admitted that yes, her daughter did smoke, but this particular honest admission was not what most people wanted. Instead, they expected to hear instant denial; her candor disappointed their expectations, making them uneasy and eventually suspicious.

At night the lake took on a different appearance. The beach was deserted, but at the other end there was a place called Hell's Half Acre, actually no larger than a couple of standard-sized residential lots, which jutted out on a point at the end of a dirt road. There were always cars full of young people who had carefully prepared their evenings to arrive at this stage. There was always noisy laughter and exchange from one car to another, but if there was screwing it was conducted away from the lake, for Hell's Half Acre contained too many cars with too many young people devoted to plain kissing and an occasional jab at a breast to allow any serious attempts at seduction.

On Sundays the farmers arrived to bathe, and the townspeople went elsewhere, for no one in town wanted to look at, or be associated with, those fish-bellied creatures, men with tanned faces and forearms, with white rings around their foreheads where the bills of their caps had fought off the sun. They would stand up to their chests in the water with their bars of Ivory soap, splashing and laughing loudly at nothing, never swimming because they didn't know how, merely splashing and yelling and soaping and dunking – actions that the townspeople felt they could have accomplished well enough at home in their own water troughs. After they had soaped all over, leaving trails of scum to float upon the brown surface of the lake, and had finished dunking their helpless, squalling kids, they would emerge from the lake and sprawl along the banks, eating their enormous Sunday dinners of fried chicken and apple pie spread out on tablecloths that their pale wives had brought with them, women who had set their permed-frizzled hair for church that morning, and who now had trouble arranging their skirts over outstretched legs, trying futilely to keep their legs crossed and their underpants concealed. Yet there always seemed to be someone who would shout, 'Hair dere, Ollie!' – mocking the Scandinavian dialect so common in the state. He might be silenced by his peers or elders, those who had learned to keep quiet in the presence of gratuitous displays of pubic hair and milk-white thighs.

Joan allied with the townspeople in their contempt for the farmers; her disdain surfaced most on those Sundays when she had to pass by the lake and witness their public display of vulgarity. Yet she was not supposed to feel superior to them, for if it were not for them she wouldn't be living in the nicest house in town in the best town in the county, by the lake, for it was to the farmers that her adored father owed his prosperity, for he helped to mortgage farms and he saw to it that the farmers got enough money to leave their land once a week for picnics and church. It was Mr. Nelson who saw to it that they got their REA and soil bank loans approved, and that they weren't deprived of the conveniences that made their lives more productive, like electrical hookups to their barns and telephone service to unincorporated areas. Her father liked to point out that although farmers were different – for example, they would rather put their money into a new barn than add rooms on to their houses – they were not to be scorned. She was never to say 'dumb farmer' the way her friends did (not that her friends were any safer from the farmers' influence than she was), and she was directed to tolerate their differences and look for their goodness.

Unlike most men of New Bonn, Joan's father had a sense of humor about the people he worked with, and he really liked calling on farmers and discussing with them the perpetual problems of corn blight and soybean worms. Many merchants, some of whom had once been farmers themselves, would not give the time of day to the farmers who shopped in their stores and bought their products, but Mr. Nelson would stop to chat with any farmer he recognized. It always amazed Joan that her father knew the family history of each one – the name of his wife, the ages of his kids, sometimes even the details of family illnesses. Joan thought such knowledge excessive, but she never would inform her father of his lack of discrimination. 'Never look a gift horse in the mouth,' was what her mother liked to say whenever Joan began to complain about the burden of association that she thought was inordinately unfair. 'If it weren't for them, we wouldn't be here.' Joan liked the implied superiority of her mother's 'them' but the cause and effect statement bothered her.

She also resented being told to look for goodness. Tolerance she could bear, but an out-and-out search for goodness was more than she was willing to pursue.

Chapter One
Locksley Hall

Joan's mother had pressed for the big house on the lake just as she had, in Minneapolis, encouraged her husband to play golf and change churches. She pressed in a special kind of way, not exactly nagging at the man, but always reminding him that self-improvement was available to all: a person could better himself without being downright pushy. Everyone knew what 'pushy' meant: Jewish merchants and manufacturers who bought up the best houses in the nicest neighborhoods, thereby making it unbearable for everyone else; Jews, and even some Catholics, who formed their own country clubs instead of being content to play on the public courses; and, most dreadfully, those Jewish women who goaded their kids into becoming professionals so that one day they could take over the practices of the gentile pioneers, women who spent hours each day playing bridge at the Standard Club and then returned home to harangue their Lutheran maids about the quality of the roast and the neglected grease spots on the wallpaper.

Not that there was anything faintly Jewish about the Nelson family – their name alone certified them as proper Minnesotans. In Minneapolis, where most of the Nelson relatives lived, Joan's mother had always been uneasy about her husband's Swedish relatives – they were still a bit 'foreign' for her tastes – but she managed to dutifully entertain them on those occasions that were reserved for family: Christmas and Easter holidays, Thanksgiving, and the occasional Sunday post-church dinner. The best menus were reserved for the business acquaintances, who came each fall to eat the game Mr. Nelson had shot, lovely pheasants and plump ducks, shot down in the fields and duck blinds of Mr. Nelson's hunting club. They were nice men, Joan thought, and she liked them all, especially the ones who paid attention to her and let her sit on their laps, when she was a little girl, while they sipped their pre-dinner bourbon highballs. Joan's mother worked on those dinners from five in the morning until the morning of the guests' arrival: a perfectly unnecessary form of drudgery, Joan felt, since they always had a maid who could serve nicely and wear her black uniform as if she were in masquerade.

These men had wives who were nice to Joan, but not in the same way. Their conversations with her seemed to begin with an obligatory question about school and ended with an inquiry about her particular grade level that fall. Maybe their indifference was because they all appeared so much older and didn't have children of their own, or if they did, their children were already grown up and away, for Joan's birth had been what her parents acknowledged as their 'little mistake'. This term usually evoked a rapid chuckle but no real laughter, as if people were not sure how to respond to such an admission.

Both her parents had been forty-five when she was born. 'She was the best thing to come out of the Depression,' her father would announce to friends who were meeting her for the first time. As a child Joan was ignorant of the consequences and era of the Depression, yet hearing her father's statement so many times eventually caused her as an adult to equate herself with historical periods. An unfortunate result of this fallacy was a kind of historical narcissism that connected sexual matters with historical eras, for she was convinced that dark periods in history were inextricably associated with perverse couplings of people long past their sexual prime. Such people, she thought, had reproduced quietly and torpidly; so resigned were they to economic deprivation that pleasure for them resided in their pathetic sexual grapplings. As an adult she also liked to examine people in crowds and speculate who was, and wasn't, a Depression baby. Among her identifying criteria were bad teeth, sallow complexions, and bony arms, like their discouraged, aging parents whose sexual energies had long been depleted by the great economic crash.

Her father's friends had nice manners, though, and seemed to take a genuine interest in the trophies she won at horse shows. Although none of them owned horses or professed interests in any kind of animal, they would ask to see her photographs and scrapbooks that were devoted exclusively to show horses. They even managed to listen quietly while she played the piano, a performance that her mother considered mandatory for every game dinner. One man, a Mr. Burkwalder, always requested *Clair De Lune*, a piece that Joan played better than most others in her repertoire because it was quiet and rhythmically tenable. He was Joan's favorite guest, and Joan missed him when he was not present, for without his request her mother would insist on 'something more lively'. Joan knew that one selection was more than enough for an evening, but she could never convince her mother that the audience had come to eat, not to listen to a kid groping for accuracy on music better left to experts.

Yet no one seemed to resent Joan for her mother's presumptuousness – and it was years later that Joan understood 'pushiness' in its wider implications. If the guests were bored they concealed it well. But this was in Minneapolis, where, despite the abundance of guests and the predictable assurance of a maid (usually a Swedish farm girl from the northern part of the state where the land was rocky and untillable, the farms too poor to support a lot of girls), Joan's mother still felt there were many untapped resources for improvement. She had established the family in the richest Congregational church in Minneapolis, which contained two sets of laymen: the ushers, who wore dark suits and were rotated on a quarterly basis; and the deacons, who were permanent and wore cutaways and were always a regular part of the Sunday procession. Everyone knew that the deacons were the benefactors, the ones responsible for maintaining the enormous church with its university-tenured organist and its paid chancel choir. Since Mr. Nelson would never earn the kind of money to be chosen as a deacon, the Sundays at church were less pleasurable for Mrs. Nelson than they were for Joan and her father. Mr. Nelson loved to belt out the dignified hymns in his robust monotone, and Joan actually enjoyed the Sunday school, where she could meet boys from other schools. They would sit in an informal semicircle, enclosing the dedicated teacher, who was always so earnest about the weekly lesson, and who tried to be oblivious to the giggling and nudging at whatever they considered the dirty parts of the Bible.

Mrs. Nelson, though, could never find much pleasure in their membership in the swanky church; although her husband was not exactly created to wear a cutaway, she thought he was at least as dignified as some who were already permanent deacons. Although she sang in the choir and gleefully contributed its weekly stipend to the church's building fund, she found little inspiration in the music. Sometimes she would cry a little at the termination of the anthem, moved not by the message of the music but rather by the futility of her own aspirations. It didn't occur to her that others might share her despair, for her desires, she was sure, were uniquely her own. It also never occurred to her to ask God to consider them – they were far too private and too worldly for Divine concern.

Not that Mr. Nelson was unrefined, exactly, for he was a smart man who had made a lot of money and could handle the income without looking vulgar, but Joan's mother sensed correctly that they had gotten as far as they could in Minneapolis, and that maybe her husband was essentially and basically a Lutheran who could never be completely purged of his origins. It was she, then, who seized upon the opportunity to move to New Bonn when her husband casually mentioned at dinner, one night, that there was a possibility of a job there.

'Why don't you take it, Bert?'

Joan's father looked around the table as if he were counting hands raised in acquiescence. 'I don't know. It doesn't sound like the kind of thing you would like. It would be for a long time, you know, and Joan would have to be pulled out of school.'

'Well certainly there are schools there. That's ridiculous. Besides, wouldn't you like the work? The change? It would get you away from the problems here, at least.' By 'problems' Joan knew that her mother was referring to the hierarchy of the bank, a system of benevolent despotism that retained her father, even promoted him regularly, but would never admit him as a senior officer, like a president.

'I don't know. I'll have to think of it more. It's certainly a good deal, but there could be problems there, too.'

Joan was alert enough to understand that the New Bonn 'problems' would not be financial ones, for the existence of a 'good deal' she could translate as more money than ever. Joan had been to New Bonn once when she was nine or ten, and she had not been impressed by its miniature pastoral nature, but she felt her own popularity in Minneapolis to be declining, decreasing at a perceptible rate, so the prospect of a move might allow her to escape the social abyss she found herself approaching. Her mother, she knew, was also aware of Joan's imminent decline – fewer visitors, fewer phone calls, no recent invitations to sleep-overs – and since Mrs. Nelson espoused the principles of popularity the way that some people dedicate their lives to worthy causes, Joan figured it was merely a matter of time before her mother would bring up her daughter's current status of social inferiority.

The clincher, though, was the reality of a horse. Like Mr. Nelson's situation as a perpetual deacon-manqué, Joan had given up on the possibility of ever owning her own horse. They were simply too expensive to keep in the city, but in New Bonn pastures and barns were as natural to the landscape as department stores and office buildings were to Minneapolis. In New Bonn Joan could begin life again, 'Give yourself a fresh start,' was how her mother put it, and she could accomplish her rejuvenation accompanied by her very own horse.

Joan's only experience at New Bonn had taken place the summer when she was at her runtiest stage. From kinder-garten on, Joan had always been the smallest in classes not particularly distinguished by large children, and as a result she had strenuously attempted to cultivate kids near her own size, but it always seemed as if the best kids, the ones who never failed to obtain perfect test grades, the ones who got the choice parts in the Christmas plays and were chosen by their peers to be class president and even treasurer, were many inches taller, and demonstrably rounder, than she. She had never learned to properly swim, either, although she had convinced her mother that she could dog-paddle well enough to travel outside the ropes at Lake Calhoun. (Mrs. Nelson was deathly afraid of water. Because of a childhood fright, she had never conquered her fear that all lakes contained hidden holes and other traps placed there to suck in innocent victims.)

That day in New Bonn had been focused upon the lake. The daughter of some family friends had taken Joan to the lake, and Joan had managed to churn her way out to the dock without revealing how frightened and helpless she felt at swimming in a place without ropes, those wonderful aids that give at least the appearance of competence to non-swimmers. She had made it to the dock, she remembered, and she was sure that her fear was not detected by the other kids sitting there. But when it came her turn to dive – there was an unofficial system where everyone took turns – she refused to get off the end of the board. She perched there for what was probably an hour, and at first the others coaxed her, assuring her that it was easy after you had gone in the first time. Some kids attempted to demonstrate how simple the initial plunge can be by putting their heads between their legs until they were almost on top of the water's surface. From that position you were supposed to slide in. After a while, when they saw that she was not going to accept their suggestions, they ignored her, almost as if they respected her fright, a kindness she hadn't expected but was always grateful for. What she didn't understand at the time was their motivation for kindness, for she was, in their eyes, a 'city girl', and therefore a novelty to be encouraged rather than ridiculed. Had she been a farm girl she would have been unceremoniously dumped.

Although Joan could not remember her exact age on that one summer visit to New Bonn (the ages of nine and ten were absorbed into the more comprehensive rubric of her ugliest years), she never forgot that long afternoon on the end of the diving board. She could still see the goose bumps that first appeared on her arms and legs, and then spread all over her body until she was shaking uncontrollably, her teeth chattering, her lips blue. Mercifully she forgot how she finally got off her perch and how she managed to swim back to shore. Did someone rescue her in a boat? Hardly likely, since there were so few boats on that tiny lake. She must have held her nose and jumped in, perhaps redeeming herself in part, but she held no memory of any sort of action.

That one day at the lake had obliterated everything else she remembered about New Bonn, and now she wondered if anyone else would remember her mortification and still consider it a disgrace. Her father had told her that the town was small and lacked the big-city resources that she took for granted, but he assured her that there would be no problem finding pasture land and a decent stall for the horse she would now be allowed to buy. Her mother assured her that they would still be spending a lot of time in Minneapolis, visiting old friends and relatives, so there was no reason to feel bad about leaving all her friends. Joan thought she heard a note of irony in her mother's judgment, for Joan's original cast of friends had been diminishing since the fifth grade, and her mother knew it. Although Joan never had to eat lunch alone at school – to her this was the most deplorable sign of the outcast – and she usually found someone to leave school with so she didn't have to walk out of the doors by herself, she was definitely not anyone's favorite, as once long ago she had been regarded. New Bonn's tiny size meant that the number of girls her own age would be proportionately small. She wondered if their queen or reigning princesses had yet been chosen, if the circle had been permanently closed.

The kinds of things her mother worried about in moving to New Bonn Joan thought unimportant, like where to find a decent piano teacher, what to do about kennels for the dog when they went on vacations, and where to buy lamb in a community that raised and sold nothing but beef, pork, and chicken. Perhaps Joan would have felt more regret about leaving Minneapolis, and the only home she had ever occupied for thirteen years, if her slam book hadn't confirmed her inexorable slide: fewer 'cutes' appeared, now replaced by 'NA', that odious abbreviation for 'not acquainted'. Such cryptic judgments were more than enough to confirm her social wane. Clearly a move was the only way to revitalize her social strengths.

*

The Nelson family left Minneapolis one day in January, a day that began with the movers stripping bare the ten rooms of their Dutch Colonial house. Only the gas range remained – New Bonn had yet to get natural gas although it had been promised for at least ten years – so Mrs. Nelson had reluctantly bought an electric stove, the most expensive one she could find as a kind of defiant gesture at New Bonn's lack of natural resources. After driving a hundred miles, the sleet they had been struggling against turned into the kind of heavy snow that sticks to windshields in huge clumps, defying the wipers in its sticky density. They were forced to spend the night in a town called Magnolia, at the Magnolia Hotel, a dinky place that also sheltered that night the crew of movers. The hotel had neither elevators nor restaurant, but the family, together with the movers, managed to locate a coffee shop just down the street, where they all had a rather jolly dinner of roast pork and home-made mince pie.

When they arrived in New Bonn the next morning, Joan's first impression was one of clear, daylight acuity, unfiltered by snow or sleet. The town consisted of what she was later to think of as three parts: the business district, called, inevitably, Main Street; the residential area that extended from Main Street; and the Lake, which had its own residential district. Main Street was two blocks long and the cars parked diagonally to the curb as well as in its center. There were two grocery stores; two hardware stores; a movie theater; a combination medical and dental office building; a variety store (like Woolworth's, her mother explained, only much smaller); a men's clothing store; a women's clothing store named after someone's favorite relative, 'Gertie's Gown Shop'; the offices of the local newspaper, a weekly; a bakery; the New Bonn Hotel; the municipal liquor store; one café, three bars, and two pool halls.

Around the corner from the Korner Kafe were the post office and a building that sheltered the fire engine and also served as a temporary lockup for prisoners waiting for transportation to the county jail, fifteen miles distant from New Bonn, located in Clayton, the county seat. (Joan later learned that the jail had been occupied only once in its history of over forty years, that one time being the occasion of a vagrant black man who had miscalculated both time and geography and had found himself stuck in New Bonn for the night. The sheriff had obligingly locked him up for the night, protecting him from the threats of irate citizens – 'for his own good,' Joan was told. Evidently somewhere on the books was a local ordinance prohibiting Negroes from loitering after dark, and the sheriff had no desire to defy community laws.)

One block from the business district was a park, containing a bandstand and a cannon. Bordering the park were a number of one-story frame houses, neat and well-kept, but definitely unpretentious. To Joan this looked like her Swedish grandmother's neighborhood, the houses counterparts to her grandmother's, with their front porches and yards containing apple and fir trees. The summer furniture of swing and castoff wicker chairs would be stored in basements until spring, when everything would be given a vigorous dusting and a fresh coat of paint if necessary.

Away from Main Street, across the railroad tracks, was

the Lake, and around its shoreline were spread some dozen or so houses: but isolated from those was the home the Nelsons were to occupy, which Mrs. Nelson had earlier named Locksley Hall. Whereas the other builders in that area had confined themselves to large frame squares or Victorians that had lately been remodeled to incorporate more windows and fewer staircases that led to nowhere, the Nelson house was a half-timbered, English Tudor. In seeing the house for the first time, Joan felt vindicated for her previous extravagant lies to her Minneapolis acquaintances when she had spun out tales of tennis courts and rooms in the double digits. She hadn't been so far off, after all. There was even a *porte cochere*, a term her mother had introduced to her during one of their drives through the classy neighborhoods in Minneapolis.

Inside there were parlors, dining rooms, pantry and kitchen, a servants' kitchen, which was like a scale model reduction of the regular kitchen. The study contained floor-length bookshelves, and a dumb waiter traveled from basement to attic on rope pulleys. Next to the dumb waiter was a fascinating gadget that showed the appropriate number whenever one of the four doorbells was rung. Upstairs there were five bedrooms and a sleeping porch that extended the length of the front of the house. Such splendor seemed remarkable within the context of an ordinary village like New Bonn, a place not exactly renowned for its luxury and ostentation.

The history of the house is well known in New Bonn, though, and bears repeating. The man who designed and built the structure was nothing more than a retired carpenter who had suddenly and surprisingly earned more money than he had ever imagined simply by speculating on some crops from acreage he had casually acquired through the years. Thus he lovingly laid parquet floors and constructed closets with double doors of bird's-eye maple three inches in width, and he erected cabinets in kitchens, pantries, and in the two dining rooms. Because he couldn't get enough of working so carefully and deliberately with the kinds of wood he loved, as a kind of final embellishment he constructed the eight-foot bookshelves on the four walls of a room that was declared, by virtue of its carpentry, the library. As so often happens in fiction and in fact, the poor man died before he could even begin to acquire any kind of book collection, and his pleasure at the construction of the dumb waiter was never fully realized, for no hired help would stay longer than a few months for his wages, and no one who worked for him ever forgave his indulgence of three sets of stairs.

As soon as he died his widow put the house on the market, but she could find no one even to rent it – the stairs had become a notorious liability – so it had been unoccupied for two years when Joan's family bought it. It could be said that it was purchased sight unseen, except that Joan's father, on one of his preliminary trips to New Bonn before their move, had looked at it and had even taken pictures of it to show Joan's mother. Mrs. Nelson was unable to repress her delight at its grandeur, although she did consider maintenance a potential problem, yet her complaints were more rhetorical than actual, for the issue of hired help was a false one: farm girls were more plentiful and certainly cheaper in New Bonn than they were in Minneapolis, and Mrs. Nelson was confident they could work out an acceptable compromise with the stairs with whoever they hired to tend the house.

Mrs. Nelson had named the house before they had left Minneapolis: Locksley Hall. When Joan had asked her where she'd gotten the name, her mother had told her it was her favorite poem written by a famous poet. 'One day you'll feel the same about this poem,' she had said, after Joan had quickly scanned it and had found little reason for her mother's enthusiasm. Joan did like the name, though, except that she couldn't understand why her mother took a name from a book rather than think up one of her own. Joan classified this method with another of her mother's favorite premises, which insisted that only when she had truly suffered would she be able to play music. 'Until then, it is just noise,' she was fond of pronouncing. Joan liked the idea of secret suffering – it seemed a fine way of allowing otherwise ordinary people special qualities – but she was suspicious of how anyone could actually test it. She didn't like the idea of merely producing noise while she played the piano, but she was not sure when and how a person ever made the exchange between sounds and authentic harmonies.

Being neither Catholic nor Lutheran, Joan was sent to the public school, where she was placed in a combination of seventh and eighth grade. On her first day of school she set out with a notebook, lunch, and her purse, which held her pencils, lipstick, and two sanitary napkins (her periods were still irregular and she knew that institutional girls' rooms everywhere were never reliable).

She had some change to buy a Coke in the school cafeteria, and although she dreaded the first day in a strange school, her worse fear was her old one, that she would have to eat lunch alone. She had already reconciled herself to a brief period of isolation and had justified it as natural to the condition of newcomer. At school she discovered that she had only one teacher, and that the two grades were confined to just one room, quite unlike the continuous shifting in her old junior high with its home rooms and study halls and room changes for each subject. Her teacher, a man with a skinny, pinched face and a chin and neck that reminded Joan of a stork, greeted her by saying, 'I know who you are. We've been waiting all week for your records.' He then pointed out her seat, which was located in the back of the room next to the blackboard. When she sat down she discovered that there was no place for her purse; books had already been placed into the recess below the desk top, and they now occupied all its space. There were three rows of eighth graders in her section, and separated by an empty row of desks sat three rows of seventh graders. She noticed two blonde girls in the eighth-grade rows who seemed to be looking at her, but it was a while before she caught their eyes, and when she did they both smiled so genuinely that she was immediately relieved.

The morning was occupied by history and social studies that she already knew, and so she was taking more time than she needed to copy an assignment from the blackboard when a siren rang out. At once everybody stood up and reached for coats that had been hung on the wall – she had overlooked those hooks and had instead thrown her own coat behind her on the back of the chair.

One of the blonde girls walked over to her and said, 'I'm Maryann and I'm supposed to walk you home for dinner.'

Joan didn't understand the sequence, but she followed Maryann out of the door with the other blonde girl accompanying them down the steps. Joan had not been introduced to the class, yet everyone seemed to know her name, and although the blonde girl didn't offer her name, Joan decided that this was probably an oversight, that she would learn all the names quickly enough.

As they left the school yard Joan asked Maryann about the siren. 'Oh, that's the dinner bell. Didn't you know? Did you think it was a fire or something?' Maryann looked down at the bag that Joan was carrying along with her purse, and at that point Joan realized that neither of the girls was carrying a purse, let alone a lunch.

'Do you always go home for, ahh, dinner?' Joan had enough sense not to inquire about a cafeteria.

'Sure. Everyone does except the dumb farmers. They

have to eat at school and they're not allowed to leave the room.'

'How long do we have for dinner?' The word seemed awkward and alien to her at this time of day.

'Two hours. Then there's another hour and a half of school.'

Joan wondered why this girl, who seemed so direct and casual, had assumed the responsibility for escorting her home, especially since the girl didn't seem to feel that there was anything unusual about the favor. 'Do you live near me?' Joan asked.

'No, but I'm on your way, and my mother knows your mother so my mother told me to make sure you got home the quickest way and to see that you didn't get turned around.'

Joan realized that it was possible for anyone to get confused, but she hadn't had any trouble getting to school that morning – her father had simply drawn up a block map for her to follow and she had been able to read it without losing her bearings. Joan didn't know whether to thank Maryann for something that appeared so offhand and casual, so she asked, instead, how she liked school.

'It's okay, after you get used to the farmers.' Before Maryann could explain this judgment, she abruptly stopped at a house a half-block from the lake, saying, 'Here's where I live. See you.'

Joan continued her walk home, wondering if her mother had even expected her home for lunch, and was surprised when she arrived to find both her mother and father in the kitchen, eating sandwiches at the table. Joan greeted her parents and took the back stairs to her bedroom, where she deposited her purse into a dresser drawer. She decided to postpone asking her parents any questions about farmers, at least for now, but her mother did volunteer later that day, as if in answer to her daughter's unvoiced question, that most people in rural areas eat their large meal at noon.

Joan wondered how she could make a sandwich last two hours. She also wondered if her family were going to abandon their lunches and start eating dinners. She hoped not. That prospect did not appeal to her.

Chapter Two

Neighbors

Joan didn't have to ask her parents about the farmers.

By biding her time and keeping her mouth shut, she soon found out that Maryann and Caroline had been eagerly looking forward to her arrival so that they could comprise a trio of eighth-grade town girls. The other girls in the eighth grade were all from the farm, but all this could change next year when the Catholic and Lutheran schools graduated their own eighth-grades and the parochial graduates were then admitted to the public high school. Until then the three of them represented the female town bloc. There were only four eighth-grade boys who did not arrive on the school bus every morning, dinner pails in hand. Of these four, only one was at all interesting: Bobby Lyons, the second son of the president of the bank, a boy with genuine golden hair and the most beautiful gray eyes Joan had ever seen. Unfortunately, Bobby was both aloof and short – at least two inches shorter than Joan, who was then only four foot eleven.

In Bobby, Joan recognized that sense of isolation that short people try to cultivate, and – to her credit – she respected it, unlike Caroline who was always passing notes and combing her hair, trying to secure Bobby's attention. Joan did allow herself an occasional moment of mooning over Bobby, but she never seriously felt that there was anything she could do about him until he grew a few inches. She was actually more curious about the parochial kids than the farmers; in a town the size of New Bonn, which had never exceeded its 1950 census figure of one thousand and seven, she wondered how it was possible for people to avoid one another. Kids the same ages, but at different schools, seemed to be stuck tightly into their own private groups. What was so powerful about churches that they could keep their parishioners under wraps?

In Minneapolis her friends had been either Congregationalists like her own family, or Episcopalians, although when she went to junior high she found a friend who was a Catholic, and she rather liked walking with her to church on Saturday afternoons and waiting for her while she went to Confession. Besides, Minneapolis was not a Catholic town; her mother said that St. Paul was for the Catholics, and the Nelsons almost never had reason to go to St. Paul. When Joan first heard people in New Bonn refer to Minneapolis and St. Paul as 'the cities' she had been shocked, for there was simply no comparison. Minneapolis was superior to St. Paul in every respect: all the money was there, the banks, the schools, the university, even the lakes.

In New Bonn the boundaries between the parochial alliances were definable and evidently impenetrable. The Lutherans not only had their own church and school, they had stores as well: Schoonmacker's Hardware was owned by a Lutheran family – twin brothers who were also deacons of their church – and its clientele consisted of Lutheran farmers and townspeople, whereas Our Own Hardware was owned by her friend Maryann's father, and it catered mostly to Presbyterians, that anomalous group of county people who, finding themselves neither Catholic nor Lutheran, and unwilling to initiate conversions, had combined together some thirty years before to establish their own church.

She found out that they had collected enough money –

bribes or blackmail? These possibilities weren't mentioned – to erect a building that was plainly different from both the neo-Gothic Catholic church and the Victorian-Edwardian pastiche of the Lutheran church. A white frame building without adornment, it reminded Joan of the pictures she had seen of Quaker meeting houses in New England, and she thought it rather unsuitable for a European denomination with its own distinguished, if not turbulent, history. That was the church the Nelson family attended each Sunday, a building that Joan felt was so lacking in inspiration that the sight of parishioners dozing throughout the service never surprised her.

Joan learned, too, that there was a Catholic dentist as well as a Presbyterian one. The Catholic dentist had scandalized the community by marrying the daughter of the owners of the Korner Kafe, themselves Presbyterians, and she had then further mortified her parents and the Presbyterian community by converting to Catholicism, a vagary that Joan later learned was surpassed in ignominy only by a Catholic-Lutheran match.

The Presbyterian church lacked a Sunday school, which didn't disappoint Joan, since she felt that she had outgrown the games and the Bible stories that never seemed to progress much beyond the Moses and the Bulrushes story. The minister, an earnest young man with the absurd name of Reverend Blue, had a frail wife who somehow managed to timidly play the organ every Sunday, but since the Sunday school was traditionally the responsibility of the clergy's spouse, the children's hour gradually vanished, for Mrs. Blue was not up to both assignments.

The Presbyterian membership was outnumbered by both Lutherans and Catholics, but what they lacked in bodies they compensated for in wealth. All of the people in town with money were Presbyterians: Bobby Lyon's family; the town physician; the druggist's family; Maryann's family, who didn't have much money but were third generation New Bonnites. The Reuter clan, or at least part of it, belonged, too. (These were four brothers who had founded the combination furniture store and mortuary, and were partners in the pool hall and bowling alley, but their religious alliances were divided. Two had taken Catholic wives while the other two remained in the Presbyterian fold. Religious conflicts aside, it was common knowledge that the Reuter clan owned most of the buildings on Main Street as well as several enormous working farms in at least three counties. They also owned a gravel quarry, and it was said that Dick, one of the Catholic brothers, had done a big business during the war in bootleg tires and selling corn to the Four Roses distillery.) Among the congregation there were a few farmers who dressed as well as their village counterparts, and in church they were indistinguishable as farmers except for faces tanned the color of mahogany and hands dark and tough as leather, which contrasted sharply with their white shirts.

Joan was not exactly new to farmers, for even when she lived in Minneapolis she would travel with her father when he saw to the bank's country investments. 'Take me with you, Daddy,' she had requested when she was about six years old, and quickly her presence during his short business trips became a kind of given. She enjoyed seeing people who appeared to be working hard while being interested in what they were doing. She had traveled with her father to western and southern Minnesota, where the bank's vastest country holdings lay, and one summer, when she was nine, she had stayed for two weeks with a family that owned an authentic riding horse. She knew that her father got along well with these farmers, for had he not she wouldn't have been received so warmly at every farmhouse.

Sometimes she got bored waiting for her father to quit talking business, but mostly she enjoyed the occasions, especially the food, for it seemed as if they were always eating things that she liked but never got enough of at home: pies, cakes, corn on the cob, fresh doughnuts, and heavy fried chicken, spread out on the table in no particular order or arrangement, so that she felt that she could eat at those various farmers' tables without being watched, safe from the obligatory domestic sequences at her mother's table, where she had to eat salad before even thinking about dessert.

Often on those farm visits with her father there was a new baby which she was allowed to hold, and even at the places where there were neither babies nor children there was usually a tire swing – erected, perhaps, for grandchildren or nearby cousins. She especially liked going with her father during thrashing time: then she could sit for hours and watch the wagons being hauled to the huge thrashing machine which took in bundles at one end and majestically deposited them at another, in the form of shiny grain, the piles of chaff having been neatly discarded to one side, rather like a horse expediently shitting the grass it continues to chew.

Of course she had never known these farmers well, had seen them only as her father's companions, and she had looked at them through his own delighted eyes, for it was in the fields, talking to farmers, that he seemed the most animated, standing with one foot on the lower rung of a barbed-wire fence, writing in his notebook while talking with authority about which crops to plant next year and where to store the barley until the prices went up, and how much to pay the bank until the beans could be sold and next year's fertilizer purchased. At those times she thought him most energetic and impressive. But that had been when they lived in Minneapolis and they always went home from the trips, when she could still go to Lake Calhoun or downtown to Saturday matinees.

In New Bonn she had to look at the farmers with her own eyes, and she was no longer convinced that those shiny workhorses which pulled the wagons to the machines were friendly pets, and she was no longer sure that the meals that the farmers' wives were always serving were actually the result of dedication – the dedication from women whose pleasure came primarily from their own well-laden tables.

In New Bonn she began to notice the farmers' names: why would people so completely indifferent to most writing other than the *Poultry Digest* and *Cappers Farmer* want to name their kids Homer or Virgil or Milton? She also noticed that they spoke German to one another, but that they never attempted to speak German to her father. Lacking literate backgrounds, why did they attempt to preserve a language that had no meaning for them? Joan decided that their insistence on speaking German was part of their stubbornness, which could only reflect a strategy to preserve their separation from the townspeople.

The town kids were given names like Dwight and Dwayne and Roger, and the girls were called Lillian or Cheryl, or some variation of Mary, particularly if they were Catholics. Not that Joan had read the *Iliad* or *Paradise Lost*, but her mother had told her that Milton and Virgil and Homer were all names of great writers of the past. Because it bothered her mother, Joan was also bothered that illiterate parents would name their children after people about whom they were ignorant; she felt that there should have been some kind of correspondence between what people knew and what they named their offspring.

Joan was beginning to experience, albeit indirectly yet with frequency and sharp pain, the kinds of conflicts that are inextricably linked to genes and soil everywhere. She was also becoming aware that solutions to conflicts of such a nature cannot be reduced to a simple formula that serves all occasions.

During her first year of high school Joan acquired a reputation as a musician, a reputation that led her to her first unfortunate encounter with the official position of the Catholic church. The parochial eighth graders, upon admission to high school, became secularized, at least temporarily, and those farm kids whose eight grades of education had been confined to one-room schoolhouses – there were three surviving structures in the township – infiltrated the school. It was clear that the farm boys were there expressly for the purpose of killing time until they were sixteen and could legally leave school for the farm. No one paid much attention to the boys; when they were in school they sat in the back seats and quietly scribbled in their books, or else they stretched out their legs and slept at their desks. The teachers didn't call on them, so they passed unnoticed and unregarded until they simply disappeared, one by one, throughout the year.

The girls all seemed to have enormous breasts and large calves, and they wore their hair in the large rolls that had been popular ten years before. They always wore dresses, never skirts and blouses and sweaters like the town girls. Like the boys, they were quiet and were usually ignored by the teachers. The only classes where they seemed to be visible and at home were the home ec. classes, the ones that Joan especially loathed because she was totally indifferent to both sewing and cooking – perhaps because she was no good at either. By now the Nelsons had engaged a hired girl – no one in New Bonn said 'maid' – who was a sister of a boy in Joan's class.

Joan had stopped taking piano lessons, not because her mother had dismissed music as an integral part of gracious living, but because there were no piano teachers in New Bonn. (There was, however, a very enthusiastic high school band.) Perhaps because Joan's mother felt that she was neglecting her commitment to cultural refinement by not pursuing all the possibilities, she inquired extensively about music teachers and finally discovered one person capable of going beyond Schirmer Book Three, and that person was Sister Mary Loretta of St. Gabriel's Convent, who taught science to third and fourth graders, but who occasionally doubled as a music teacher, primarily choir director. After considerable bickering over terms that included the Mother Superior, two other nuns, and the parish priest, the nun finally agreed to administer lessons to Joan for $1.50 apiece, on the understanding that the lesson fees, and anything else the Nelsons wanted to contribute, would go to the church's building fund.

Sister Mary Loretta was nothing like Joan's Minneapolis teacher, a university graduate who drove to her pupil's houses, charged $5 an hour, and sponsored jolly year-end recitals, and who would let Joan play actual compositions in addition to the compulsory studio exercises. Joan was unable to impress Sister Mary Loretta, either with charm or with technique; nothing she played was good enough, although Sister would never openly chastise her for her mistakes. Technically she played without fault, but she was never given the opportunity to advance to the next level, nor was she ever given more interesting pieces to play as rewards for her technical facility. One day Joan summoned enough nerve to ask the nun to play the piece the way it was supposed to be played, but Sister refused, her voice thick with hauteur as she stated, 'I can't learn for you, you know. You have to play for yourself.'

When Joan left her weekly lesson, which took place on the second floor of the convent, she had to pass a life-size statue of the Virgin Mary, an ugly cream-colored lady dressed in clothes that looked more appropriate to a young housewife than to the chief female protector of the religion. If Sister went first, she always knelt and crossed herself, and then Joan would walk awkwardly by, eyes averted, embarrassed because she was so unsure about her own kind of acknowledgments. Sometimes Sister would remain at the statue, on her knees and whispering to herself, which forced Joan to sidle past both figures in the narrow hallway.

One day Joan decided that it might be to her advantage to imitate the nun's reactions. As she approached the statue she paused and began to descend to her knees. Immediately she felt a sharp pain between her shoulders, and as she turned to discover the source she felt another blow, this time on the cheek. She stood up quickly and faced Sister's blows, delivered with the same ruler that she normally used to beat time on the keyboard. After the first rush of smacks they decreased to almost ritual taps, but the nun's face, normally the pasty color and texture of freshly laid cement, had become scarlet with rage.

'Never, never, never, let me see you doing that again! She is not yours!' she screamed.

Joan had the good sense to clatter down the stairs and to run out of the doors without stopping to collect her coat and boots from the downstairs coat rack. Walking home and sobbing – the nun had more than stung her with her first outraged blows – Joan wondered if Sister had thought she was being mocked. At first she pondered the wisdom of reporting the incident to her parents, but she decided she could probably use the event to her advantage since it looked like a sure way of getting out of the horrid lessons. Besides, her parents would expect some explanation of her missing coat – the boots she could explain away easily enough, but a coat was something people didn't ordinarily leave behind them. She decided to tell them immediately, but she was in no way prepared for the depths of their outrage.

Her father's reaction was as immediate and as illogical as the nun's. 'What the hell did you expect?' he roared, but to his wife, not to Joan, and without waiting for any more explanations he stormed out of the kitchen, uncharacteristic behavior in such a soft-spoken man.

Her mother appeared less shocked. 'What did you do that for?' she inquired of her daughter in tones that were similar to those she often used whenever Joan had cut her finger or banged her knees.

'I honestly thought she might like me better, that she might tell me how to play better instead of the way she always sits there with her ruler beating time and looking at her lap.'

Mrs. Nelson looked pained, her mouth a straight line, her eyebrows pulled tight across her forehead. 'Of course she isn't going to like you any better,' she sputtered. 'That's not why you're taking lessons in the first place. Anyhow, it was the wrong thing to do and you should have known it.'

Joan was ready to cry again. 'How could I know it when no one told me?' She also sensed another futile argument, that the words she and her mother were exchanging were not really about the incident itself.

'I'll see to it that it will never happen again.' For a minute Joan had visions of her mother storming the convent, screaming curses at the offending nuns. In the event of a rescue, she wondered how her mother was going to tell the nuns apart, for all of them (and there were either a half-dozen or a dozen) were exactly alike, each as ugly as a starling and without any distinguishing markings. Her father had seemed most angry, the most dishonored and injured despite Joan's physical evidence of assault. 'Never mind,' her mother had stated, 'you won't have to put up with it again,' as if seconding her husband's fury.

Joan heard her father leave the house, banging the door with a slam completely uncharacteristic of his customary quiet departure. She left her mother in the kitchen and went upstairs to her own room, where she managed to shed enough tears to permanently stain the green satin bedspread.

Later she learned that her father had gone directly to the priest, old senile Father Sturm, who agreed that the good nun had been unnecessarily harsh, but that she was, he hinted, legitimately upset with such ridiculous posturings. Mr. Nelson had demanded to see Sister Mary Loretta, but Father Sturm had told him that it was absolutely forbidden by the order for the nuns to communicate with anyone after 6 p.m., male or female. Mr. Nelson suspected the actuality of such an ordinance, but he did respect the unfathomable nature of a religion that encourages its own religious to beat up helpless Protestant girls while performing acts of piety – misguided but sincere, he insisted. So the matter was never resolved.

At best the Nelson family acquired new strengths to bolster their formerly half-hearted Presbyterian inclinations, and Joan acquired a new coat and boots, both fur lined. The boots were a replacement for the plain, serviceable ones she had left behind in the convent cloakroom. Perhaps these were donated to needy orphans or to some remote mission. Secretly Joan liked to think that they were passed back and forth by the nuns, who couldn't resist embellishing their own dreary habits. After hours, Joan was fond of thinking, when the convent had settled into its evening routine, then maybe they would toss around the boots and take turns wearing the coat, maybe even marching around their barren rooms, humming militant-sounding melodies, beads rattling, mouths pinched in perpetual reproof.

Chapter Three

Musicians, Performers and Clowns

One morning Joan's mother burst in on her while Joan was still asleep. 'How dare you?' she screamed at Joan, who hadn't the faintest idea what her mother was talking about. Joan woke up quickly at the sight of her mother standing by her bed, her face crimson with rage, her voice so shrill the high tones disappeared as if carried away by the force of her rage.

'How dare you? How could you?' her mother shrieked.

'How dare I what? What are you talking about?' Joan was used to her mother's fury, which was usually directed at someone or something else. This time she was mystified, and she couldn't think of any recent acts that could possibly account for this kind of outburst. 'What are you so mad about?' she asked her mother, careful to keep her voice sounding neutral.

'Only the Peace rose you so thoughtfully picked, grabbed right off the bush. That's all.' Again the familiar sarcasm, but this time directed at Joan, not at external targets. 'The only one blooming, and I was waiting for it to open up. How could you have been so thoughtless?' By now her mother's color had returned to normal, her voice less strident, now more wheedling.

Joan had to think for a minute until she could place the

flower and its appropriate bush. She had plucked it the night before, not thinking of reactions, only knowing that its creamy gold and soft pink colors constituted a combination she often admired. There it stood, in a water glass, on her desk, as if to confirm her guilt. 'Honestly, I'm sorry. I didn't realize it was the only one. Or that it meant so much to you. Really, I'm very sorry,' she repeated, and immediately burst into tears.

The episode left Joan not much wiser about her mother's disposition, but at least she had learned not to pick the flowers without permission. And in some way it set the tone for a lot of their future communications.

After a month without piano lessons, Mrs. Nelson learned of a teacher from Sioux Falls, South Dakota, who gave lessons in Worthington twice a week. Worthington is at least eighty miles from Sioux Falls and twenty-five from New Bonn, but the man was said to have a unique reputation. In Worthington, he conducted his lessons at the home of his sister, where twice a week he serviced the musical needs of the community. He was fond of saying that his extensive commutes were a matter of love, not money, for he rarely lost an opportunity to proclaim his love of music. 'I do this for love, you know,' he would state to Joan, or her mother, or anyone who was listening.

Joan liked Mr. Schlage – she had been instructed to call him Herr Schlage by her mother, but she couldn't bring herself to articulate this label – but thought he looked a lot like the New Bonn farmers: large and gawky, he had a loud voice and an accent that was plainly Hun, but he lacked the outdoors look of the farmers and his clothes always looked elegant to Joan: white-on-white shirts, paisley ties, and brightly colored vests. Joan especially liked his bold colors. She liked the drawing room of his sister's house because it contained two grand pianos and no other furniture cluttered it up, and she liked the way he hummed and strode around the room while she played. He never seemed to notice when she faked the bass in the Liszt, and invariably when she finished a selection he would proclaim, 'Very good!' in robust tones. Occasionally he would sit at the other piano and they would play two-piano Beethoven pieces. He didn't play much better than Joan, but his enthusiasm for the noisiest parts was equal to hers, and on those occasions when they finished a piece together, on the same measure and beat, he would respond with a smile of such radiance that she knew he was approving himself as much as he was endorsing her.

Thus Joan's reputation as a serious musician was verified, for why would anyone drive or be driven over fifty miles once a week unless there wasn't some compelling reason for musical excellence? As a result of her musical importance she was asked to play the piano for the glee club and the mixed chorus, and on those rare occasions when an accompanist was needed, she played for the band. She also took up the clarinet, a choice that was determined less by its musical appeal than for its marching size. A flute or piccolo would have been preferable, but her friend Maryann already held that combined chair and Joan didn't want to openly compete with friends.

The New Bonn musical groups were composed of town students. The reason for this segregation was simple – the school buses left every day at 3 p.m., and most musical events, including rehearsals, were held after school hours. The same was true of sports, which was not so much of a problem with basketball but which worked against the school in football, for there weren't enough town boys to supply a full football squad. As a result, New Bonn was limited to six-man teams, a tedious arrangement that is like a slow parody of real eleven-man games.

The band attended all the games, and Joan learned to enjoy playing the marches and pep songs. The only position that Joan failed to secure during those early high school years was that of cheerleader. She tried out once but discovered that she could not yell, jump, and look convincing at the same time. She also suspected that she lacked the breasts for the cheerleader costume with its prominent display of the red letter 'N' and 'B' on each boob against the black background of the tight sweater. She was not terribly disappointed, however, for she felt that the rallies of the cheerleaders were, for the most part, unheard and unappreciated, especially compared to the band, which was always applauded. And she did associate big breasts with farm girls who never seemed to wear the correct size bra, and who also never seemed to realize how conspicuous they were when they jiggled across the room.

The school music teacher was supposed to have just graduated from the University of Minnesota and its classy music department, said to be among the top ten in the nation, at least in band instruments. He had a hump back but didn't seem to notice it. The students called him Shorty behind his back. Joan liked him because he was a Presbyterian and because he gave her so many musical responsibilities. He had long fingers, which she thought were very sensitive, and although his instrument was supposed to be the trumpet, he still was very good at giving her clarinet lessons.

One day during a lesson she developed a nose bleed that wouldn't quit. At first they tried to wait it out, and then when she was unable to stop the clots that kept running from her nose, he told her to ignore them and play as well as she could. 'Just forget about it,' he advised. 'Keep going as if nothing is wrong.'

They finished the lesson and she was still dripping gobs of blood on her skirt, but he ignored them as if she had produced a substance that had nothing to do with them or their music. At the time she was rather uncomfortable about this episode, especially since she had made such a mess of her clothes, but she rather liked his ability to act as if there were nothing the matter with her.

Joan's mother was not exactly displeased with the clarinet, but she would have preferred that Joan spend more time on the piano. Since the music required a lot of extracurricular time and meant that Joan got to meet more and more people, Mrs. Nelson was pleased because Joan was spending less and less time with her horse. Sometimes, for days at a time, Joan's riding clothes continued to hang undisturbed in their special place on the back porch, along with her boots, in an area that was able to absorb the pasture smells without contaminating the rest of the house. The horse, itself, was an issue that always threatened to disturb the surface of their labored tranquillity, for clothes and friends were involved, two essential ingredients of Mrs. Nelson's formula for her daughter's character.

Mrs. Nelson had always made sure that her daughter dressed as well as her friends. This had not been a problem in Minneapolis, where Joan's friends had mothers who also did not approve of ostentation. Nice clothes, they were fond of stating, did not have to be expensive, and dressing well didn't necessarily demand a wardrobe full of dresses, shoes, bathrobes and slippers, and three kinds of winter coats, replenished annually. Joan's biggest problem with her mother and clothes occurred with her continual request for riding clothes, a separate ensemble completely unrelated to church clothes or school clothes. Mrs. Nelson never balked at school or church clothes, but she did resent equestrian paraphernalia, mostly because Joan's interest in riding had nothing to do with friends. Yet Mrs. Nelson liked to attend the horse shows and see her daughter collect trophies, so she usually conceded to Joan's requests for new boots or a bowler, and she had even seen to it that Joan had gotten her hunting coat, the required gear for the hunting class, although Mr. Nelson's last-minute protestations – based on safety, not fashion – almost kept his daughter from showing in that class.

These concessions from her mother did not come painlessly, of course. There were always pleas and recriminations, and sometimes bartering regarding piano practice and dishwashing duties – it had been Joan's duty to wash and dry the dishes on the maid's night out – but Joan never entered a horse show improperly dressed for the events. Although Joan knew that her mother disapproved of her interest in horses and her stables routine, she realized that her mother enjoyed seeing her win. Denied by her father's income from actually owning her own horse, she nevertheless possessed all the expensive gear that was part of riding one, whereas in New Bonn it was almost as cheap to own a horse as it was to maintain a dog, and since there were no shows to enter, the expensive wardrobe didn't have to be replenished. Without this strain, Joan and her mother should have gotten along better, but they didn't.

Although Joan could never prove it, she did suspect that her mother was more interested in her winning something than she was in seeing that she performed her duties over the dishes or overseeing the Czerny exercises and Chopin etudes. Joan had no way of knowing that her mother was, at heart, as unconventional and as pretentious as the house she was presently supervising. The daughter of a small-town doctor, Mrs. Nelson had herself attempted to study medicine but was discouraged by both family and university. She settled on Latin, instead, although she could have also taken a degree in German. Joan's father had never been to a real college, except for a business school with dubious credentials and some night-school classes in property law, and he was rather in awe of his wife's formal education.

Joan and her mother got along in much the same way that Joan operated with her father's business friends; she was polite and quiet most of the time, although sometimes there were occasions when Joan provoked outbursts from her mother that resulted in several days of quiet, unstated hostility. These occasions usually arose from some event that was only partly understandable to Joan: a phone call that she had neglected to report; a forgotten piano lesson; an errand she had neglected to run. Mrs. Nelson never seemed to pick at messy rooms or dirty clothes, which made her anger often mysterious and unpredictable to her daughter.

Unlike many women who victimize their children out of boredom, Mrs. Nelson was obviously not bored. She worked at everything she did and seemed to have loads of energy left over. She never complained about her physical ailments the way that some of the mothers of Joan's friends tended to go on and on about their female complaints. The only time that Joan knew without question that her mother would attack were those rare Saturday afternoons when she preferred to stay at home rather than spend time with friends. 'You'll ruin you eyes with your nose stuck in a book all the time.' Joan had heard this prediction since she had learned to read, and by now its only value was the signal that an assault was about to begin. Yet her mother read all the time, and not only the current best-sellers, but novels and poetry, sometimes in German.

In addition to the familiar reading admonition, she liked to stress another maxim that Joan, years later, found inscribed on the wall of a San Francisco bar: 'It is easier to be liked than to be disliked.'

Since Joan knew so little about her mother's feelings (assuming that they were more unpredictable than trustworthy), she was able to establish a working arrangement with her in practical ways only. Few complaints, modest demands (the riding clothes were an early exception), and no raised voices or crude expressions. 'Shut up!' was an offense to decorum that Mrs. Nelson regarded as inexcusable, and it might easily send her into a week of polite indifference to both Joan and her father. In New Bonn, Mrs. Nelson belonged to a bridge club, the Reading Club, and the Presbyterian Ladies' Aid. The bridge club alternated meetings, which obligated each member to entertain four times a year. This club was one of the three bridge clubs in New Bonn and was considered the best because it was the oldest; perhaps its age exempted it from having a name. (The others were called the Fortnightly Club and the Queen of Hearts Club.)

Since the Lutherans were forbidden to play cards and to dance, except for folk dancing – whatever that was – the membership of the bridge clubs was limited to Presbyterians and Catholics. Mrs. Nelson's club was exclusively Presbyterian, although there were both in the other two clubs, and Joan often wondered how much it differed from the Presbyterian Ladies' Aid.

There were no farm women in any of the bridge clubs, for the farmers preferred to play whist in mixed pairs in the evenings. Two old-maid sisters had helped to found the bridge club, and they were not only its charter members but the club's perpetual source of disguised glee. Now in their early seventies, everyone called them the Goldust Twins, although their actual name was Smith. They were targets of ridicule and topics of conversation, not because of their age and its possibilities of senility and other weaknesses, but because they cheated at cards, and evidently they had been cheating for years. They cheated by contriving a series of signals that were so old and transparent that no one, not even a novice player, could fail to observe them. It became a game among the members of the club to try to separate them, to prevent them from playing partners. Once Joan's mother thought she had discovered the perfect strategy by insisting that everyone whose names began with a letter after N in the alphabet should take a partner whose name started with the preceding letters – a standard potluck formula that the Goldust Twins easily thwarted by insisting that first names counted as well, and thus Sarah Smith ended up playing with Ada Smith as usual.

Some people said that they were called the Goldust Twins because they were rich and had stashed their money away in cash under mattresses and in the closets of their huge messy house. Others claimed that their name came off the label of a common brand of household cleanser. Probably both explanations were correct, for they were both rich and witchy-looking, better suited to an era when women wore long, loose-fitting dresses and allowed their hair to sweep down their backs, unrestrained by combs or pins. These sisters never went anywhere except to their bridge club, not even to church at Christmas or Easter, and they had years ago stopped entertaining the club on their required days. They were never asked to account for their exceptional claims; they were simply allowed to neglect the traditional obligation of hostessing and all the problems and trouble it entailed, perhaps because charter membership in anything, even a small-town bridge club, carried certain precious privileges, unstated but nevertheless understood. Their groceries were always delivered to them, and they were seen at home only on their front porch, where they would occasionally occupy twin rockers in the evenings. Their yard had long ago turned into weeds, yet they were never censured by the townspeople for not maintaining their property. In fact, people liked to bring them vegetables and fresh strawberries and apples, and one Monday Joan's mother sent Joan to their house with an elaborate flower arrangement that had graced the Presbyterian altar the day before. Hoping to get a peek inside their house, she was instead summarily dismissed at the doorway as she handed over the flowers, a muttered 'thank you' the only acknowledgment of the church's generosity.

Once a year, at spring time, they would hire a school boy to clean out their cistern, for which they paid him $4, a sum that had evidently been fixed years ago and had never been altered. If any boy had expected an inspection – even a glimpse – of their house he was always disappointed, for every year the boy was ushered to the cellar and left to his job, then escorted out by way of the same cellar steps, so that his vision was always confined to the periphery of the cellar. According to the series of boys who had performed that annual cleansing, often times brothers within a family, there were no bodies buried within sight, nor was there any sign of treasure, contraband or legal.

Those who presented the sisters with gifts – children and adults – were treated the same way: they were met at the door and cursorily thanked, then quickly dismissed. Joan used to ride her horse past the house, hoping that at least one of them might respond to the novelty of the noise, but she never knew if they heard her or cared that she was approaching on an animal not ordinarily seen in the community. They had a telephone but no one talked to them, for they simply let it ring until people abandoned calling them, yet they always showed up for the bridge games and they were never late. They always knew of last-minute substitutions, too, ones that were too late to appear in the paper. No one could figure out how they knew all these things, cut off as they were from everyone else. On the afternoons of the bridge club meetings, they would arrive in their old Packard and walk briskly up the path of the hostess's house. They carried canes, but neither seemed to suffer from arthritis, and they always strode quickly as if they were determined to confront and conquer disagreeable forces. Their Packard was another source of mystery, for it was never serviced and was seen only on the bridge club days. No one could figure out where they bought their gas since they were never seen at the local gas stations.

Another member of the bridge club who was considered a community curiosity was Lorraine Grofhelder, the town's only divorced woman (there were no divorced men). She lived next door to the Nelsons in an enormous white frame house, at least one hundred years old, which really belonged to her mother, Mrs. Arnold, a sweet-faced elderly widow who was, along with the Goldust Twins, a charter member of the club. Her mother's position undoubtedly accounted for Lorraine's acceptance into a circle that would have ordinarily closed ranks upon the ignominy of a divorce. It was common knowledge that Mr. Grofhelder (long ago vanished) had been no good. He had left his wife and three children with nothing except the protection of the kindly old Mrs. Arnold. By the time the Nelsons had arrived in New Bonn and had bought Locksley Hall, the two sons had already been to college, served in the military, and were married and living in other parts of the country, which left only the youngest offspring of this pathetic jilting, a daughter called LoJane – named after her mother (Lorraine) and her grandmother (Jeanette). LoJane was a year older than Joan but was a year behind in school – Mrs. Arnold and her daughter didn't believe in 'pushing' youngsters, they frequently claimed. Joan couldn't stand the girl but her parents had insisted that she be especially nice to her because they were neighbors, and because she lacked what everyone else in the community was supposed to possess – a resident father.

LoJane was a tubby redhead whose mouth always seemed to be lined with spit around its edges whenever she talked, which was incessantly and without direction. Like her mother, she giggled all the time but had no sense of humor. She had a strange talent for absorbing whatever was said to her, and then she would repeat the statements almost verbatim, but they were invariably reiterated without their original logic or purpose. Like many mimes, she had a tricky knack for syntax, but intellectual efforts taxed her to the point of aberration. Her mother was the night operator at the telephone company, a job that had few demands, which enabled her to sleep on the office cot and still honorably collect her salary. If people questioned Lorraine's ability to maintain a house and daughter on the salary of a night operator, they did so without any real interest in the topic, for most people in town realized that Lorraine's major source of income came from the regular visitors who could be seen at times in the Grofhelder kitchen drinking coffee with dear old Mrs. Arnold. These visitors varied: one was the local franchise-holder of the Buick-Chevrolet-Pontiac agency; another was an elderly farmer who bore the name Homer Senior, a convenience solely to distinguish him from his oldest son. Another, although not nearly so regular, drove over some Sunday afternoons from his home in Clayton, the county seat, where he was Justice of the Peace.

All of Lorraine Grofhelder's visitors were respectable, non-drinking men, earnest men whose only flaw appeared to reside in their marriages to women who had no intentions of divorcing them. It was through Lorraine that Joan first heard the expression 'living together as man and wife', which was something that Lorraine's visitors evidently did not do. Although the town found a little amusement in speculating about Lorraine's next conquest – among a few of the men she was the source of some crude jokes – there was little vicious gossip about her habits, perhaps because her feelings about alcohol were felt to be more important than the vagaries of her cautious adulteries. Had there been a catalogue of sins among the town's populace, listed in descending order from the most unforgivable to the least contemptible, the sin of drinking would have ranked number one as the most despised. Of course there would be variations among the sins of the lesser natures, ranked according to religious indoctrination; the Lutherans would tend to rank dancing close to the top, for example, whereas the other denominations would probably reserve it among the more harmless sins. But according to the unofficial code of the community, Lorraine's conduct couldn't be too strenuously condemned, for she entertained her callers at home and not at some sordid, clandestine drinking place; she never appeared in taverns; and her selection of admirers was economically impeccable.

When Joan arrived at the age where she began to question the fairness of community sanctions and priorities, she was able to understand New Bonn's relative indifference to a teetotaling mistress. What she couldn't understand, though, was Lorraine's attraction to men who seemed, although dull, at least capable of judging surface appeal, for Lorraine was skinny in the kind of way that suggested a lack of body fluids, and she had atrocious taste in clothes. She wore either drab browns or grays or else outsized floral prints. She was also incredibly dimwitted, with her perpetual giggle and her trite conversations that never focused on anything other than the weather and her own kin. If she felt guilty about her own conduct she never revealed it. In church she was the first to glower at a squirming child, and at home she openly recoiled in horror over any kind of remark that could possibly contain sexual overtones. It was especially difficult for Joan to be nice to LoJane, the dim daughter of the town's genteel whore, and often she was ruder to her than she intended to be. Yet of all the girls near her age, LoJane was the only one to display an interest in Joan's horse, and although Joan appreciated any interest in him – she was secretly dismayed at others' indifference – she nevertheless refused to let LoJane ride him.

Not that she could have, for he was a spirited horse which liked to balk and to run away, and Joan could never accurately predict his moods. At first the English saddle amused people, and the way that Joan rode provoked considerable derision, for she continued to ride in strict conformity to the rules of dressage, but after she abandoned her formal riding gear and began to substitute jeans for jodhpurs and an old jacket for her tweed coat, interest in both horse and rider evaporated. Joan knew that LoJane would fall on her butt the minute she let her on the horse, and Mrs. Nelson agreed that the risk was far too great. 'It would be your fault if she fell and hurt herself,' she had averred, and although Joan thought this assumption was absurd, she was grateful for an excuse not to share her precious possession with a person whom she had been ordered to befriend.

Lorraine, in addition to owning the position of the town's most refined whore, had the strongest claims to its championship in the gossip sweepstakes. Because she was a second-generation resident with a respectable heritage, and because there were two families living in town to whom she was related, she had access to previous historical information that was generally unknown. Her position at the telephone company served to increase opportunities to pursue present goings-on. She could monitor every telephone call, incoming and outgoing, and she often did. Since the young people were the most frequent users of the telephone after 10 p.m., she was uniquely informed of the lives of New Bonn youth, and because she was too obtuse to realize that she was violating in any serious way a professional ethic in revealing her sources, she used her information the way a farmer uses his dogs to cull out unwanted animals from the common herd.

It was she, then, who was mostly responsible for aborting an elopement between an underage girl and a farm lad from Clayton: one call from the frantic girl to her admirer was enough to tip off the girl's unsuspecting parents. She was subsequently whisked away from the village and sent to live with an aunt three states away until she could return home safely some six months later.

Since the Nelsons and the Grofhelders were next-door neighbors, and because the Nelsons believed that the ability to get along with one's neighbors was an essential key to the individual character, LoJane spent a lot of time in Joan's room listening to records and reading magazines, whereas Joan often ate supper next door, delicious meals that always began with a grace that mortified Joan, for the Grofhelder-Arnold family insisted upon a blessing that circulated around the table, with each diner asked to contribute a pious suggestion as at least a partial explanation for the evening's fare. (One might say, 'We thank thee, Oh Lord, for this wonderful pie that Mama spent hours preparing,' and the next person might add, 'We can't neglect LoJane's efforts at slicing the apples.' Innocuous stuff, but it served to include everyone present.)

Joan was embarrassed at what she considered a violation of religious decorum; to her any sort of public display of piety was outrageous. Thus she cringed when Catholics would make a point of crossing themselves before every meal, and the mild grace that her devout friends mumbled also made her uncomfortable while it was being said – usually a matter of no more than thirty seconds. Any personal testimony that asked for an analysis of God's claims upon a perfectly ordinary dinner reduced Joan to uncharacteristic stammering. The suppers at the Grofhelders were delicious, though, for both Lorraine and her lovely mom liked to bake, and so there were always choices of desserts – unlike the Nelson table, which often eliminated desserts altogether for the sake of health. The homemade bread at the Grofhelder table was spread with the sweet cream butter from the farm of Homer Senior.

New Bonn's other known fallen woman was far more

mysterious than Lorraine, yet she was also the object of almost total community indifference. She was the mistress of one of the Reuter brothers and had borne him three illegitimate children, all daughters who looked exactly like Cheryl, his licit daughter (and only child), the unfortunate product of a Catholic–Protestant marriage that was naturally doomed. The mysterious woman lived two or three miles from town in a well-kept house, surrounded by a small flower garden. The most consistent and continuous reminder of her isolated, ignominious state was heard in the cries of her peacocks, which roamed all over her garden and along the driveway to her house. Her name was Mrs. Heinz, but everyone called her the Peacock Lady, and the existence of her peacocks seemed to appeal far more to people's imagination than her status as mistress to one of the wealthy Reuter brothers, for this was a situation that the community had long ago accepted as perhaps the best and most acceptable alternative to a marriage which precluded its partners living together as man and wife.

No one saw the Peacock Lady; she remained isolated in the same way that the Goldust Twins had managed their separation, and no one Joan knew had ever visited her house. The three bastard daughters did not go to any of the schools, perhaps because the parents could never conclusively determine their religious affiliations. Occasionally a naïve new official would attempt to correct their violation of the Minnesota Compulsory Education Act, but the complaint was never legally executed, for no one with the legal authority wanted to change the conjugal arrangements of a family that appeared innocent of community offense.

Mrs. Heinz and her three daughters would probably have been completely ignored save for the nightly screeching of the peacocks, with their spooky noisy cries that sounded like 'Help!' which took at least a full minute to articulate. Nor were the peacocks treated as a public nuisance and shot, as had happened to so many harmless pets, dogs and cats, whose only offense was running in the streets. These creatures would suddenly disappear, only to be found later with twelve-gauge shot lacerating their bodies. In a community of hunters, the peacocks remained the only birds who had not been shot at. Perhaps they were preserved as a kind of memorial to their owner's anomalous position, kept alive as a kind of unofficial historical monument.

The presence of the Peacock Lady bothered Joan because she had become friendly with Cheryl, the beautiful legitimate Reuter girl. She thought that maybe Cheryl would sometime reveal the secrets of her father's tastes, or 'extra-curricular activities', as Mrs. Nelson labeled adulterous alliances. But Cheryl never disclosed her feelings about either her parents' loveless marriage or her father's second family (another term of Mrs. Nelson's, and more acceptable than bastard, she claimed). Eventually Joan decided that Cheryl had been kept ignorant of her father's dalliances, an unlikely situation if not impossible, since the relationship was almost as old as Cheryl. Although people had grown indifferent to it – 'water under the bridge' was a typical comment about it – no one tried to conceal it, either. Joan wondered if Cheryl might have adopted the same kinds of indifference that others claimed. She seemed independent and was certainly beautiful, and her father indulged her to the point of absurdity, buying her a car when she was not quite fourteen and ineligible for a driver's license for two more years, and calling her 'Baby' and inscribing her checks with that name, even after she had graduated from college and had been married twice.

Joan was not unfamiliar with loveless marriages. She considered her parents' marriage, when she considered it at all, as typical in that whatever disputes occurred seemed to be focused upon money, or else there was a difference of opinion regarding the disciplining of her – rewards, punishments, postponed decisions – the necessary but stupid conflicts she supposed every family put up with. She knew that her uncle, who lived in Chicago and was very rich, had ceased 'liking' her aunt (he had told her as much), but she didn't understand how any community could accept these kinds of marriages as a matter of course. Her own parents had spent what seemed like endless hours discussing the possibilities of Uncle Sid's divorce and what would happen to Aunt Abby and where the property would go and how the money was to be divided. In New Bonn, however, there was no divorce – Lorraine was the exception, but she'd been deserted – and it appeared that men came and went whenever they pleased, whereas the wives remained at home and assumed a position comparable to that of an old maid.

All of the women in the community were identified by their husbands' names: Joan's mother was called Mrs. Bert Nelson, or sometimes Mrs. B.K. for short (there were three other Nelson families in the township alone), and even those women whose husbands were only technically so were still designated by their spouse's names and initials. Those women who were married 'in name only' tended to be the most bitter and vituperative critics of their own children's conduct. Of course they had not yet the advantages of modern science to show them that their resentment was based on a sexual dependency that they abhorred, but would it have mattered if they had been aware of the theoretical basis for their commonplace behavior?

Clearly their resentment was obvious to them regardless of its lack of modern terminology. What they needed was not so much a label for their unhappiness nor an explanation for its existence, classified and codified with appropriate names of Latin and Greek derivations. What they needed, and did not get, was an alternative to their sadness, a sadness that was nourished and reinforced every day by their children and friends of their children, but which was stimulated most profoundly by the boisterous camaraderie of the town's male population.

It was not unusual, for example, to see a cuckolded husband conducting a business deal with his wife's lover, and there seemed to be no real deception involved in their mutual negotiations of terms, for they were conducting their business lives in much the same ways they conducted their marital lives, where commodities and chattels were often exchanged with the same sense of acceptance of a practice that was fundamentally contemptible. Lovers and cuckolds together formed an unspoken alliance while conducting their own affairs of money and finance, and undoubtedly it was this appearance of solidarity – of conspiracy, even – that proved the most painful to their wives, innocent or guilty.

Chapter Four

The Doctor's Daughter

Mrs. Nelson, although not a partner to a loveless marriage, was frequently treated the same kind of way that the isolated Peacock Lady had received before the town settled upon its truce of apathy. When the Nelsons had first moved to New Bonn, someone – Joan could never discover who it was – had dubbed her mother Mrs. Browning, and although this was a senseless label, it remained. Once Joan asked her friend, Maryann, who was always honest with her when she did know the truth, why her mother had been given this strange name.

'I dunno. Maybe because it has something to do with poetry.'

Yet Joan's mother didn't spend all her time reading poetry, and she certainly had never written any.

'Well, maybe it's because she should be writing poetry, or something,' was all Maryann could offer. The connection between Locksley Hall, their home, and Robert Browning was a forced one, indeed, which made Joan wonder what the 'something' meant. Besides, the village itself was notoriously inaccurate or whimsical with its labels: the owner of a grocery store which didn't do much business because both proprietor and hired help were so indifferent to both products and customers was called 'Infallible', a name whose dictionary definition conveyed no explanation for this particular label.

Poetry was considered a kind of stupid frivolity that no one engaged in, either actively or passively (an attitude that is certainly American and by no means limited to the Midwest). Knowing the general incompetence of the community regarding names, Joan nevertheless decided to do some research on Mrs. Browning, feeling that she might discover a clue to whatever it was that her mother possessed that had inspired her weird name.

Joan didn't want to read Mrs. Browning's poetry – the famous 'How do I love thee' sonnet, which her tenth-grade English teacher had force-fed the class, had turned her off from further investigation of more, and she was not interested in the life of her husband, so the information she did find gave her little satisfaction. Mrs. B., she learned, was known primarily for her marriage to Robert Browning, one of England's greatest, and she had left a sickbed in order to marry him, defying her own papa and exiling herself to Italy. Joan rather liked that part of the story since it indicated Mrs. B. didn't lack gumption, that her will was strong enough and she possessed enough guile to deceive her own doting father – something Joan found unthinkable – but there the interest faltered. Nothing in the lives of the famous Brownings corresponded to the reality of the Nelsons, whose marriage had been conventional and without drama.

Joan was not attracted to scholarship nor to additional work of any kind. It was enough for her to get by with relative ease in the not very demanding high school curricula, so she was irritated about her time spent pursuing a futile search through boring pages of the *Brittanica* and the Great Poets series that was kept in the school library. Yet the label nagged at her, for in her own eyes she felt she was clever enough to interpret and solve most minor community mysteries. She decided that she had better become more alert to gossip that might give her a clue to her mother's position in New Bonn, for she was gradually becoming aware, to her great dismay, that her own identity and that of her mother were not, after all, mutually exclusive.

To most of the people in New Bonn the Nelsons were objects of consternation. Mr. Nelson (B.K.) was the kind of man who could get along with everybody. He was genial and courteous. He always remembered people's names and the ages of many of his clients' children. He was not a handsome man – his nose was too long, which gave him a remarkable resemblance to Harry Truman, a coincidence that rankled his Republican sensibilities. He was a short man but extremely graceful, and he played a good game of golf. He continued to belong to a hunting club whose membership was composed of eleven Minneapolis businessmen, and he liked to improve his hunting collection with an occasional purchase of a gun or some new duck decoys. He was a gentle man, though, and could not stand to hunt deer – he had gone deer hunting only once – and his appetite for hunting seemed satisfied by three or four annual trips to the duck blinds with his club.

He wore well-cut suits without appearing overdressed or foppish. Even when he was talking to the farmers on their own soil with his tie and coat conspicuous next to their bib overalls and dirty work shirts he did not look incongruous. He had a resonant laugh; genuine sounds emerged from his torso which seemed to correspond to the crinkle lines around his eyes. His hair was white, and in the summer his face was deeply tanned so that in that season he looked especially healthy and robust. He did everything in moderation, smoking no more than six cigarettes a day, drinking at most two highballs before dinner. His idiom was correspondingly moderate: a few 'hells' and 'damns' were the strongest epithets that most people had ever heard from him. He had the highest respect for music and religion, two areas of experience that he considered himself totally ignorant toward but which he held in great esteem, if not awe. He liked to listen to Sunday afternoon radio symphony broadcasts, and he rarely missed a Saturday Metropolitan Opera broadcast. Nothing gave him more satisfaction than listening to his daughter's attempts at the piano reduction of the Pilgrim's Chorus from *Tannhauser*.

His formal education had ended at high school. He had hoped one day to study at Carleton College (at that time the best private college in Minnesota), but his older brother had followed the traditional bad example of eldest sons by attending Carleton and squandering his old man's money on a four-year education without the reward of a degree. Mr. Nelson finally forgave his older brother for spoiling his own chances, but he never succeeded in ridding himself of his residual bitterness, so there was always a coolness and strain between them, and he couldn't help feeling that his brother's eventual financial success had been purchased with his own future. He still believed in higher education, though, and perhaps one of the reasons he had been attracted to his wife was her degree. Certainly the attraction would be hard to explain in other ways because he was not the kind of man to be impressed merely because she was the doctor's daughter.

Although the families of doctors enjoyed the same kinds of veneration in the early part of the twentieth century as they do today, Mrs. Nelson (nee Carrie Clifton) was not the daughter of the typical American country doctor who often serves as both village father and rural saint. Dr. Clifton was a competent doctor (and there were many who testified to his lifesaving talents), but his sexual conduct was extremely unorthodox. He had divorced his first wife, Carrie's mother, herself the daughter of a Methodist minister, when she was not yet twenty. At seventeen she had been pulled out of the icy edges of a half-frozen lake by the young physician, and in less than eight months after this heroic rescue Carrie was born. Their divorce was considered by most people of their community, a rural area in the southeastern corner of the state, more scandalous than their marriage. Nevertheless, it left them free to pursue other courtships, something that their marriage had not allowed. Carrie was raised by two sets of grandparents, the Browns and the Cliftons, both of whom had hoped that their duties to their children had long since been served and satisfied when they had left home.

Carrie spent no time with her mother and little with her father until the year that her father remarried; by then she was nearly fourteen. Many years elapsed before she learned the reason for her father's remarriage, when she found out that he had been blackmailed into marriage by his Masonic brothers who were tired of his attempts (some successful) to seduce their wives (and in some cases their daughters). At the age of fifty-two, Dr. Clifton took a mail-order bride, a woman who had been described in several rural publications as being of 'good disposition' and willing to travel. He took a train to the small town in Oklahoma where she lived with her enormous family, and within a week they were married in her Southern Baptist church. She was twenty, which was perhaps the most attractive thing about her, for her age suggested to Dr. Clifton that a baby or two would help him out of his problems with the Masons – and by extension, with the rest of the community. His problems actually amounted to a conflict way beyond the boundaries of the Masonic brotherhood, for many people felt that all ailing women were fair game for Dr. Clifton's licentiousness. Why he resorted to a mail-order arrangement when he could have had his pick of the local eligible women was never satisfactorily explained, although there was plenty of speculation regarding his motives.

Carrie had been overjoyed at her father's remarriage, for

she was confident that it meant a permanent, suitable home for her. A genuine drawback, he would explain to her when he visited her at her grandparents' homes, was his bachelor environment and its unreliable, unstable life. Carrie had no way of knowing that an Oklahoma girl of twenty would not welcome her husband's fourteen-year-old daughter, and when she did visit the newlyweds several weeks after their marriage she found a lovely young woman with an atrocious Oklahoma twang who talked very little but who was nervous and jittery about tornadoes. It took her little time to install a tornado cellar, something few Minnesota houses had at that time. Lily, short for Lillianne, did nothing to welcome Carrie, who actually returned to her grandparents earlier than the intended termination of her visit. Nothing at that time was mentioned of other visits or even of a special room that Carrie could call her own.

Lily, with all her mail-order naïveté and unspoiled rural simplicity, was clearly not the woman to effect the good doctor's sexual salvation, and perhaps out of admitted failure she began to spend more and more time in Oklahoma with her folks. Every winter she would take the train just a few days after Christmas, and she would stay in Oklahoma for at least three months, 'waiting out the winter,' as she called her custom of winter departures. When she did return in the spring she failed to produce the child that might have consolidated their marital partnership.

Growing up away from her father and never hearing from her mother, even at Christmas time, allowed Carrie almost unlimited funds from her father. She was given money whether she asked for it or not. She was sent to Carleton College, where she graduated with honors, but she could never convince any authority, paternal or academic, to allow her to study medicine, something she had wanted to do as a little girl. She joined a sorority – one of the 'top three' – which immediately supplied her with the female companionship she had lacked the first eighteen years of her life. Her sorority sisters also helped to gratify Dr. Clifton's chronic roguery, which by then had diminished to the level of passive observer. He liked to spontaneously drop by the sorority house whenever he was in town, and he would take as many girls as were available to dinner at the best restaurant in town. During the summer Carrie was encouraged to entertain the sisterhood at the cottage her father owned on Lake Alexandria, and it was at this time that Carrie felt that she had finally established a stable home with her father, for Lily by then was very much out of the picture.

Since Lily was so lazy and such a terrible housekeeper and cook, Carrie happily performed the daily chores while Lily sat in a lawn chair, fanning herself with a palm leaf, and groaning and sighing from the heat. Carrie was at her happiest during those times: she cooked, she cleaned, and she entertained her friends. These girls, who considered themselves the Sisterhood, would go for boat rides and evening swims, mostly ignoring Lily, who seemed content without an audience for her complaints.

Despite her dedication to household drudgery, Carrie was a college graduate and she was a doctor's daughter – albeit a doctor whose feet were decidedly mired in clay – so her reasons for marrying B.K. Nelson were never clear, either to Joan or to most people in New Bonn. She did not lack suitors (no sorority girl ever does), and she was not desperate to marry because of advancing age or dark forebodings of spinsterhood. Although Bert was charming, he certainly didn't measure up to her more sophisticated suitors who could negotiate charm in the same easy ways that a child can so easily manipulate a group of adults. Perhaps it was his dignity, his sense of his own accomplishments in respect to others, that enabled her to perceive him as the one man who could supply her with security of both matter and location, for he was, above all, precisely and ineradicably stable. His laughter was predictable, his reactions to occasions judicious and controlled. They were married the year she was twenty-five, in her father's garden, in a summer ceremony presided over by the local Congregational minister, with two of her favorite sorority sisters as attendants. They honeymooned in Chicago, where for a few hours they visited her mother, who was then living in a railroad flat on the South Side with her third husband. The next year Dr. Clifton and Lily adopted a baby girl.

Chapter Five

C Sharp Minor

There were minor rebellions at this time, too, like smoking, but since everyone else was smoking and getting caught at it, Joan's mother did not consider smoking as much more serious than a waste of money, unlike the Lutherans and many Presbyterians, who felt it was linked with Original Sin, especially among females. Joan's parents even allowed her to smoke at home, which her friends promptly used to their advantage. Some afternoons her room would be full of girls puffing on their last cigarettes before returning home, secure in the smoky refuge of the Nelson household. They then would have to return to their homes where their clothes proved their actions. Rebuked, they would tell their own parents that they could call Mrs. Nelson to confirm where they had been, which then meant that Mrs. Nelson received the wrath of outraged parents. 'I don't want Susan or Sally or Marian' – or, the calls were generic – 'hanging around your house smoking cigarettes any more,' would be the message.

'I thought you knew Susan et al was here and that she had your permission,' Mrs. Nelson would reply, handily casting the blame on the parent who was supposed to know where and how her daughter spent her spare time.

Despite the opposition, Mrs. Nelson liked to have Joan's friends around because their presence confirmed Joan's popularity. What she didn't like was being the only adult held responsible for what was surely a communal lapse. Joan and her mother discussed the matter frequently. 'I can't have those girls coming here every day and smoking, smelling up the household,' was Mrs. Nelson's standard objection, delivered about once a week.

'But why not? Under the circumstances don't you think it's better to bring it out in the open than to hide it somewhere in a car or something?' Joan and her friends had carefully assessed the possibilities for smoking and they always came up with the same result: there were few places other than cars, which were too easily spotted and identified, for New Bonn lacked secluded side streets or dense thickets. The girls' locker room at school was out as a full-time resource, since it was too risky, and the dock could only serve during the limited months of Minnesota summers.

'It's one thing to be out in the open and another to do it here where I get all the blame for your friends.'

What these discussions revealed was that Joan and her mother were actually involved on the same side in the same battle, for once, a novelty that pleased Joan so much that she felt compelled to seek out a solution that would harm no one and still allow them all to smoke.

'Maybe you could talk it over with them all together and sort of talk it out,' Joan suggested, which at the time sounded nicely democratic, but which was eventually rejected as unrealistic because of Mrs. Nelson's previous conversations with each mother. (The fathers were not involved in this issue. Like so many that pertained to conduct, except for sexual conduct, the fathers considered themselves exempt from participation.) Finally Joan suggested that her mother bring it up at the next Reading Club meeting, an idea that stimulated Mrs. Nelson into mapping out a strategy. The bridge club as a forum was impractical because not all Joan's friends' mothers belonged to the club, but all the women in New Bonn who could skim through the current best-sellers and who possessed a bookshelf, even if it was covered with figurines, belonged to the Reading Club, so it was this resource that Joan's mother decided to use.

Since the Reading Club was open to all – it granted membership to a woman once she had stated her desire to join – its composition was larger than any of the other organizations in New Bonn (with the exception of the Catholic Ladies' Aid, which was the largest group of any kind), and the size of the group usually determined its location and occasion of meetings. Nobody wanted to read and report on a book once a week, and since the reading-and-reporting procedure was the one the club always followed, the meetings were held monthly, usually in the basement of one of the three churches, on a rotating basis.

The meetings were serious in purpose. Three women were assigned one book which they would read and then they would combine as a trio to present their observations about the book. The reading list was usually obtained from the Minneapolis Sunday *Tribune*, which published weekly its list of best-sellers, as well as a separate list of other books of current worth. Sometimes there were book reviews written by university professors, which were very helpful to New Bonn club members, who were careful to commend both the interview and source in their discussions. Although a few women plagiarized the reviews, nicely paraphrasing the more difficult or rather gamy passages, this practice was considered lazy, even a bit subversive. Although the reviews provided valuable short cuts, the university, itself, was considered by many people in New Bonn as a questionable place of authority, its faculty populated by commies, not necessarily card-carrying, who displayed an alien political ideology that had no place in Minnesota, especially in its rural outposts.

During the first part of the meeting, the readers who had been assigned the book would describe it a little, and then the discussion leader was expected to ask the first leading question, which was designed to break the ice. It was a time-honored convention for the wife of the Presbyterian minister to function as the club's president and its discussion leader. The reasons for this arrangement were obvious, for the Lutherans were discouraged from most kinds of social life that involved non-Lutherans, and the priest, of course, was unattached. Since Alice Blue, the wife of the current Presbyterian minister, was chronically ailing and had some time ago been absolved of her traditional duties as Sunday school supervisor, her hold on the presidency of the Reading Club was a curious one. Perhaps she felt guilty about her weak show on Sundays, or possibly she had literary pretensions that her feeble church work could not gratify. Unlike her predecessors, however, she delegated most of the responsibilities of the job to a cluster of women who were always eager to tamper with her directions, and with the normal course of the arrangements.

Mrs. Nelson regularly attended the Reading Club, and she often asked questions, even past the discussion hour when most women preferred to get on with the social hour, so she considered herself one of the more powerful and conscientious members. It took little persuasion from the hospitality committee for her to volunteer Locksley Hall for the next meeting, which coincided with the Christmas meeting, an occasion that the members tried to make festive and memorable.

Instead of the ordinary cookies and cake, there were specially baked delicacies donated by the baker's wife, also a member, and instead of the usual choice of coffee and tea, there was always a cold punch and tiny sandwiches, triple-layered and filled with cream cheese and tuna and deviled egg. Since this was to be a Christmas meeting, Mrs. Nelson decided it would not be amiss to provide some kind of entertainment after the discussion, and so she asked Joan to play the piano, both for the discussion of the book and then afterwards, as background for the refreshments. Her purpose was twofold: the club had selected a book on modern music which gave Mrs. Nelson the perfect opportunity to display her daughter as a serious girl of worthwhile qualities who would, through her musical knowledge, vindicate herself to all those condemning mothers who based Joan's character on her cigarette smoking. Mrs. Nelson felt that the authority of Joan's music – she pictured her as a kind of interpreter-guide – couldn't help but communicate her serious nature, thereby relegating the minor sin of cigarette smoking to its proper place, a kind of dustbin of moral trivia.

The book assigned was one on modern music written by a University of Minnesota musicologist who felt compelled to explain to his audience the essential legitimacy of a mystifying post-war arrival of alien sounds that happened to be mostly Russian. At that time the book was enjoying a spurt of popularity, but it was read mostly by Minneapolis symphony-goers whose ears were being assaulted (or so they thought) by these noisy works. The book made no invidious comparisons; it merely attempted to make respectable some strange sounds that most people felt were simply not music. (It was rumored that the book had been commissioned by the Communists, an unfair accusation since its author was completely innocent of political motives or affiliations. He was simply tired of restive audiences and their predictable groans that always accompanied the first measures of a Stravinsky or Prokofiev selection.)

Joan's mother was both hostess and one of the reviewers, and the plan was that Joan was to demonstrate on the piano, while her mother talked about certain passages of

Stravinsky and Shostakovich so that the club members could follow the structure of the text. Mrs. Nelson, herself, privately thought that the 'new music' was mostly noise, but she swallowed her disgust and picked her way through every page of the book, and even took extensive notes. No music store in either Worthington or Sioux Falls stocked the records of any of the modern Russian composers, so she had to send to Minneapolis, where she could get only one Stravinsky orchestral work, 'The Firebird', but she had better luck with the Shostakovich cello concerto – it was not only available, she had a choice of performers and orchestras. Joan's piano teacher, Mr. Schlage, had better luck in finding sheet music. 'Perhaps he has ties to the Communist underground,' her father suggested, a joke that Joan thought rather lame considering all the work that she and her mother had undertaken in order to illustrate one dumb book.

Joan rather liked the music, not because of its origins in the folk tradition (one of the major points of the book), nor because it provided new alternatives to the harmonics of the conventional chromatic system – she had been trained enough on scales and harmonic inventions to be satisfied at letting things stand as they were – but because the new music allowed her to make mistakes without detection. Once in a while even the least attentive or most tone-deaf listeners could detect a sour note in Chopin or Liszt – composers she felt were easiest to fake – but this music was almost free from chromatic development, which permitted her to strike an A chord when a B chord was written with no one being the wiser.

Mr. Schlage was amused by her new interest. Unwilling to tell him the whole story behind her mother's choice, she did describe the Reading Club and her role in its Christmas meeting. Mr. Schlage thought that the music was a temporary craze that would pass as soon as conductors quit playing it, but he did applaud her mother's project as worthwhile because it attempted to account for a temporary silliness. 'Fools will always be taken in by anything that sounds different,' was his judgment. Since that was not exactly her mother's intention, nor that of the man who wrote the book, Joan thought her music teacher's reaction rather curious. He was usually so unemotional about music, even the kinds he said were the greatest ever written, but he did promise to help her after she had promised him that she would not push the New Noise, as he called it, to any audience after the club's Christmas meeting.

Together they worked on a piano reduction of the Shostakovich Stalingrad Symphony, and within a day or two she was able to make the notes correspond to the crashing crescendo that signaled both the end of the battle and the termination of the piece. Joan had no intention of spending any more time than she needed to learn the piece, and once she discovered that the movements had no definite key area, she spent little time practicing. Key areas were essential clues to error detection, she knew, but without a definable key she felt free to err as she pleased. Thus she was really unprepared for a musical demonstration of unfamiliar sounds, and while this bothered her a little, she felt that the untrained tastes of her audience were definitely to her advantage.

On the afternoon of the party, Joan and two of her smoking friends helped her mother make the dainty sandwiches, while her father made the punch, threatening in a joking manner to spike it and give some life to the party. Joan had not thought it wise to inform her friends of her mother's strategy since, in her own imagination, the plan had assumed a kind of conspiracy. She feigned martyrdom at having to play what she acknowledged as hard music just to indulge her mother in one of her whims. She showed the manuscript to her friends, both of whom had a slight knowledge of notation, and it did look formidable, with all its sharps and abrupt metric changes and strange-looking clefs.

As a special favor her friends were permitted to remain for the evening, a deliberate transgression of the rules that Mrs. Nelson thought was justifiable, given the festive nature of the occasion and the high seriousness of its purpose. The girls helped to arrange the chairs into a horseshoe, which gave the parlor the look of a provincial salon. Joan liked the effect; the baby grand piano was placed to one side so that it looked important but not overwhelming. She thought the holly and the candles provided just the right kind of Christmas observance without narrowing down the whole function into just another Christmas gala. The guests seemed to share Joan's approval, too, for each woman, as she removed her coat, would glance around with apparent delight at the soothing light of the candles and the glistening holly in the shiny silver bowls that Joan and her mother had laboriously polished for the occasion. Some made direct comments: 'Oh, how pretty it looks,' and 'How Christmassy your house looks tonight,' were the most stated ones. Only one woman observed that playing by candlelight could ruin your eyes, but Joan dismissed her remark with a gracious smile and an assurance that this particular occasion was unique, that she saw to it that she always had plenty of light when she played.

The two other women who formed the trio of readers had not responded to the book with the alacrity or zeal of Mrs. Nelson. The first reader, Mrs. Larson, delivered her presentation in a half-sitting, half-standing posture, as if she were so unsure of herself and her judgments that she couldn't make up her mind whether to sit or stand. She confessed that she was 'way over my head with this book', and added to her humility with the confession that she was tone-deaf. Joan thought this an admirable admission and hoped that the second presenter would be as accommodating. However, when the second reader, Mrs. Handslip, stood up and looked at Joan, who was sitting at the piano waiting for her mother's presentation so she could demonstrate the knowledge she had so adventitiously acquired, Joan felt uneasy. She felt uneasy because she was her best friend's mother, and because she was, of all the other mothers, the least inhibited about voicing her own disapproval of her daughter's habits, which of course extended to the vagaries of her friends.

Maryann Handslip had never told Joan how much her mother held her accountable for Maryann's corruption, but Joan had often heard Mrs. Handslip's strident denunciations of her own daughter's conduct, and it was clear from what she said to her daughter that Joan was indeed the culprit, the real corrupter of youthful morality that was threatening the heart of New Bonn, Joan had once heard her say. That was how she talked, in large rotund, oracular sentences that took sin for their subject and responsibility and blame for their verbs.

So Joan should have known that what was coming from Mrs. Handslip was completely in character, and she shouldn't have been shocked at the woman's opening words, when Mrs. Handslip raised her hand as if to quiet an unruly mob, and said in tremulous tones that were surprisingly audible to those at the back of the room, 'I think this music is wicked.' Perhaps Joan was shocked because Mrs. Handslip, to her knowledge, had never heard the music and was supposed to only have read the book. Joan looked at Maryann, who was looking out of the window with such intensity, as if there were exotic animals or animated spirits out there, instead of a yard empty of everything but six-foot snow drifts.

The women in the audience seemed intent on Mrs.

Handslip's next utterance. Although not exactly stunned by her announcement, they did seem eager to hear her full description of wickedness. After a pause of at least a minute, Mrs. Handslip continued in a voice that seemed steadier and more controlled. 'This music is wicked because the men who wrote it were wicked and because it has no real musical value. You can't whistle it or hum it, and it does nothing but make a huge sound to the point that you want to hold your ears if you don't want to go deaf.' (Had Joan read the book she would have recognized this attack as an almost verbatim repetition of the first chapter, which carefully set up the standard arguments against the music, with the subsequent chapters a methodical and enlightened repudiation of them. The originality of Mrs. Handslip's attack lay in the judgment of the composers' characters, not in the noises they were alleged to have created.)

'I know it's old-fashioned to think about wickedness nowadays,' she continued, 'but I can't help it. I can't help it, I can't help talking about it because what this book talks about is music that is written by bad men to make other men worse.'

Joan noticed that Mrs. Handslip held a bundle of notes in her hands but was not referring to them. Her hands were shaking badly and her voice once again cracked on the third 'wicked'. Joan wondered if she were getting ready to burst into tears. She looked at her friend Maryann again for unspoken support, but Maryann was still gazing out of the window at whatever phantom was cavorting in the snow.

'I can only say that I wonder why people have to listen to this kind of noise when there is so much beautiful music in the world which we don't have time enough to listen to in the first place. Why do we have to listen to this terrible stuff when we can all benefit from familiar music that we all know and love and that everyone agrees is beautiful?' With her rhetorical question asked, Mrs. Handslip took her chair, a seat next to the piano, where she could look at the wicked music and watch Joan's hands as they attempted to span its impossible chords.

Joan cast a furtive look at Mrs. Handslip while her mother was giving her presentation. The woman sat with eyes downcast, her glasses notched slightly lower than usual on her beaky nose, a slight, barely perceptible smile of victory on her stern, uncompromising face. Joan's mother was making an effort to rise to the occasion, but it was clear that she had been upstaged by the second reader. Mrs. Nelson looked intently at Mrs. Handslip and then smiled bravely, 'I know how you must feel, Anna, at these kinds of unfamiliar sounds. And I must admit that at first they didn't seem pleasant to me at all, either.' She cast Joan a look of such transparent indulgence that Joan blushed. 'I must admit that all Joan's practicing hasn't made them especially pleasant for me.' This got a slight titter from the audience, approving sounds that undoubtedly gave her confidence to proceed. 'Yet we are not here to really judge the music. We're here to try to understand the book, and that's why I've asked Joan to play some of the music so that at least you'll get a better idea of why the ideas, or the themes – I guess that's what they are – these themes that went into the music make the music sound the way it does.'

Aside from the rather conciliatory lameness of her deference to Mrs. Handslip, Joan thought her mother had carried off her retort with admirable calm, and so her concluding comments seemed satisfactory. 'The man who wrote the book didn't like the music either, or at least not very well, but he thought it important for us all to keep abreast of the times.'

Joan was used to this argument, a favorite of her mother's, but she usually heard it when her mother was trying to stuff some unpalatable assignment down Joan's reluctant mental craw, and in the case of the particular book her mother was defending, Joan was not sure this traditional appeal even applied. Keeping abreast with the times seemed to Joan an especially maternal concern, certainly not worth writing a book about, even a dumb one. The audience seemed to go for her mother's comments, though, for they responded as if they were being summoned for duty. Joan, who was ready to begin the selection as soon as her mother finished her prefatory remarks, felt their appreciative glances as she waited at the piano, hands poised.

'Shostakovich wrote this symphony as a tribute to his country after it had survived a terrible series of battles and setbacks that seemed at the time to spell certain defeat for Russia.' Now her mother was reading from her notes with determined and confident tones. 'Today we might not like Russia and all that it stands for, but we can admire, can we not, the loyalty and patriotism that this composer felt for his country?'

Aware of the essential profundity of her words, Mrs. Nelson continued in a voice that was modulated by appropriate feeling: 'I'm sure we have all felt the same kinds of deep patriotism that the composer felt, but none of us have been able to put it into words or music, have we? And because we have all felt love for our country, we can identify with the composer's feelings, even if we can't admire his country. We don't even have to admire his politics.' Mrs. Nelson smiled benevolently at the assembled women: 'Let us think of the composer's feelings, his love for his country and for those men, women, and children who were lost in the terrible war, while we listen to the selection that Joan will now play.'

With these words Joan's mother sat down, smiling a mixture of almost perfect triumph and aesthetic bliss, and Joan began the first measures of the Russian cacophony that had just barely escaped conflagration by a congregation of frenzied harpies, for that is the way she played now, as if she were playing the piece for the first and last time before its final siege.

She banged the bass as she had never done before and refused to even acknowledge the few passages that requested 'pianissimo'. She played every measure at 'forte' and 'fortissimo' until she had accurately reconstructed, for herself, a genuine battle with its horrendous loss of blood and lives. The idea of mistakes did not occur to her, and the notation was so subordinate to her purpose that it could have been removed and she would have scarcely missed it. She crashed and thundered until she heard all the armies fall, a fall that fortunately coincided with the dying notes of the piece.

When she had finished she heard a small gasp, but she refused to look at her audience, adopting, rather, the downcast gaze towards the keys that her teachers had instructed her to employ. When she finally did look up, she noticed that most women looked only mildly interested, and some looked fatuously bored. Only one, though, Mrs. Handslip, looked openly disgusted. As Joan rose from the piano bench, her mother said, 'Thank you, Joan. That was very nice,' and only then did the ladies respond with their applause. As Mrs. Handslip was leaving the room accompanied by Maryann, who had managed to disengage herself from whatever she had been previously fixed upon outside, she said to Joan in a voice coated with treacle, 'Joan, next time why don't you try "The Warsaw Concerto" for us?'

Although their attempt at cultural refinements did not produce the effects that Mrs. Nelson and her daughter had desired, it did provide an occasion for frequent reminiscence as well as immediate community gossip. Joan's musicianship had never been in question – this had never been an issue – but the morality of Mrs. Nelson encouraging such an enterprise was analyzed with morbid zeal. Mrs.

Nelson had attempted to prove to the community that her daughter was a talented girl, and therefore a good girl, despite her relatively innocuous habit of smoking. Yet possession of a talent could not bear the weight of the equation, for people now directed their indignation at Mrs. Nelson's weird choice of music. Curiously, most people did not begrudge Mrs. Nelson her presumptuousness in showing off her grand home, in converting her living room into a conservatory. Most Midwesterners felt that if you had it, you showed it, so long as you kept everything within the bounds of good taste, and the community didn't really disapprove of Mrs. Nelson using her daughter as a showcase for talent and opulence. But everyone remembered the outrageous music, and people eventually spoke of sounds so awful that it made them literally sick to remember what had been played that night. For people ultimately felt that this had not been music at all but was something that Mrs. Nelson and her daughter had conspired to seize for their own advantage and then had created something horrible out of it.

Why not 'The Warsaw Concerto'? they later asked, until the evening assumed the dimensions of an episode in which the Nelsons – even Mr. Nelson could not escape censure – became the tyrannical perpetrators of a plot calculated to destroy the musical equilibrium of the community. People were convinced that Mrs. Nelson had hatched the plot and they had gone about selecting the book by which she accomplished her strategy, forgetting all about the Minneapolis *Tribune* best-seller list as conveniently as they forgot the few realities of the episode.

In a sense, though, Joan's smoking lost its moral impact. Instead, it was considered a symptom of a larger, more serious vice, that unforgivable vice of defiant heterodoxy.

Chapter Six

Rock of Ages

Shortly after the Christmas of the Shostakovich episode – an event that Joan labeled years later with a painful measure of self-conscious irony – Reverend Blue's wife was hospitalized with a prolonged bout of her mysterious ailment, which meant that there was no one to play the organ for the Sunday services. Joan agreed to Reverend Blue's suggestion that she fill in until Alice could get on her feet, perhaps because she was eager to experiment with an unfamiliar instrument, certainly not because of excess piety, for she found the Presbyterian services increasingly dull.

Reverend Blue knew that Joan couldn't play the organ, yet he was not the sort of man who offers easy salvation to any of his flock, so his motives for asking Joan to play must have been complicated by a number of pressures. Yet it was practical to take the best pianist in the congregation and make her an organist. He gave her a couple of books and told her to learn for herself, advising her to do the best she could. 'Try your best, that's all we can ask or expect,' he instructed her.

The instrument was not that much different from a piano, after all, for it was a modest organ with pipes only for show, and there were only two keyboards and very few stops. He also told Joan that the organ music wasn't much different from the music she regularly played on the piano – a delicate evasion of the Shostakovich incident, Joan thought. He claimed that the most important thing to remember was that the congregation merely needed support for their hymn-singing, and the choir could sing a capella until Joan was sufficiently trained to accompany them. 'You can play the prelude or the postlude from your own piano pieces,' he advised, 'but play them very quietly because the mood of peace is more important that your choice of composer. Bach, Beethoven, it doesn't matter as long as it's done quietly and in good taste.'

Joan thought she heard a warning in his voice, but she decided that playing the organ might provide her a quick road to power, if not vindication, at least until Mrs. Blue recovered.

Joan took her place at the organ one Sunday without announcement. She quietly slipped into place at the instrument, thereby replacing the temporary pianist who could play only hymns written in the key of C. She liked the feel of the pedals as she knocked on their oak surface with her sandals (her first practice session had shown her that it was impossible to play with high heels), and she enjoyed pulling out the flute stop and the dulcet stop; together with the tremolo they made a whistling noise that she thought blended well with the more mawkish hymns. She found that one reedy stop, plus a low double dulcet, combined to provide the ideal peace that Reverend Blue had hailed. She liked the challenge of the prelude, too, when she had an audience of blue-suited farmers as well as the stiff-backed women who wore their Sunday hats like battle dress. The postlude was a loss, however, since there was no enforced listening, for everyone was in a hurry to leave once the recessional was over. Joan decided that she could play just about anything for a postlude without the audience caring, and one Sunday she had attempted a legato rendition of 'You Are My Sunshine', set in a minor key. She had prepared a defense in case Reverend Blue should recognize the melody and raise hell about it, for 'Sunshine', she decided, could literally refer to Jesus's golden rays, but he never acknowledged her musical deviations. She soon abandoned the practice of improvisation and similar liberty-takings when she realized that there was no one with whom she could share the joke.

One afternoon Reverend Blue came to the house bearing music that his recuperating wife wanted Joan to have. No one was home except Joan, and she hesitated before she asked him in, mostly because she didn't know what to serve him. She knew that to ignore a minister's visit was an unforgivable breach of conduct, at least by New Bonn standards. She had often seen him at the kitchen tables of her friends drinking coffee and eating doughnuts that seemed as if they had been especially created for him. He was a large man with an enormous jutting jaw that made him look a lot like Dick Tracy, and he always wore dark suits but disdained the clerical collar, which gave him a sleazy, mortician's look.

Joan decided to offer him lemonade, a concoction she considered harmless and refreshing, and she thought he might welcome it as an interesting variation of the traditional handouts his parish served him. When she had brought him his glass of lemonade, he suggested that they adjourn to the piano where she could run through some of the new music, and together they could select the next few weeks' musical fare.

When Joan had played the first few measures of the first selection, a theme and variations on the 'Old One Hundred', she remarked, 'This will never work. The congregation will think it's the Doxology and get confused.'

Reverend Blue's smile vanished. 'I suppose you're right. But it would be at a different time, you know. Besides, it's a tune they're all familiar with and could like.'

This was as close a recognition of pleasure as Joan had

ever heard from the clergyman, whose major function in life, Joan thought, was to remind people of how lousy they really were, but how they could improve somewhat – enough to get by, maybe – if they only set their minds towards improvement. With God's help, of course, and guided by regular prayers.

'I could play the theme and variations of "A Mighty Fortress" instead. It's written by Bach.' She expected the minister to be automatically charmed by the magic of Bach's name. She did not expect the strength of his response.

'Never, never, never, play that piece here!' he roared at her, his jowls shaking, his voice traveling up and down the register of human rage.

'But why not? What's the matter with Bach? I play Bach all the time in the preludes.'

'My dear,' he now almost whispered, 'don't you know that tune is too close to the community and might cause a terrible row?'

'Why? I don't understand why a tune that everyone knows would bother people at all, especially in a church.'

'Take my word for it. It's *not* to be played.' His tone of finality eliminated any possibility of more questioning. Indeed, Joan wondered if she hadn't gone too far, especially since his outburst seemed so unrelated to music and her manipulating musical choices. He departed soon after they had agreed on several bland selections for the coming services, leaving Joan more than curious about the source of his objections.

Joan thought she could solve the mystery on her own by consulting the family encyclopedia under 'Bach' but found nothing that would correspond to a congregation's horror at hearing his music. There was no entry for 'A Mighty Fortress' either. She was reluctant to ask her mother, since her mother usually responded with an attack of her own:

'What did you do to make him so upset?' she was bound to respond. She knew that her father would try to help her but she hated to introduce a topic that might be sensitive to his alliance with the farming community, for Joan was convinced that the taboo had something to do with farmers.

She was unable to find any written source that could enlighten her, and short of playing the damned thing and waiting for an audience reaction, she was afraid she was always going to be in the dark about the tune. Yet the idea of a forbidden piece tickled her. She knew that in Catholic churches they weren't allowed to play Schubert's 'Ave Maria' (or was it Gounod's?) because the composer wasn't a Catholic, but she knew that Bach was a Lutheran, and therefore should be safe for all Protestant ears. She was aware of the continuous antagonism between Catholics and Protestants – they were always sniping at one another, usually through marriage – yet one time a family of eight children and their parents appeared at Sunday Presbyterian services, deliberately ushering themselves into the front pew, which they continued to occupy (and monopolize) on subsequent Sundays.

This miserable family, with their potato faces and nose-picking kids, had turned out to be the losers in a fight with St. Gabriel's priest, Father Sturm, and they had evidently decided to dump their Catholicism the way that farmers dump sacks of feed to their chickens, quickly and with just one resolute movement. The Presbyterians felt the family's acceptance of their new faith was commendable; some even considered it a triumph of faith, although many privately wished the family was better groomed and less eager to occupy the most conspicuous place in the church.

In spite of the depths of Catholic–Protestant antagonism in New Bonn, Joan decided to ask her history teacher about the tune. Even though the teacher was a Catholic, Joan thought she could safely survive ridicule by phrasing her questions obliquely, in as neutral a fashion as possible. 'I have a question for you, Mrs. Dewey,' she began. 'I guess it's more an historical question than a musical one.'

Why hadn't she asked the music teacher, who was twice as smart as the history teacher, and who wasn't a Catholic, either? Joan realized that it was too late to extricate herself from her strategical error, and that if she didn't watch it she could easily commit herself – and, by extension, the entire Presbyterian congregation – to Catholic censure. 'I was wondering how, I mean why, there is this one melody that many composers have used, and keep using all the time, and maybe you can tell me why it's so popular.' Joan hoped this lie was convincing, although there might have been other composers than Bach who used the tune.

'Which tune is that, dear?'

'I'm not sure of its name, exactly. I think it's something like "Our Mighty Fortress".'

'Our Mighty Fortress? You mean "A Mighty Fortress". Don't they teach that in your church?'

Joan felt less like vindicating herself than boosting the parish. 'I'm sure they do. I may not have been listening, but I'm sure they do.'

The teacher frowned, her forehead wrinkling like an astonished rabbit. 'Well, Joan, I'm going to give you a library assignment and maybe you can correct some of that ignorance that seems to have rubbed off on you.'

A strange statement, Joan thought, for how can ignorance rub off of nothing to begin with?

'Go to the library and look in the encyclopedia under Martin Luther and you should have your answer.'

Mrs. Dewey delivered her mandate with a mixture of intellectual confidence and righteous indignation, a combination that made Joan regret her request in the first place, but after she had checked out the Luther volume, she knew she was on to something, and as an added piece of luck she found a bibliography that appeared untouched although its date of publication was 1911.

Joan's introduction to Martin Luther verified impressions that she had formerly felt only vaguely when she witnessed the sneers in some adult conversation. And while she was discovering the formal basis for schisms and protests, she acquired modern information that made the religious nature of New Bonn more comprehensible. (Of course she never told Mrs. Dewey how much she had learned, and she would have been mortified to know that the teacher had denounced her ignorance to the Catholic Ladies' Aid. Joan's ignorance was considered typical of the most insipid kind of Protestantism; any Lutheran would have known the answer to the question, was the consensus, regardless of schism and synod.)

Through her reading, Joan learned the official motives for Protestantism. She also learned that Martin Luther was a man who could not control his lust and had to form his own church because of it. (Her 1911 bibliographer had been a Catholic whose contribution bore the imprimatur. Joan admired this elegant seal of approval, and later, when she discovered the index of forbidden books, she was thrilled at the intrigue involved.) 'A Mighty Fortress' was Luther's battle cry, then, and its reaction had been known to have changed audiences into bloodthirsty mobs eager to dismember their Catholic victims, especially women and babies. It was understandable why a Catholic audience would always be offended at its rendition, perhaps even to the point of staging a riot, but Joan had never proposed playing it to anyone other than carefully screened Presbyterians. She decided to ask a Lutheran friend if the hymn was ever played in her church, and it was her Lutheran source who finally revealed to Joan the raw nerves that the town had never completely healed as a result of Luther and his emblematic hymn.

AnnaLisa, her Lutheran friend, was two years older than Joan, but she shared Joan's vice of smoking, and she also used to sneak off to dances in peripheral towns. Always anxious about being caught at either or both of her vices, she seemed happy to unburden herself of the particular period of the community's history. Perhaps she felt that by discussing New Bonn's early vagaries her own would seem less conspicuous. She said that the 'whole thing' (and by this Joan took her to mean the town's sensitivity) would never have happened if New Bonn hadn't been settled by two kinds of Germans. According to her, the earliest residents were farming people who created a village in the same kinds of way that villages were erected in the Old Country. The very first New Bonn natives, mostly Rhine-landers, stayed on their farms but built a church which they could all attend at least once a week, locating it in a place central to their own farms. Thus the first building had been the old St. Gabriel's church, and then the town had developed gradually, much like a child's tinker toy project, with a central structure and later additions according to need. The first farmers had been Catholics, but eventually the word spread among their relatives in Germany that here was land that was both cheap and fertile. A few families arrived from the northern German provinces, and they were mostly Lutherans. A few converted to Catholicism, but most felt too strange in an alien land to completely repudiate their religious heritage, so they, too, built a church in a place that was by then beginning to resemble a town – its original hamlet look had gradually disappeared.

AnnaLisa described the early days as tranquil. 'Oh, they got along quite well, although there was a certain amount of bickering and some really serious quarrels. Some offspring were disinherited, even, but most of the time they managed to get along.'

Joan was impressed at the combination of necessity and

virtue this alliance presented. 'What happened, then? What upset the apple cart?'

'Well, they continued to speak German and to conduct services in German which gradually developed into a kind of dialect – I think it's like Plattdeutsch, or an Americanized version of it.' At Joan's questioning look, she explained, 'The reason I know this is because we had to learn it in school, in catechism mainly, and I had to study the language even though no one in my family speaks it much anymore, except my parents when they want to hide something from us kids. Anyhow, the Presbyterians hadn't arrived yet, you know the bankers and merchants, when the great eruption happened, and like most eruptions it began in a kind of mild way.'

AnnaLisa's narrative then described how a very rich farmer named Otto Fingster came to church one Sunday with his wife and six sons, and during the long Lutheran service – at that time they were often over three hours long – one of the sons, perhaps the youngest who was no more than a year old, began to get restless and started to cry. At first the pastor ignored the baby's lament, but as the wails increased in volume he became more and more distracted from his traditional Sunday tirade. (Later on, no one could explain his conduct, for certainly he was accustomed to squalling babies and nervous adults; perhaps he had felt that this particular Sunday his words were uniquely essential to the spiritual vitality of his parish. His motives remain a mystery, AnnaLisa claimed.)

Pastor Schneider, St. Paul's Lutheran first spiritual leader, became florid with rage. Slamming his massive German Bible onto the floor, he bellowed, 'Shut that baby up or leave!' Joan's friend swore that there were people in the church who actually heard the pastor's voice ascend from baritone to soprano.

Otto Fingster had then looked at his chastened wife and

six blond sons, all healthy products of this new American soil, and he grabbed the boys who were sitting next to him and shoved them out of the pew. His meek wife followed with the rest of the brood, a gaunt woman with engorged varicose veins that no thicknesses of woolen stockings would hide.

Unusual as Pastor Schneider's conduct was on that particular Sunday, no one thought that permanent damage had been done to St. Paul's parish, even when the Fingster family did not show up for services. 'I think everyone expected them to stay home and lick their wounds for a while,' AnnaLisa maintained. Some people regretted the pastor's outburst, but most felt that in time the Fingster family would either forget the offense or else start attending St. Gabriel's. The family farm was about three miles from the new village of New Bonn, and although this was not a large distance from the town, most farmers were self-reliant and did not often appear in town except for church or an occasional visit to the hardware store or the blacksmith's shop. Since there were no immediate neighbors to account for the family's movement and behavior, and because the incident in church was so transitory, the family so unremarkable, the entire brood was easily forgotten. 'Folks were busier then and had more on their minds than worrying about a farmer and his passle of kids,' Joan's friend remarked. 'Besides, there were better things to gossip about,' she added knowingly.

It took a full three years before the family was mentioned, and then only because someone commented that 'something funny' was going on at the Fingster place. Whoever reported this symptom could not describe it in detail because he had been shot at by what appeared to be a high-powered rifle when he had gotten out of his wagon to look, but he did see enough to notice a huge white building being constructed near the site of the barn, which itself appeared now to be torn down. Coinciding with this rumor, new faces began appearing in town, all of them men who looked as if they were related and who spoke the local German with just a shade more precision.

They would arrive in town in pairs or threesomes, always male, and they seemed to be buying farm implements and construction tools. Their purchases were always in cash, and they were usually friendly but aloof. They limited their conversations to the weather, a topic much respected by a community of taciturn people who frequently chose not to discuss their crops or their children. 'They weren't that much different from everybody else,' AnnaLisa said. 'Oh sure, their German was a little strange, but they looked all right and paid their bills, which was what everyone cared about the most, natch.' About three months after people began noticing this new crop of men, a notice was delivered by hand to all of the members of St. Paul's church. The notice was invariably delivered at dusk by a young man who was unusual only because he wore a felt hat instead of the regulation cloth billed cap that every farmer wore on weekdays. Once a young boy of about ten delivered a notice, but he was as close-mouthed as the older messengers, limiting his remarks to the weather and stating a desire that each member of the family please carefully read the notice. Written in elegant-looking Gothic script (but grammatically almost illiterate), the notice announced the erection of a new Lutheran church, located on the property of Otto Fingster, and all were invited to attend services, which would begin at exactly 9 a.m. next Sunday.

The attendance at St. Paul's the following Sunday was pathetic, for most of the parish traveled to the Fingster farm to see for themselves this personal affront to accepted authority. Nor were they disappointed. Although most went out of horrified curiosity, no one felt cheated, for Otto Fingster, with the help of one dozen German immigrant families, had erected a church on the grand scale. Some said it was modeled on the magnificent cathedral at Cologne; at least it gave that impression to a few.

The steeple was a full forty feet tall and contained a bell that had been personally delivered by Otto's cousin from Asselbach. It had been forged and hammered, and then inscribed, by another cousin from Bremen. The bell bore the inscription 'God Is All' (in German, of course) and had angels of silver embossed all around its circumference. The altar had been constructed in Germany, too, out of the thickest of ash, and the altar cloth was of such deep purple velvet that it looked as if it belonged in the castle of some Rhenish prince. The pews matched the wood of the altar, and although there was no organ there was a Bechstein piano that had accompanied the bell on its steerage-class voyage.

But the most impressive contribution to this instant parish was its pastor, the Reverend Schoonmacher, a man of at least sixty-five, who spoke the kind of German that only the oldest of New Bonn natives remembered, a colloquial, metaphoric German that evoked immediate memories of paternal villages and churches that most people thought they had forgotten. This man was assumed to be related to Otto Fingster, but he quickly announced his true heritage by informing the congregation that he had learned of this promised land and had wanted to partake just a bit of it before he was summoned by that great and just God who had personally supervised the erection of this marvelous new church.

'*Ich bin auf Hamburg*,' he proclaimed, and there was an audible murmur of approval throughout the crowded new building that seemed to reverberate and echo its own approval.

'*Ich bin auf Hamburg*,' he repeated, and then continued, in his avuncular German, 'and I consider it an act of God, a miracle, that I have come here to live out the rest of my days in these marvelous fields. I came here not because my kin – my brothers and sisters – sent for me, but because I felt a strong desire in my heart of hearts to travel to America and be with those brethren whose bodies crossed the waters but who had left their spirits with me. I am here now to reunite body and spirit, and I do so in this first sacrament of communion in our magnificent new church.

'Let this, then, be an occasion of great joy for all of us,' he concluded. 'And let me say that this is the happiest occasion of my life, which I now share with you to make it your own most joyous of days.'

The gawkers, as well as the merely curious, were immediately converted to Otto Fingster's version of Fatherland, with those who had participated in the first sacraments that Sunday remaining to form the nucleus of the Fingster church. Of the original St. Paulites, fewer than a third returned to the fold, which left the growing village of New Bonn with two Lutheran churches within a three-mile radius. The loyal St. Paulites – the First Lutherans as they were sometimes called – remained in their original parish mostly because of consanguinity – both the Reverend and Mrs. Schneider had an abundance of cousins – although there were a few non-relatives who were intimidated by the fruity tones of the Fingster pastor's German. Those remaining few also felt that there was too much 'old country' and not enough of the advantages of America in the manner and authority of the old German pastor at the Fingster church.

The congregation of St. Paul's became so pathetically decimated that the empty pews and thin sounds of the hymn singing embarrassed the faithful, yet it took almost a year for the elders to devise a counterattack. This plan was so ingenuous and obvious that after it was enacted everyone wanted to claim credit for its success. First there was an announcement, a cryptic notice that did not attempt to compete with the Fingster Lutheran's Gothic elegance, that stated the availability of Sunday school, every Sunday, completely independent of the biweekly catechism classes that were offered after services. This meant that adults were free to engage in two or three hours of Sunday piety, uninterrupted by the demands of their children. The success was immediate; families returned for perfectly sound reasons that did not violate their sense of honor or their allegiance to their heritage, for they were attending to their children's spiritual growth in ways that no institution in New Bonn had previously provided. The success was so great that within a few years the original St. Paul's was torn down and replaced by its present structure, a large limestone building with a tall steeple that displays a copper-colored cross.

Adjacent to the church, in the same block, a full-sized school, capable of educating and preparing children through the eighth grade in German, was constructed.

The Fingster church, after its initial burst of glory, dwindled away. After the old minister died there were problems replacing him because of the unofficial nature of the church itself, for it belonged to no synod and had never received bishopric sanctions. Technically it wasn't even a church, for it had never been officially recognized, but despite its lack of institutional endowments it continued to oblige those few who cared little for American refinements. Perhaps its continuation lay in those original Fingster brats who had so fortuitously been led away by their intransigent father, for all six sons married comely farm girls who generously reproduced until the church became full of Fingster heirs-apparent. They multiplied energetically, and eventually came to be known as the Fingsterites.

To the Fingsterites, unaffiliated with any of the Lutheran synods, the credentials of their ministers were of little importance. There was an informal arrangement that one of the smarter sons – and one least adept at farming – would go to a non-credentialed Lutheran college and take just enough courses to keep the congregation informed of liturgical changes. This endeavor usually took less than a year. One semester was the average stint for the minister-to-be, and one year there were as many as three Fingster sons enrolled at the same Iowa institution.

By the time Joan arrived in New Bonn the legend of the Fingster schism had lost its interest and appeal, which was the major reason she had such trouble tracing the path of her original query. The former renegades were now considered merely a close-knit clan of rural eccentrics. She was warned, though, that she should not ride her horse near the church property unless she wanted to be shot at, so their reputation was not completely harmless. None of the Fingsterites attended schools, and none of the series of county truant officers had tried very hard to persuade them of the values of education. They were prosperous, though, and had managed to form themselves into a township, which entitled them to material improvements like regular road maintenance and electricity.

AnnaLisa's grandparents had been among the original St. Paul loyalists, which meant that her knowledge of the schism was thorough as well as colorful. She enjoyed recounting the origins and histories of the first families, and she even referred Joan to other people who, she insisted, would be more than willing to give their own impressions of the events. Yet her explanation of the hymn's taboo sounded extremely illogical to Joan. 'Don't you see? That hymn would only bring back bad memories. Feelings that people have tried to forget.'

Joan was puzzled and tried hard to accept her friend's logic.

'Do they feel ashamed, then, for having one of their

pastors starting such a mess?'

AnnaLisa considered for a moment the ideas of shame and responsibility. 'No, I don't think so. But people like to think they have made something of themselves, and this hymn only reminds them of how German they really are.'

'Doesn't anyone play it ever, not even on special occasions like Martin Luther's birthday?' Joan hated the idea of unsung music.

'No, and don't you try it, either. It would be a disgrace to remind people of something they've tried to forget. Even Presbyterians.' AnnaLisa looked grim, her tone menacing. 'Look. The Presbyterians may or may not be Germans, but there are a lot of them who are related to people who are, and it would get back to them, and then there would be hell to pay.'

Joan accepted this threat as sound advice. She had no desire to witness any version of a New Bonn or German hell, and she did respect her friend's historical accuracy, crazy as its underlying logic might be. To Joan, AnnaLisa seemed about as un-German as a person could be; she didn't speak the language and she refused to admit an understanding of it despite her parents' use at home. Joan also sensed some sinister implications in AnnaLisa's threat, for what she told Joan suggested that the town had still not achieved stability and peace. Instead, it looked as if a new rebellion were possible, one more far-reaching, for now there were Presbyterians to enlist and take positions.

Joan stuck to her Bach renditions of chorales that contained only laments and ministrations of suffering. 'Oh Sacred Head Now Wounded' was her favorite, whereas the congregation appeared to prefer the theme and variations on 'Jesu, Joy of Man's Desiring'. It pleased Joan to feel that whenever she played the harmless Bach she was contributing, in a modest way, to the uneasy truce of the community.

Chapter Seven

Wedding Dance

Linda, the hired girl whom the Nelson family employed, was only three years older than Joan. She was a cheerful farm girl who had seven brothers and three sisters. One of the sisters had gone to beauticians' school after she had saved enough from her maid's wages, and another was allowed to remain in high school because she was considered the family brain. Linda's goal was to emulate her beautician-sister, and her name was one that she had recently chosen for herself. Baptized and called Mary Margaret, she considered the name Linda more appropriate to her prospective vocation than Mary Margaret, a double saints' name she thought awkward – 'a mouthful' was her description – but that she retained until she had gotten a job and had moved to town.

Unlike the Nelson's Minneapolis maids, she tended to neglect her servant's training by doing such irritating things as setting the table in the kitchen. Mrs. Nelson attempted to gently reprove Linda for her carelessness, but her words must have lacked authority, for Linda could never be convinced of Mrs. Nelson's convictions that dining rooms were designed for consumption of ordinary meals, including breakfasts. She continued to repeat her mistakes until Joan wondered if Linda might, perhaps, be playing some kind of game with her employer.

Most people refused to accept Linda's new name and

persisted in calling her Mary Margaret. Of course Linda knew that her own parents would never come around – they would stretch out every syllable until the day they died, she often remarked to Joan – but Joan felt that her own mother should be more generous in recognizing Linda's attempts at independence and should be regarded with a consistent 'Linda' rather than an occasional one.

Joan was fascinated by Linda's insouciance. Physically she was rather uninteresting; she had a bony face and long, strong legs, but no tits at all, and her hair was thin and wispy. 'A hell of a beautician she'll make,' Joan's father one day observed, much to Joan's amusement. Joan imagined Linda as more the professional waitress type, definitely not the housewifely kind. She seemed to have no family feelings at all, for when she spoke of her younger brothers and sisters it usually involved some kind of denigrating comment about their work habits. To her they were all irredeemably lazy, which included her own father as well. Joan had never heard her speak warmly about any member of her family, and although she occasionally thought it fun to have a lot of brothers and sisters, she did sympathize with Linda, since she appeared to have been on her own practically since her conception.

At Locksley Hall Linda slept in the bedroom directly over the kitchen, but she did not spend time in her room as had the Minneapolis servants. Instead, she liked to sit in the kitchen, near the table, listening to the radio and sewing flouncy, gauzy dresses that she wore to Saturday-night dances. Linda felt the greatest contempt for the feed-sack dresses that were standard attire among the farm women, and she spent most of her first wage on the flowered print materials that were always on special at Gertie's Gown Shop. Joan thought the prints were atrocious and no real improvement upon the more subdued designs of the feed sacks, although the splashy flowers did display animated colors, and the texture was finer and softer than the muslin sacks. Linda smoked, too, which Joan's mother considered rude since Linda had never attempted to secure her approval or permission to smoke in the house.

Joan speculated a lot about Linda's sex life. She knew that she succeeded in picking up a man whenever she attended a dance, even though no one ever called her for a regular date. Sometimes Linda came home at three or four in the morning, and Joan would wake up to rustling and giggling noises that sounded like unconvincing protests. The Nelsons were aware that their hired girl did not keep respectable hours, but Mr. Nelson would not allow his wife to scold her. 'It's really none of our business how late she stays out. We are not responsible for her after hours.'

'But she stays out half the night,' Mrs. Nelson protested.

'Let her. It doesn't make any difference how late she stays out as long as she gets her work done.'

Joan admired her father's practical application of the laissez-faire principle, and resolved to use it herself when the occasion arrived.

Joan and Linda didn't talk much to each other, mostly because Linda wanted to talk about movies and fashions while Joan preferred to gossip, and Linda was too close-mouthed and stingy with information of any kind, even though she had relatives all over the county and could have been a veritable fount of scandal. Linda puzzled Joan; she could never quite make her out. She knew she wasn't pious – although she faithfully attended Mass – for she made no display of her religion; her room lacked even the regulation crucifix and Sacred Heart. She was interested in clothes, but that didn't explain her lack of gregariousness, which Joan considered abnormal in a female. Joan finally decided that Linda must be a sex machine and simply clammed up about almost every topic for private reasons. (Joan learned that uncharitable term at the beginning of her sophomore year in high school – this year – when she discovered that girls were identified as either virgins or sex machines.)

On Saturday in the late fall there was a wedding dance at the town hall that celebrated the union of two renowned farm families. The son and daughter of two equally land-hungry farmers were formally united, and they had publicly invited, by means of an announcement in the weekly newspaper, the entire community to share their mutual good fortune. Wedding dances had long been established in New Bonn and were embedded in the rural domain, where they had originally been held in someone's barn. Only later had the locations been moved to town, perhaps because of fire dangers. A common ground at least kept them safer, less at the mercy of sleepy fire department volunteers. In New Bonn the common ground was the community hall, a frame building resembling a roller rink, with outside privies. To the town people, wedding dances were considered strictly rural celebrations, and not even quaintly so. In fact, they were to be avoided 'like the plague', Joan's mother had asserted, a statement that echoed the sentiment of almost every anxious village mother.

This wedding dance was an exception, however, for the farmers were rich enough to be more than respectable; for example, the groom's father owned two buildings on Main Street. There were always bands of a sort at wedding dances, usually amateur fiddlers and drummers from adjacent farms who played for pleasure and free booze, but this wedding dance promised the well-known and expensive Six Fat Dutchmen, a group of Bavarians who played and sang impeccably in two languages. Often the wedding dances would last all night. The bride and groom, after swirling around the floor in full regalia for the first few dances, would leave for their honeymoon – most often at the Twin Cities – which left the rest of the crowd to continue dancing while openly flaunting the sin of public drunkenness. There was usually a fight or two, harmless skirmishes that attracted crowds but provided little physical injury, for drunken adversaries are rarely effective, regardless of the vigor of their motives. Someone usually puked in the street, and after a while the men did not bother waiting in line at the crowded privies; instead they peed in doorways or in the street, or alongside a conveniently parked car.

It was for these vulgar acts that Joan and her village counterparts were prohibited from attending any kind of wedding dance, and ordinarily Joan would not have been disappointed at being denied the privileges of an observer given her contempt for rural rituals of any kind, especially those that used music. Nothing offended Joan's musical sensibilities more than the 'oompah oompah' sounds of the tuba, which she felt precisely duplicated juicy bathtub farts, and the monotonous bass drum with its two-beat plonking rhythm, as accompaniment to the folksy wanderings of the trumpets and trombones sounded to her simpleminded to the point of idiocy.

There was a reason she wanted to look at this dance, though, although she had no intentions of actually attending it. Linda had been working on a dress for two weeks, carefully preparing herself for the event, and she had shown the dress to Joan, a lavender organdy affair with long, ruffled sleeves and a contrasting mauve sash that tied in the back, giving her butt the appearance of a recently sprouted hump. Also Linda had hinted that she was having a genuine date for this dance, and she had made many phone calls, which Joan had overheard, to discuss the evening's plans. Joan thought this occasion might afford a test of her sex-machine theory, and she desperately tried to think of an approach that could secure her parents' permission to look in at the dance, but not to attend, a delicate distinction that she was afraid they would neither understand nor respect.

Her attempts to exonerate the Six Fat Dutchmen from her earlier contempt sounded lame. Rube music was a strain she had always ridiculed, so now her change in position fooled no one.

'Why do you want to hear something now that you've always hated?' her father asked her.

'Well, people can change, can't they? I mean you're always saying there has to be some good in everyone.' (Actually, these words were her mother's, but she didn't think he would object to their association with him.)

'I'm not talking about everyone, I'm talking about music you have never liked and have always ridiculed. And please don't try to persuade me that you've suddenly become interested in farmers at this late date.'

Her father's mention of farmers inspired Joan with what she saw as the perfect solution. 'Why don't you come with me, Daddy, and that way you can talk to your farming friends and protect me as well?'

Her father beamed at her with amusement and pride. 'How smart of you, my sweet, to come up with the perfect answer. How can I resist such brains and cleverness?'

Although he was being sarcastic, his pleasure was genuine at having been included in his daughter's scheme, and though this solution was by no means ideal – going to a dance, even just to look, was not the best way to go – it was still preferable to not going at all, and Joan was still too young and too untested to be able to sneak off by herself – that kind of duplicity would come later.

If Linda had a genuine date for the dance, he was not visible at Locksley Hall at 7 p.m., for at that time she drove off with two of her brothers in their pickup truck at precisely that hour, one hour before the dance was scheduled to begin. Joan thought Linda looked more like an oversized Easter bunny than a girl launching out for an important evening, sandwiched as she was between her two brothers on the front seat of the truck. The brothers looked handsome, though, and not too farmerish. They both had on dark suits, and their white shirts and dark ties contrasted nicely with their tanned faces and hands. Karl, who was either the second oldest or the oldest – Joan couldn't keep them straight and doubted that Linda could either – saw Mr. Nelson at the kitchen window and not only waved from the pickup but got out of it and came to the door to shake hands.

Mr. Nelson greeted him. 'Going to the dance, I see. It should be a corker. My daughter and I plan to take it in ourselves.'

If Karl was surprised at this announcement, he did not reveal it. Instead, he smiled and said, with detectable measures of warmth, 'Hey, that's great, Mr. Nelson. Is Mrs. Nelson coming, too?'

'I'm afraid not. She doesn't care much for dancing or crowds.'

Joan recognized this lie as a deception designed to protect Karl's feelings as well as those of his friends and family, since Joan's mother actually loved to dance and was surprisingly good at it, but there had been little occasion for dancing since their move to New Bonn. As for crowds, Joan remembered that of all the people she had known, her mother seemed least threatened by Minneapolis rush-hour traffic, holiday airports and railroad stations, and rowdy mobs at university football games.

Joan felt a stab of uneasiness at going off and leaving her mother at home by herself. 'Do you really want to do this, Daddy? Maybe it will be too crowded.'

'Nonsense. It was your idea, wasn't it? You're not going to back out now at this late hour, are you? Anyhow, it won't get too crowded until late, way after we've left.'

Joan wondered for a minute who was using whom. The situation seemed to have become reversed, but it was too late now to back out gracefully, and it had been her idea. She wondered also if there might be the equivalent of a Peacock Lady in her father's own life, someone who could turn up at this dance by coincidence. Horrified at her nasty private thoughts, she immediately put them out of her mind.

Although Joan and her father arrived at Main Street well before eight o'clock, there was no place to park. The street was full of sedans, pickup trucks, and the occasional half-ton truck, which forced Joan and her father to park two blocks from Main Street. This dance suggested a banner event judging from the magnitude of vehicles assembled. 'Wow, this is almost like Memorial Day, or Turkey Day,' Joan remarked to her father. (Memorial Day produced a parade every year as well as a community celebration sponsored by the American Legion. Turkey Day was responsible for the inaccurate label New Bonn had acquired as being Turkey Capitol of the World. The celebrants included the high school band, led by a drum major sporting modified Pilgrim's clothes, and an enormous multitude of farmers who chose the occasion to display their new tractors and combines. Unlike any other parade that Joan had attended or participated in, there were no horses, only turkeys, the sole creature represented. Each year the farm machinery consumed more and more of the parade whereas the number of turkeys diminished. No one liked these turkeys, including their owners, but they were profitable birds – if they managed to live to maturity – and those farmers who had taken so many risks in raising them to maturity saw them through their ritual maturation on Turkey Day.)

The community hall was packed with people waiting for the wedding party to arrive, and the band was already on stage, tuning up and tootling their rehearsal melodies. The band members looked stunning. Each musician wore forest-green lederhosen and a contrasting Alpine hat, each with a pheasant feather stuck in its brim. Their white shirts were embroidered with flowers, edelweiss and mountain lupin, perhaps, and around their necks they flourished brilliant, scarlet scarves. Though not exactly dignified, they didn't look like clowns either, and apparently they were well known to some in the audience, for they were chatting in German with a few older men who seemed to be in high spirits as they passed around their pints of whiskey while going through the motions of trying to persuade the band to begin playing before the arrival of the wedding party. (Later Joan was to remember the unique orderliness of this crowd. Unlike other waiting audiences she later encountered, this audience bore its period of waiting with patience and without the customary restive wandering that characterizes audiences who aren't sure about the performers' reliability.)

Joan recognized no one in the crowd other than a number of farmers she had occasionally seen with her father. She was still peering around, trying to get a look at Linda, who must have been lost among the hundreds of patient people, when the wedding party entered. The band struck up 'Here Comes the Bride!' and the crowd let out a roar that made Joan's flesh tingle.

The bride, one of those buxom farm girls who resembles a plump version of a Rhineland travel poster, picked up her satin train with one hand, handed her bouquet to a grinning older woman (surely her mother), and clasped her new husband's arm. The groom grinned at her with such unmistakable pride that the audience responded with a second, louder roar. The pair proceeded to the middle of the dance floor and waited until the song ended; with its conclusion they smiled at the audience and kissed. Their kiss then signaled a subsequent action that Joan was not prepared for: money, in the form of quarters, half-dollars, and bills weighted down by paper clips, nails, and even wads of chewing gum, began to fly at the couple, who continued to stand full center amidst the deluge.

The storm of money must have lasted for two or three minutes, which gave Joan the opportunity to look around the audience. She noticed that her father removed from the breast pocket of his suit a five-dollar bill which had been folded into a silver money clip in the shape of a horseshoe. The uproar, the continuous shouting of the crowd, made it possible for Joan to ask her father about this unusual procedure without being overheard. 'Do they always do this? Don't they give presents like everybody else?'

'Of course they do, but this is just like throwing rice, which they already did at the church. This time it's more fun because it lasts longer and you can do something with it.'

When the crowd finally stopped yelling and quit tossing coins and bills, the woman who had taken the bride's bonnet nudged a little boy of about ten onto the floor. With his broom and dustpan, which someone had thoughtfully adorned with a white satin bow, he swept up the loot with amazing speed. Evidently this little boy had been in the wedding party, for he had on a blue suit and wore a white flower in his buttonhole. Joan thought he looked like a miniature groom, or maybe Tom Thumb. The crowd seemed to enjoy his antics with the broom almost as much as they had enjoyed showering the wedding pair, for they cheered every swoop of his festooned broom as if he were a magician performing wondrous tricks with a magic wand.

'Do they ever throw anything else?' Joan had seen her share of slapstick movies and could imagine pies or old shoes.

'They used to sometimes toss out baby clothes – bottles and stuff like that – but I haven't seen anyone doing that for a long time.' Mr. Nelson was obviously prepared for this occasion, which annoyed Joan that he had neglected to tell her what to expect, forcing her to ask questions about procedures everyone else knew.

'Do they need all the money or do they use some of it for bills, like paying the band?' The Six Fat Dutchmen were not cheap and she was curious about their financing.

'Of course they keep it. They put it into a special account that the bank has already set up for them. If they are careful and mind about their expenses, they'll keep adding to it.'

This mundane outlet for the shiny loot that had just been so ceremoniously collected seemed anticlimactic to Joan. 'I wouldn't put all of it in the bank,' she observed. 'I'd spend it on a honeymoon or a long trip. I wouldn't just deposit it in a bank without spending some of it, anyhow.'

'It's really not your concern, is it? You're hardly in a position to decide how you are going to spend your wedding money.'

Mr. Nelson was clearly irritated by his daughter's questions. 'Since you don't know what's going on, why don't you just keep quiet for a while?'

Joan recognized his irritation and accepted it as legitimate; nevertheless she was hurt at this curt dismissal of her opinions, for she knew that although they were not exactly informed or sophisticated, they still belonged to her, his daughter, and not to some upstart girl asking questions merely to hear the sound of her own voice.

When the band began its first song, the bride and groom danced alone around the periphery of the floor until they signaled to the rest of the wedding party to join them, so suddenly there were sixteen people dancing. On this chilly October evening they looked like an incongruous spring bouquet with the women attendants in their yellow, blue, and pink organdy dresses. Only the men, in their dark suits, seemed appropriate to the season. Joan was relieved that none of the women had on lavender; she was afraid that Linda might be outclassed, but now it didn't seem to matter since Linda was nowhere in sight. She did spot both of her brothers, though, who waved at her from the crowd of young men they were standing with. Joan was tempted to ask one of them where Linda was, but she decided they were their sister's source of transportation, not her chaperons.

After the first set of tunes there was a pause, and then the groom took the stage and announced his gratitude for the wonderful turnout and for everyone's kindness to his bride and himself. 'Now, everyone dance!' he concluded. There was an immediate rush to the dance floor and the band began a livelier tune than those the wedding party had danced to. Her father dutifully asked Joan if she wanted to dance.

'Of course not. I can't dance to this kind of music.'

This statement was true, for Joan really couldn't dance to polkas, schottisches, waltzes, or two-step variants. Her knowledge of folk-dancing began and ended with the Virginia Reel, a dance she had learned as a Brownie Scout in Minneapolis.

'Well, do you mind if I do, then?' Joan was surprised that her father would have any desire to participate in this kind of musical atrocity. She also didn't want to be left standing by herself, and she wondered who her father had in mind as a partner, but she felt obliged to concede to his request. She stood by one of the chairs that lined the walls, feeling less like a wallflower than an inexperienced novice who was being denied entrance to an unusual rite. Not that she wanted to be admitted, but she did wish she had a choice. She spotted AnnaLisa's older brother, Walter, a young man of twenty who was as firmly Lutheran as his sister.

'What are you doing here?' she asked, a question she

knew was more rhetorical than actual.

He looked as if she had spoken to the wrong person. 'I'm old enough, aren't I? I don't need a permit to get out of the house after dark.'

'I mean, you're not supposed to be dancing, are you?'

'This is not the kind of dancing we aren't supposed to do. This is folk-dancing, dumbhead.'

Joan noticed a bulge in his jacket pocket that could only contain a pint of whiskey. She looked at the other men around him and observed that these bulges were as standard to their clothes as the suits and ties that belonged to the occasion. To her horror, Walter reached into his pocket, pulled out the bottle, which was protected by a brown paper bag, and offered her a swig.

She longed to say, 'Don't mind if I do,' but the idea of sharing with the crude brother of her friend restrained her. 'No thanks. I'm with my dad and he wouldn't like it. In fact, he'd raise hell.'

She wondered where her father had gone. She couldn't see him among the hundreds of people dancing, and she was still concerned about his choice of a partner.

'I know you're with your old man. I saw you come in. Go ahead, have a quick one. He's dancing out there in the middle of the floor and can't see you.'

Joan wondered why Walter, who never paid any attention to her, nor to any girl under eighteen, was suddenly so solicitous about her pleasure and safety. 'Okay, but just a little one.' She had never tasted whiskey straight; in fact, she had only tasted it in the well-iced ginger ale highballs that she sometimes surreptitiously sipped from her parents' drinks.

She took the proffered bottle and stuck her tongue in its hole so that she got only a trickle, but it was enough to make her immediately gag and cough. The tears came to her eyes and her gut heaved convulsively. Walter burst into laughter that sounded rawer and more malicious than anything Joan had ever heard. He grabbed the bottle and walked away, chortling with lewd satisfaction. Mortified, Joan remained by the chair, fervently hoping that no one else had witnessed her conduct.

Joan finally spotted her father on the dance floor, dancing with the wife of a farmer whose dinners she had sometimes eaten. Usually a tired-looking woman with the typical farm women's varicose veins and ill-fitting house dress, tonight she appeared animated. The feed sack had been replaced by a gown of velvet the color of the band's lederhosen. Her hair was pinned up on her head, resembling a coronet of squirrel tails, and her protruding veins were concealed by russet-colored nylon stockings. She also wore a gold chain around one ankle, a sporty touch that Joan admired. She seemed to be enjoying herself because she was laughing and talking at the same time, action completely unfamiliar to Joan who was accustomed to taciturn farm wives who spoke only when they were spoken to, like good children. When the music stopped, Mr. Nelson did not return to his daughter. Instead, he remained on the dance floor, ready to resume dancing with this transformed farm wife. Not exactly a Cinderella, Joan thought, but she could easily be model for the 'after' part in a 'before/after' ad for some beauty course or fashion makeover.

Joan needed to go to the bathroom, which, she remembered as she was heading toward the restroom sign, was actually an outdoor privy courteously placed thirty feet from the rear entrance of the hall. The line outside was impossibly long, and Joan, whose bladder tended to correspond to her anxiety, felt desperate. She decided to walk behind Main Street to a corner house that she knew was fairly safe because of its extensive, unpruned shrubbery, a barbary hedge that extended the three sides of the lot. Nicely concealed, she was squatting on the grass when she discovered a purple satin ribbon, a ribbon that could only be Linda's since she recognized its filigreed borders that matched the bodice trim on Linda's lavender dress. She was pleased at discovering it, for now she had an excuse to seriously search for Linda. The ribbon, she knew, was indispensable to the harmony of her outfit.

When Joan heard the crack of a twig, she looked over the hedge at the prospect of a lavender circle spread out beneath a deciduous oak that was all but barren of leaves. On top of this circle was a man, lying face down, who seemed to be heaving himself up and down, and was doing so with great difficulty, for his hands kept slipping on the grass and his shoes slid back and forth, creating tiny furrows in the ground, like two miniature plows harrowing tillable land. Joan could see Linda's face. Her eyes were shut, almost as if she were asleep, but her legs were spread out like the lower branches of the tree, and her underpants had evidently been tossed by this heaving mound of a man, for they rested on a branch of the tree that was at least twelve feet from the ground.

Joan was both appalled and amazed. Linda looked so tranquil, almost as if she were taking a nap, with her arms at her sides and her fingers stretched out full length. In contrast to her, the man looked busy. Although he made no noise he kept frantically pumping up and down, but he didn't seem to be in a hurry. Since neither of them seemed concerned about being discovered, Joan felt she was safe, and although she knew she was witnessing a private act and had no business being there, she also felt that Linda's air of indifference represented a kind of permission to observe. She remained there for two or three minutes without seeing any variation of the thumping and pumping – Linda's eyes never once opened – before she noticed the three men standing about ten feet away from the pair, on the other side of the tree. They were saying nothing, and looked as patient as the earlier audience awaiting the arrival of the wedding party.

The man who had been injecting Linda with what he must have considered strong and powerful doses of his own masculinity suddenly quit. He made no noise in quitting; he simply stopped, got to his feet, dusted off his knees, and zipped up his fly. He didn't speak, either, not to Linda nor to the other men, one of whom had now detached himself from the rest and knelt down while unzipping his pants. Joan saw him remove his tumescent organ and she thought its pinkish color an amazing complement to the lavender of Linda's gown. Without a word he thrust it between Linda's outspread legs; she twitched slightly and flinched, but made no sound. The two remaining men continued to wait beside the tree, saying nothing. Joan recognized neither of them, and she wondered if they weren't bored standing there, having so long to wait for an act that appeared to consist mostly of drudgery.

The second man took less time than the first, and after he had finished Linda sat up, her eyes still closed, and spoke for the first time. 'What time is it? I have to get my ride at twelve.' She addressed no one in particular – she looked as if she might be talking to the tree – except that her eyes were closed and there was a slight tone of exasperation in her voice that suggested impatience.

'Don't worry. You've got plenty of time. It's only ten thirty.'

The man who had responded to her question took his place on the grass, and once again Linda lay back, but this time she brought her legs up to her chin.

Joan hurried away. The mention of time created in her a sense of urgency when she saw by her own watch that it was actually eleven thirty. Her father would be waiting for her, and it would be difficult to explain how she had spent the past half-hour or so.

It was only when Joan was returning to the dance hall that she remembered that Linda had not danced at all that evening, and undoubtedly she wouldn't. Joan threw the purple ribbon into a gutter where it landed next to a pile of empty whiskey bottles and cigarette butts. As she approached the building she could hear the Six Fat Dutchmen playing 'The Tennessee Waltz' as if it had been composed with them in mind, but that was one of their talents – they could take any piece and transform it into an oompah triumph.

Inside the hall people were openly and visibly drunk, and the noise was deafening. Couples were leaning against the bandstand and sitting on the chairs, kissing and hugging and giggling inanely. Walter had obviously emptied his bottle and the results showed. His face was splotchy and his eyes were glazed. He smiled stupidly and made no attempt to get out of people's way. One couple was dancing to the music – swaying, actually – the girl singing the lyrics to the song while her partner rested both hands on her broad rump. Mr. Nelson was standing in a corner talking to a farmer he knew, but he seemed relieved when his daughter walked up to him.

'Ready to go? Have you had enough?'

He didn't listen to her answer as he escorted her to the door through the crowds of people who politely made a gap for them to pass through. Fortunately their car was parked at the opposite end from Main Street, away from the hedged yard with the giant oak, and the only people they encountered on their walk to the car were families of tired, wailing children and women trying to persuade their reluctant spouses to hurry. A few of these squabblers greeted Mr. Nelson, but most were too preoccupied with their own bickering to notice Joan and her father.

'Did you have a good time, Joan?' Her father sounded

worried, as if he had taken on too much in escorting her to the dance.

'It was okay.'

She would have liked to question her father about the purpose of the whole thing. Other than an occasion to get drunk and look stupid, what was the point? Yet she knew this kind of question was likely to be misinterpreted, taken as a derogatory judgment upon farmers and that was not really what she had in mind. Farmers were part of it, of course, but what really bothered her was the purpose of the wedding, itself. Was that wealthy farm girl who had found an equally wealthy husband going to spend the rest of her life with him on the top, heaving and pumping? Was she going to lie beneath him with her eyes shut, with smiles only for the people she met in public? Of course Joan knew what she had previously assumed: that Linda was a sex machine, and she was not so naïve to assume that ordinary sex involved a line of extra men.

But if it gave so little pleasure, what was the great fuss all about? She thought she hadn't learned very much from the wedding dance. No answers, and now a whole new set of questions, other than that her suspicions about Linda had been proven.

Yet for many years she dreamt, with disturbing regularity, about a lavender circle, amorphous in the moonlight, and a pair of nylon panties swinging from the topmost branch of a giant oak tree.

Chapter Eight

Courtships

Evidently Joan's parents were aware of Linda's reputation as a sex machine, for one morning, when Joan had stayed home from school with vague flu-like symptoms, Mrs. Nelson came into her bedroom on the flimsy pretext of checking her temperature. Joan had immediately spotted this phoniness since not an hour earlier she had argued with her mother about missing school and the necessity for regular attendance. Now her mother sat on the bed as if she was settling in for one of those cozy mother-daughter chats that magazines for growing girls recommend.

'I wish you'd tell me when there's something wrong.'

Joan sensed the question underlying this request, but she was damned if she'd acknowledge it. 'I've already told you. My throat is scratchy and my head aches. I think I'm getting the flu.'

'Yes, I know. But that's not what I mean, exactly. I mean, I wish you'd tell me if there's something wrong around the house.'

Now she was getting warmer. Joan felt obliged to string along, not only to bide time, but to try to find out how much her mother knew. 'What do you mean, "around the house"? Everything's okay.'

'Does Mary Margaret talk to you much?' Clearly her mother was becoming uncomfortable.

'Talk to me about what? And I wish you'd call her Linda

like she wants.'

'Does she talk to you about her dates?'

Mrs. Nelson stumbled over the word 'dates' as if it were a forbidden term.

'She doesn't have dates as far as I know. I mean no one ever comes to the house to pick her up. At least I haven't seen anyone, have you?'

Mrs. Nelson, although a genteel woman, was not a dumb woman, and she knew enough about her daughter to recognize coyness and evasion. 'You know what I mean,' she said slowly. 'Does she ever talk to you about the boys – ah, the men – she goes with?'

'No, she never mentions them to me, but then she never talks to me much. Why? Has she done something wrong?' This loaded question caused Mrs. Nelson to make a face that resembled a caricature of disgust.

'I don't know if she's done anything wrong but there's a lot of talk about her around town.'

So Linda's lovers were not restricted to farm lads – she had crossed the barrier between town and the land! Joan wondered if she should stall around some more and then sensed a convenient alternative in a generalized, high-minded denunciation of idle talk. 'What have you heard? You know there are a lot of people in this town who do nothing but gossip, and nothing they say is true.'

'I've heard enough to know that she is not a *nice* girl.' There was no mistaking Mrs. Nelson's equation of 'nice' and sexual conduct.

Joan wanted to steer her mother away from the topic of sex, especially as it related to Linda, since Joan felt uneasy about Linda's conduct. Seeing her in action that night had made Joan feel that she had become part of a conspiracy, although she was by no means sure why she felt that way, let alone what her role in its design amounted to. Why did she feel guilty? She wished she knew, or at least could forget the question. 'She doesn't drink, does she?'

'I don't know if she drinks. That's not what people are talking about.'

'What are they talking about, then?'

'People are saying that she goes with men all over town and does things with them that no one should ever do unless they're married.'

Mrs. Nelson's accusations were painfully uttered, for her face turned pale, making her features more pronounced. Joan would have liked to summon the sanctioned village whores who played married games with impunity, but she knew that pointing out this accepted hypocrisy would only make matters worse for Linda.

'Well, what if she does. I mean, I haven't heard anything about it, and I'm sure I would if it were true. I can't see what difference it makes, after all. It's really her business, isn't it?' Joan was not sure about whose business it was, but she felt that there was something obscene about discussing a person who was not around to defend herself, someone who was not even a friend or a relative, only a servant who attended to meals and housework and did the grubby things that no one else wanted to do but that had to be done. Joan admired Linda's lack of domestic discrimination: she approached cleaning toilets or emptying mouse traps in the same way she approached the construction of a Sunday dinner, and she did as she was instructed without complaining about menus or plumbing or unseemly chores.

Mrs. Nelson appeared to have recovered from her earlier uneasiness, for she plunged ahead with a firm tone. 'If she is the kind of girl that people say she is, she can't stay here. We are, after all, responsible for her while she is under our roof in the same way that we are responsible for you.'

Joan knew that the responsibility for Linda that her mother claimed was really badly disguised bullshit, for her mother had spoken to Linda's parents only once, and that was after she had been interviewed for the job and the Nelsons needed parental approval, or at least they thought they needed it to satisfy some long-established custom, for Linda had already been hired and had agreed to work that same day. 'Are you going to fire her just because of what you've heard? Don't you think you need a little more evidence, some kind of proof?'

'Of course not. I don't need proof. I can fire her because she's sloppy and lazy and doesn't get things done on time, and she resents my directions and won't listen to my suggestions to improve herself.'

For a minute Joan wasn't sure that her mother wasn't referring to her own daughter, for who else fitted better her mother's formula for dismissal: sloppy, lazy, and a procrastinator – Joan was certainly all of these – and her capacity for self-improvement had been rapidly shrinking. 'I hope not. I hope you won't fire her. I really think she means well but hasn't had much of a chance. You know, that farm and all those kids at home and no school.'

Joan could tell by her mother's pursed lips how lame her excuses for Linda were received. 'Everyone is responsible for how they act,' her mother declared. 'No one can excuse disgusting behavior just because a person happens to be poor or uneducated or has too much work to do at home.'

Joan was familiar with this kind of high-minded analysis, yet she wondered if her mother had ever applied it to the conduct of her own father, Dr. Clifton. She was tempted to counter her mother's judgments with a reference to her grandfather, but she held back, knowing that her mother could easily redirect her accusations of laziness and slovenliness at her. As if her thoughts were being read, her mother stated, 'And by the way, a little bit of work at home is what you need right now yourself. You never do anything around here. You don't even make your own bed unless I'm here to remind you.'

Mrs. Nelson left the room, her feathers obviously ruffled. Joan sighed; her throat did feel sore and her muscles were beginning to ache. She hadn't meant to defend Linda so strenuously, but she felt that her mother had forced her into a position of strange alliances.

Mrs. Nelson did not have to fire Linda. Instead, one evening just a few days after the mother-daughter altercation regarding Linda's scarlet reputation, Linda announced, while she was washing the evening dishes (Mrs. Nelson could never adjust to 'supper' for 'dinner', and Linda was equally reluctant to alter her own vocabulary, so 'evening meal' became their compromising term) that she was going to get married and would be leaving next week.

'Mary Margaret, that's wonderful,' Mrs. Nelson trilled. 'And who is the lucky young man?'

'I don't think you know him. He's not from around here. His name is Joe Schultz and he has a farm near Chandler.' Linda stated this information as if she were about to embark on another business venture, Joan thought. Perhaps as a waitress this time instead of a maid.

'No, I don't know him,' Joan's mother remarked, 'but I'm sure Bert has heard of the family. I wish he were here now to share the good news. Have you set the date yet?'

Joan looked for a ring on Linda's appropriate finger, but her hands were plunged in the dishwater. She also looked at places beside the sink that might contain a ring but she could see nothing.

'We don't know exactly when it will be yet, but some time after corn-picking.'

Joan could tell by the look on her mother's face that the unasked question had already been answered. After corn-picking meant at least another month, which meant that Linda was not pregnant.

'Well, I'm happy for you. We'll miss you, too, but that

can't be helped. We always knew you couldn't stay with us forever.' It was as true of New Bonn as it was of Minneapolis: servants never stayed. At most they spent two or three years with a family before they left to marry, and rarely did they return after marriage, for they settled immediately into their own households, like ordinary nesting birds who adapt and build wherever a location looks possible.

Joan finally asked her question without looking at her mother. 'Why are you leaving next week when you won't be married for at least a month, probably longer?'

Linda looked at Joan with undisguised contempt. 'I want to spend some time at home, and besides, I have my trousseau to make. And I haven't even started on it yet.' Linda pronounced the word 'true-saw' with conviction, conveying with it images of flimsy nighties and daring underwear.

'I expect you'll be pretty busy with that, then. A month is really not too much time.' Mrs. Nelson seemed genuinely pleased at Linda's announcement, which made Joan even more irritated at her mother's previous sanctimonious judgments of their servant's conduct. She couldn't resist saying to Linda in front of her mother, 'We'll have to give you a shower.'

This breach of etiquette was not lost on Mrs. Nelson, and Joan was curious to see how she would emerge from such an overt flaunting of approved custom, but Linda didn't give her mother a chance to respond.

'You don't have to do nothing for me. I'm happy the way I am.' There was not a hint of surliness or anger in Linda's reply; it was simply a statement of rules. No obligations or ceremonies were expected, nor were any to be welcomed by either party.

Linda's reply ended the conversation, with Mrs. Nelson abandoning the room after once again congratulating Linda. 'I know you and your Joe will be very happy.'

Joan toyed with the idea of offering to dry the dishes so she could stay and chat about weddings, even though Linda's noisy humming discouraged any sort of conversation. She imagined Linda's trousseau; she would sew it herself with maybe her mother helping her when she was too tired to finish a last hem. Would she have black lace nighties and matching bras and girdles, or would she restrict herself to feed-sack housedresses and flannel nightgowns that sagged at the knees and the rear, as befitting a properly married woman? Were there to be nylon slips with appliquéd roses covering both nipples, or would she instead construct loose petticoats that didn't even need a bra?

And who was this Joe Schultz from Chandler, a town removed from New Bonn by at least thirty miles, and how had Linda met him? Was he one of those patient men in line that night, or was he some dupe who had never heard of Linda's fame as a sex machine?

It took some time for Joan to learn enough to construct any kind of pattern, but she finally discovered, after listening to the local gossip and filtering out the probable from the impossible, that Joe Schultz was an independent farmer, which meant that he owned his own land and did not farm with his family. His holdings were considerable: one full section and an eighty in another township that was being farmed by a tenant.

Joan also discovered that he was forty-eight years old and had just converted to Catholicism as a tribute to Linda.

He was a widower without children and had been looking for a wife for at least four years to provide him with an heir, or so everyone thought. He had met Linda through one of her brothers who had helped him with a machinery breakdown. The story was that Linda's brother, Jim, who was a mechanical wizard, had repaired Joe Schultz's combine when it had broken down in the middle of the thrashing season, and Joe had been so grateful to Jim for having saved him his crops – parts ordered from Sioux Falls would have taken days to arrive – that he drove to New Bonn one night to personally give Jim a bottle of whiskey as well as to pay him for his work. That was when he had met Linda and had evidently sized her up as being promisingly fertile.

If he knew of her reputation it was not important to him. And although the people of New Bonn cynically ridiculed Joe Schultz's resolute blindness to Linda's moral worth, they were hard-pressed to explain his conversion to Catholicism.

Most people felt that it didn't matter how much a person's religion personally counted other than the required attendance at the obligatory occasions, but everyone agreed that it was unthinkable to convert to something so irrevocable as Catholicism unless there were some compelling – and usually morbid – contingencies that demanded an immediate conversion. So far these occasions had been limited to shotgun weddings and incidents of malicious family feuds.

Joan, herself, decided that Joe must love Linda a lot in order to go to such extremes. She was closer to the truth than anyone else realized, including Linda. Joe had first viewed Linda as someone a little too small in the hips for easy childbearing. Then he saw her as a rather crude, but easily manageable, prickteaser. Eventually he saw her as an example of womanhood so malleable that it would take almost nothing on his part to keep her the way he wanted her to be – slightly sulky but nevertheless satisfied with her lot. In order to get her to agree to the terms he proposed setting up for her, he agreed to relinquish his mild beliefs in an erratic Protestant god, accepting in their place the superiority of a Jewish virgin and her doomed son. Joe's acceptance of Catholicism was like his acceptance of

Linda's sexual sophistication: he took it without letting it bother him very much because he knew there were always going to be more important issues to deal with.

One night at New Bonn's local liquor store – the only place in the county it was legal to buy mixed drinks – a drunken lout insinuated to Joe that he had impressive potential as a cuckold.

'Won't be long, Schultz, before you'll need to check under the bed every time you come home unexpected.' A guffaw and leer accompanied his unoriginal prediction.

Joe deprived the drinking audience of a rousing fight, which was what they had expected, by smiling sanguinely and refusing to take the bait. More distressing than his rejection of the challenge was his apparent indifference to adultery. Sitting at the bar in his blue work clothes, his thin hair stretched across the shiny dome of his forehead, Joe's imperturbability confused the other drinkers.

'Any son of a bitch did that to my wife I'd kill him. Kill her, too. Kill them both. Why else do you always keep a loaded gun under your bed?'

The raucous chortle over this exchange didn't seem to register on Joe, who acted as if he were listening to talk from another country and not from his own neighborhood.

'What are you planning to do, Joe, stick it to her once and let the rest of the county take their turn?' Joe refused to look at his interlocutor, and had it not been for the appearance of the bartender, who was also the town constable, the teasing might have continued until everyone had contributed an insult.

'Knock it off, you guys. I don't have none of that in here.' Then, to soften his admonition, this burly bartender, whose mouth was ordinarily as foul as the rest of the lot, added jovially, 'This here is a respectable joint, with ladies present.'

Everyone knew that ladies were not only never present,

they were virtually eliminated from the clientele, for no woman, regardless of her background and conduct, would subject herself to the masculine domain of the town's only liquor store.

Joe finished his whiskey and began to walk out of the door, while the group of drinkers at the bar stared at their drinks or nervously swished them with their fingers. 'Goodnight, Joe,' the bartender muttered, but more to himself than to the departing man.

'Goodnight,' came the reply, and then a quick half-step back into the bar. Joe looked at the line of men at the bar and announced, 'I want to take this occasion to invite you to my wedding.' His glance included everyone, with no distinctions made between those who had attempted to taunt him and those who had maintained an amused silence. 'I mean it. All of you. I'll see to it that you get an invitation. I want all of you to come.'

No one expected this courtesy, and because no one expected it they all felt obliged to assure Joe that his wedding would be faithfully attended by all of them, even the foulest of them all, the man who had originally attempted to provoke a fight.

That bar room conversation had not been especially bizarre by New Bonn standards, for discussions about sex were not limited, in New Bonn, to gossiping adults who were worried about the effects of promiscuity upon their growing children. Indeed, sex was probably discussed there more than anything else; it is just that its terms of discussion were so unusual. Among the farmers and the adult townsmen, sex was considered exclusively in terms of fucking, and fucking, itself, carried its own terms, usually associated with land values and ancestors. It was common to hear one man say to another, 'I hear you've been getting into Bill Smith's daughter,' and the second man might respond, 'Not Bill Smith, Frank Smith's daughter. Bill sold out six months ago and moved to Worthington.' Thus no one denied that a daughter of Frank or Bill was getting screwed, but it seemed that the location of the girl's ancestral home was more important than any particulars of romance. The incident in the New Bonn liquor store involving the future conduct of the second Mrs. Schultz was hardly unique, for men did joke crudely about adultery and the very real possibility of wearing horns on their heads.

What was unusual about the incident was the involvement of an outsider, a man from an area with no previous ties with New Bonn, and a man who possessed more land than most, and who thus had established an identity separate from those young upstarts at the bar, many of whom were still attempting to work out some arrangement with their own families that would allow them enough independence to cast out on their own. The most they could ask for was a quarter section to farm, which if it yielded well and reliably would enable them to some day marry and be on their own.

The fact that Joe Schultz had not been provoked into a fight, and had instead retaliated with an invitation to his own wedding, added power to his strong supply of resources, so that it became a kind of gentlemen's agreement to attend the wedding among the Saturday-night rowdies who patronized the bar. Many would have been asked regardless of their patronage, because Linda's family was large, but others would never have been considered.

On the day after Thanksgiving an invitation was received, picked up at the post office by the daytime bartender. It was addressed to 'Patrons: Municipal Liquor Store, New Bonn, Minnesota.' It requested the attendance at the wedding of Mary Margaret Baumhauser to Joseph Schultz, Jr., on December 11, at 10 a.m., St. Gabriel's Catholic Church of New Bonn. There were the expected number of ribald remarks at its reception, but many of the patrons felt rather awed. 'Of course I'm going. That guy needs all the friends he can get at a time like this,' was the comment of the auxiliary bartender – there were two in duty for the post-holiday letdown. The invitation was prominently displayed, stuck into the side of the ubiquitous mirror that is regulation equipment in every American bar. Occasionally a man would come in and ask to see it, and eventually people would simply point to it without having to ask for it.

'I wouldn't miss it for the world,' said one sad-eyed young man. 'She's had her last piece from me, I can tell you that.'

Those standing at the bar within earshot of the sad young man nodded sympathetically. There was no talk about the future of the couple – their prosperity or possible happiness. Instead, it centered around the necessary cessation of Linda's sexual activity, as if the rites to be celebrated were burial rites rather than nuptial rites.

The Nelsons received their invitation two days before the wedding was scheduled. Mrs. Nelson, offended by their servant's lack of gratitude towards the family, was still smarting when the invitation arrived. 'You can go if you want to,' she said to her daughter, 'but I wouldn't give them the time of day.' This was literally true, for she refused to honor the marriage with a gift, not even one of the supply of candle snuffers she kept on hand for emergency gifts. Joan wanted to go. She wanted to see if Linda would wear white. She was also curious about how Linda had managed to talk the priest into a church wedding, for senile and incompetent as he appeared, he was notoriously aware of his young parishioners' sexual reputations, and had refused at least twice to marry brides in the church itself whom he knew to be non-virgins. These brides, both visibly pregnant, had to settle for the vestry, which was considered more desirable than the reception parlor of the rectory, another refuge for non-virgin brides.

There was to be no wedding dance, which Joan thought curious until her father suggested it might be too much for the groom. He said this with such an unmistakable leer that Joan wondered if he had been reading her mind. 'Are you going, Daddy?' Joan inquired, hoping that she would have an ally during the alien ritual of the Mass.

'I don't think I can make it. I have to be out of town all week. But you go ahead and go. I think Mary Margaret would like to see at least one of us there representing the family.'

Joan had one Catholic friend, Mary Frances, who never missed Catholic weddings. (Anyone could go to a wedding; it was the reception that required an invitation.) Joan had little trouble persuading her friend to go with her, and they agreed to meet in front of the church ten minutes before the service, yet when Joan arrived at the church twenty minutes early there were already small groups of people forming together on the steps. No one seemed in a hurry to go in, except for one old woman dressed in black who was jiggling her rosary beads as if they were car keys. Most of the people were unfamiliar to Joan, although she did catch sight of two of Linda's brothers who were smoking their last cigarettes before taking their positions in the procession. These were the two handsome brothers who had picked up their sister for the wedding dance, but this day they looked less handsome, for their summer tans had faded, leaving an ugly yellow color that clashed with their plain brown suits. Joan wondered which of them was the catalyst that had set off the sequence of events that had landed Linda and her betrothed at these doors. Jim? Or were these Karl and Jack, and could there be another brother as best man?

Mary Frances arrived at the point when Joan had almost

decided to give up and flee. She had a missal in her hand and a rosary stuffed into a coat pocket. 'Here,' she announced. 'I brought this for you. I thought you might need it to follow.' She held out the missal to Joan, who looked at it with embarrassment. 'Come on, take it. You'll be lost otherwise.'

Joan knew that Roman Catholic churches conducted their rituals in Latin, a language she had already studied for one year, but she was not aware that people really used books to follow the procedure, especially people who had been raised in the church and had been attending regularly all their lives. She followed her friend up the stairs and into the building, clutching the book in both gloved hands.

Joan had not expected the grandeur of the church's interior. On the outside the church was a large but modest red brick building, but inside there was a life that seemed independent of its exteriors. The ceilings were high and vaulted, and there appeared to be hundreds of indentations in the walls where statues commanded flowers and hundreds of flickering candles. One of her mother's familiar scornful comments about Catholics, 'They pray to the saints, you know, to the statues,' she instantly understood and as quickly dismissed as insensitive and beside the point.

Each window, and there were at least a dozen of them, contained glass panels illustrating episodes that were unfamiliar to Joan's Presbyterian eyes: The Ascension; The Assumption; the Annunciation; and their colors were so scarlet and so cerulean that they literally flashed out before Joan's eyes. Although she knew a little about the Virgin Mary, she had no idea of how many images the Virgin could occupy in one building. Everywhere she looked she saw a smiling Mary, a sweet young mother far too girlish for all her responsibility, a girl who smiled from every corner of the building with a face that suggested high hopes and very little sadness.

But the most brilliant and astonishing object that Joan saw was the golden radiating disc elevated upon the altar with candles burning immediately beneath it. Its shine cast a brilliance upon the ceiling and upon the stained-glass windows behind it so that it seemed to emerge from itself and stand isolated and independent of its surroundings. While Mary Frances knelt in the pew and mumbled unintelligibly, Joan gawked as if she were to be limited to one brief glance of resplendence, then forever shunted away and relegated to the plain, varnished oak of Presbyterian sabbaths. The people sitting around Joan, recognizable Catholics with their missals and beads, all seemed to be staring at the altar with unfathomable spirituality, counting their beads as if they were participating in a private mode of spiritual exchange.

A group of about twenty men entered and took seats near the front, and they, too, sank to their knees. If anyone recognized them as the liquor-store faithfuls there was no sign; they could have been ordinary allies of the groom, occupying space on the groom's side that otherwise might have been embarrassingly empty.

Joan had never before experienced the total silence of a magnitude. Everyone, without exception, was spiritually occupied and quiet, a condition that she had never known to exist. She wanted to cry, and she was afraid she would lose control, unaware that she was in a state of aesthetic shock. She was saved from tears by the chronology of the ritual, a formal pattern that has served the institution and its patrons for centuries. First a bell rang, then the priest and two altar boys appeared; then a chord sounded from the organ and the wedding procession began. All of this happened quickly, almost simultaneously, which gave her an opportunity to recover her emotional balance. She could even manage to adopt a more aloof manner towards the ritual, for what followed seemed more like a pageant than a mysterious, sacred episode.

The ushers escorted the mother of the bride – the groom being both widower and orphan – to the front pew. The sight of Linda's mother brought Joan back to earth in a hurry, reminding her of the baser realities of motherhood. Her legs were slightly bent inward so that she walked as if she were getting ready to squat on the ground. Her satin dress was of a color that was probably labeled Autumn Russet in the Sears catalogue, but to Joan it resembled a pumpkin that had been bitten by a hard-killing frost. Her shoes were of a contrasting color in suede, with absurd silver buckles where laces belonged, and her hat produced both ostrich and pheasant feathers, also in contrasting tones of burnt orange. Her face seemed grim and joyless, compressed into a knot of a smile that concealed her badly fitting dentures.

The bride and her father were preceded down the aisle by three girls who were either Linda's sisters or cousins, or both. The bridesmaids differed from the maid of honor only in their lighter shades of green and in their bouquets, which were small arrangements of chrysanthemums and asters, flowers with so much pungency that there was a definite clash with the permanent odor of incense. The bride, leaning on her father's arm, seemed amused at her nervous handmaidens, whose bouquets shook visibly. Linda, by contrast, looked as if she were preparing to feed the chickens or start work upon a basket of ironing. She refused to take the small, measured steps of the bridesmaids, and her hands were not so much clasping her white bouquet as they were pushing it ahead of her. Joan noticed that her white satin dress could be classified as 'off white', and felt sure that this was an intentional admission. The groom, surrounded by the ushers at the altar, appeared more anxious for the wedding procession than for his bride, and for a minute Joan wondered if he would reach over and shake the hand of the bride's father.

Joan found the Mass difficult to follow, even with the help of the missal, which seemed as incomprehensible in English as it was in Latin, but she liked the way the priest turned his back on the congregation and intoned what sounded to her like telephone numbers, and she liked the way the altar boys popped around looking helpful. She thought it generous of the priest to accept their help when they were so obviously capable of handling the whole works by themselves. It looked to her like a good way to appear important without being conceited. Joan also liked the way the altar boys looked in their short black and white gowns, with their hair so freshly combed that the water lines still showed. She knew these little boys, and she had always thought they were nothing but ugly, pesky little urchins, foul of mouth and mind, who let the snot run down their noses and half the time forgot to zip up their flies. Now she had to allow them a respect because they were so obviously concerned with the significance of their task, which was to serve rather than to control.

The only aspect of the ritual that disappointed Joan was the music. Unlike the Protestants she had known, and the many kinds of Protestant services she had attended, these Catholics took no interest in singing. The only music came from a reedy organ that produced major chords as interludes to the priest's incantations, accompanied sporadically by a trio of two sopranos and an alto who did little more than repeat the priest's Latin phrases into a register of quavery trills that sounded more like wailing than genuine musical echoing.

Joan kept a watchful eye on the bridegroom, for it seemed as if he and she were the only aliens in the church, despite his recent conversion. At one point she thought he looked as if he might be wavering, or at least having second thoughts, when it came to his turn to receive the Host, for there was a decided pause before he lifted his head, almost like a man checking the time before ordering his last drink of the evening. Linda's movements were less rushed than they had seemed on her arrival – the Mass seemed to have quieted her down – but they did appear mechanical, almost as if she were performing by proxy.

At the conclusion of the Mass the bride lifted her veil for her husband's kiss, and it was only then that Joan saw what might have been tears in Linda's eyes, yet she wasn't sure, for immediately Linda (still Mary Margaret in the confines of the church) grabbed her new husband's arm and pulled him along with her up the aisle, looking at no one, including her new mate. The standing congregation, who had been expecting at least an occasional smile or a jolly wave of the hand, was clearly disappointed. 'Well, I never,' exclaimed the elderly woman who had stationed herself one pew behind Joan.

Mary Frances grinned at Joan. 'How'd you like it? Nice, huh?' Although Mary Frances was a devout follower of weddings, Joan was unsure of the depths of her piety, and of what she was referring to.

'I loved the Mass, if that's what you mean,' Joan replied.

'No, that's not what I mean, but I'm glad you liked it.'

Joan suspected that Mary Frances was looking for signs of Protestant weaknesses. It was well known among Protestants that the rewards Catholics were given for capturing lost or strayed souls were sumptuous. She had also heard that one convert was worth at least as much as three strays.

'What do you mean, then?' Joan wondered what her friend was getting at, whether she was being teased into some kind of personal admission.

'Didn't you see the way she dragged him as if she couldn't get away fast enough?'

Joan decided to play dumb, a technique that usually

worked better on her friends than on her mother. 'Why should she want to get away fast? There's going to be a reception, isn't there?'

'Oh, for heaven's sake, Joan, you're hopeless. Wouldn't you want to get away? Would you want to show your face after all that's gone on?'

Linda's reputation was obviously not being protected by her fellow Catholics. Joan wondered how the priest had been duped, for it was clear that he must have been tricked to allow such a display. 'If she got away with it, I mean if she's done such bad stuff, why would everyone want to come and see her, and why would they allow her to get married in public this way?'

'It's not exactly public, you know.'

Joan recognized the maneuver of her friend, selecting one slightly inaccurate word and then presenting it as a separate statement. She did the same thing sometimes, her mother did it a lot, especially with her father. 'I don't mean public, exactly, but out in the open like this. In church, with a big wedding and reception and all.'

'Why don't you ask Linda, then? After all, she lived at your house.'

Joan heard a blanket indictment of the Nelson family in her friend's rhetorical question. 'I'm not going to ask Linda. That would be rude.' Joan knew she had hit home with her thrust at manners, and continued: 'But why don't you tell me how she managed to bring off a big church wedding when there are at least two girls we know who got stuck with weddings in the priest's house?' (Joan hoped she wouldn't be attacked for her use of 'house'.)

'All I can say is that money talks, and I probably shouldn't say that much.'

Joan was horrified. The idea of buying rights to a church ceremony was so improbable to her that she could only shake her head and say, 'I don't believe it.'

'What did you expect?'

'I don't know. I thought there might be a way of tricking the priest into making him think that she hadn't really been fooling around. That it was all vicious gossip or something.'

'Priests aren't so easily fooled,' responded Mary Frances. 'And why should they be? It would set a terrible example to the people. But I'm sure that when Joe Schultz converted he contributed a sizable chunk to the building fund.' There was a hint of triumph in the girl's grin which Joan found exasperating.

'Why did she go to all this trouble for a church wedding, then, if everyone in the world knows what she's done?'

'I don't know. I told you to ask her. Maybe it's because she's a Catholic and didn't want to be cheated out of her own rightful wedding. Maybe her parents would be disappointed, though that's not very likely. Maybe, just maybe, he wanted it that way. I really don't care. It's their business.' Mary Frances assumed an air of exhausted weariness, as if she had just been through an arduous routine of teaching the alphabet to a retarded child. It was this smugness that irritated Joan the most, and which provoked her into asking the question she normally would have left unvoiced.

'Why did you come, then, if you disapprove so much? And since you're so sure it's a phony setup?'

Mary Frances's reply was part snarl, part shout. 'Why did you come, you horse's ass?' She stalked off, missal in hand, her features set into a mold of preserved outrage.

Chapter Nine

Celebration

The departure of Mary Frances left Joan hanging around a church to which she didn't belong and feeling as if she were in a foreign country waiting for a mysterious stranger to rescue her. She wondered how she could gracefully sneak off without being detected. Most people, she noticed, had already begun their descent into the church basement; she saw their movements as a cover for her escape. She was rounding the corner opposite from the church basement when Karl, one of Linda's brothers, grabbed her arm.

'You're Joan, aren't you? I have a message from Mary Margaret.'

Joan gaped up at him, a giant of a farmer who stood over her by at least a foot. 'What is it? What does she want?' Joan's first thought was that Linda somehow expected her to help her escape. Perhaps she even wanted Joan to provide her with transportation and money.

'She said to tell you that she expects you at the reception, and they have a place for you at the head table. You're going to sit next to me, as a matter of fact, and that's why she sent me to tell you.' If Karl felt unfairly burdened by his task he didn't reveal it; rather, he gave Joan such a flashy, benevolent smile that she internally melted. In his suit, despite the seasonal pallor, he did look handsome and friendly.

'Okay. Sure, I mean, I'd be glad to. I didn't know that

Linda wanted me so much or I'd have been down there already.'

Like Joan's mother, Karl seemed able to detect lies with little effort, but unlike her mother, he seemed not to be offended. 'Well, you had no way, did you, to know that she wanted you especially. And that's why I'm here, so let's go. There's going to be a tremendous feed.' Despite the vulgarity of his description, Joan was happy to follow Karl. 'There's lots of booze, too. I expect everyone's got half a load on by now.'

The promise of alcohol didn't appeal to Joan so much as the novelty of its being served in a church. No champagne, but even ordinary bourbon in such surroundings seemed exotic.

When Joan arrived on the arm of Karl – she was actually clinging to his strong, farmer's hand – people were milling around the basement. Four enormous tables had been set up with a smaller one placed on the stage. This table was intended for the wedding party and the family members. A card table near the doors to the kitchen was heaped with wedding presents. Green and white crêpe paper was fastened to the ceiling lights and cascaded to each of the four tables, where it was tacked into place underneath vases of white chrysanthemums and hideous green carnations. There were rows of unlit green and white candles on each table, but there were no name cards, which indicated no special distinctions among tables or positions at the tables.

In contrast, the wedding party's table had fewer candles but more flowers, and no crêpe paper, and there was a genuine cloth, adorned with silver ribbons that wove around the flowers – a rather harsh contrast to the paper tablecloths of the lesser places.

The St. Gabriel Ladies' Aid was responsible for the wedding feast, a time-honored custom that no one cared to challenge, and so there were dozens of motherly women wearing white aprons bustling in and out of the kitchen. Each woman wore a white carnation pinned over her left breast, either a gift from the bride or the results of looting the altar's flower arrangement. The ladies were busy but happy-looking as they scurried around, smiling as they placed baskets of rolls and plates of butter on the tables. Many of them wore hair nets, which gave them the mien of professional waitresses.

There was no regular bar, but there was an arrangement of a dozen or more bottles of whiskey clustered on a counter, along with paper cups and bottles of Seven Up and Squirt. Off to one side, almost hidden by the card table laden with gifts, was a keg of beer and a stack of glasses. Joan knew few people and by sight only, but many people seemed to know her; at least they knew her name, and several asked why her father was not with her. (No one mentioned her mother.)

She thought she would be stranded with no one to talk to after Karl left her to get himself a drink, but a group of farmers who had clotted together opened up to include her, almost as if she were one of them. One man grasped her elbow and said to the others, 'I'd like you to meet Bert's daughter,' but he offered no names in exchange. 'Any daughter of Bert's is like one of my own, isn't that so?' Joan, always eager to be identified with her father, beamed a grateful smile and shook hands with two or three of them.

The farmers were talking about crops, not about the wedding, and since Joan was fairly well educated in bushel yields and the vicissitudes of weather upon most crops, she didn't feel excluded from the conversation. She thought of asking the friendly man, whose name she still didn't know but who continued to hold on to her arm, how his corn had turned out, but she decided that the purpose of this talk was to discuss possibilities and not to compare results, so she continued to smile at the group but didn't speak.

When Karl joined the circle he gave her a paper cup, which he said was Seven Up with just a dash of whiskey for taste. Remembering her gagging over the whiskey at the wedding dance, she was reluctant to even smell it, but it looked mostly clear, like plain Seven Up, so she downed it in two gulps. It tasted soothing; the usual insipidness of Seven Up was made hearty by the addition of the few drops of whiskey that allegedly resided in her weak drink, and when Karl asked her if she would like another she automatically handed him her cup. She noticed that most of the farmers were drinking out of cups, which meant whiskey, while the beer keg appeared unvisited. She looked around to see what the women were drinking, but it was impossible to tell if their paper cups contained whiskey or plain soda pop. It was clear, however, that no woman was drinking beer.

Linda and one of her bridesmaids were busily attacking the mound of gifts. Linda would open one and her attendant would record the information from the card into a white satin notebook. A little girl of about eight, wearing a pink organdy dress with rows of ruffles traveling up and down the skirt, was attempting to coerce groups of people into signing their names in a white satin guest book – a larger version of the notebook – but since she had neither enough strength nor authority to plunge into the crowds, she remained on the fringes, a slightly frantic sulk flawing her pretty, dimpled doll's face. Joan thought she looked too much like a rural version of Shirley Temple, as if too many people had reminded her of her precious look-alike, and now it was too much for her. Her patent-leather Mary Janes suggested tap-dancing and music and other occasions that didn't go along with her role at this time.

Linda's parents were busily engaged in a discussion with the priest, a discussion that seemed animated although no one was smiling. The priest seemed to be explaining something to the older pair, and they looked as if they were listening but not agreeing. After downing her second drink, Joan edged closer to the table of gifts, which was diminishing in size. A great mound of excelsior paper and ribbons rested on the floor, and Linda was feeding it with her discards the way monkeys are tossed peanuts in a zoo; frequently she was off target but her zest was unmistakable.

'Hey Joan, come on and help me here. Open some of these and Katie can go find someone with a broom.' Joan's interest in wedding presents had until now been limited to the theoretical – she had been much more concerned with the idea of Linda's trousseau – but now she dug in with an enthusiasm that is often seen in people when they are looting from stores selling exclusive designer clothes. Most of the paper was white with silver wedding bells – she was able to notice their designs as she tore off the wrapping paper with a speed that amazed her. She did notice some gifts wrapped in the kinds of neutral flower designs that hold good for most occasions, but the silver bells wedding motif dominated the choices.

One of the aproned ladies brought in another card table for display, and Katie, Linda's sister, began setting up lamps and irons and blankets and sheets and crystal and dishes without regard for function or appearance. There were a number of envelopes containing checks, and these went on the tops of convenient flat surfaces, like plates or tablecloths, with the card opened to indicate the donor's name and the check attached to it with a paper clip. (Were paper clips something that everyone brought to weddings, Joan wondered, or did the good ladies of St. Gabriel's furnish these, too?)

Among the envelopes was one which bore the unmistakable handwriting of Joan's father. Inside was a suitable parochial wedding card, complete with spiritual advice, and a check for $100. Joan questioned her father's taste in the card more than she questioned the size of the check. Who had helped him select such a horrid card? The size of the check, she noted, was generous but not magnanimous, and the signature on the card bore only his name, which she thought was unfair to her. Linda's reaction to her former employer's gift was similar to the way she reacted to the other gifts, for she was obviously having more fun opening things than inspecting their contents. Once a gift was unwrapped or an envelope unglued, she lost interest.

Her bridegroom was standing nearby, drinking beer from the keg and talking to a man who was wearing summery-looking clothes, a cream-colored jacket and powder-blue pants. He looked a little like a musician in a traveling dance band except that he seemed too old to be junketing around the country playing one-night stands. Joan was loosened enough by her drinks to ask Linda who the man was.

'Oh, that's Joe's cousin from Sioux City. Not exactly his cousin, he's really a cousin of his first wife, but he's the only relative he could dredge up. He's at least sixty but he thinks he's still a lady-killer.'

Joan looked at the man for signs of roguery but saw nothing but a beery face and eyes that didn't focus very well. When Linda opened the last present, a wooden clock in the shape of a double-masted ship, she placed it among the vases and candy dishes and embroidered silk pillows and announced to Joan, 'Finally! At last that's over. Now we can eat.'

Joan nodded her head at the direction of the sizable heap on the floor. 'Don't you want me to help clean up?'

'No. Let someone else take care of this crap. I'm starved. I couldn't have breakfast, you know.' Linda started to walk toward the raised table, then stopped as if she had forgotten an object among the gifts. She walked over to her husband and tugged at his suit jacket. 'C'mon. Let's eat. I'm hungry,' she commanded. The groom lifted his beer glass and clinked it against the raised glass of his relative. 'Here's to sin,' he announced. The relative leered appreciatively and followed the nuptial pair to the stage. Just then Karl appeared at Joan's side and actually put a guiding hand under her elbow to help her up the stairs.

'Never can tell what a few drinks can do when you're not used to it,' he explained.

Joan liked his solicitous arm but felt he was going out of his way to be smug. 'I'm fine, perfectly fine. Besides, there was practically nothing in those drinks, you said so yourself.'

'Okay, okay, I believe you,' he replied. 'You're fine, and I'm a pig's ass.'

Joan knew that Karl must be drunker than he looked, but other than a slight loopiness in his eyes, his walk was steady and his speech was not slurred. She hoped that he would stop teasing her, at least during the meal. Sitting next to him would be difficult if he insisted on trading insults. When the wedding party had finished taking their places and were arranged behind their chairs, the priest muttered a mercifully short Grace, asking only that God protect the couple on their long path in marriage, and the five tables sat down as one.

The Ladies' Aid of St. Gabriel served quickly and well. Plates of creamed chicken and buttered peas and mashed potatoes were in front of the diners almost as soon as they had sat down, and the jello and Waldorf salads appeared immediately. The conversation at the head table was limited to requests for rolls and butter and salt and pepper; only once did her husband address Linda, and that was to ask her if he could get another beer.

'I don't see why you need another one now when we're eating,' she replied, 'but maybe we can ask one of the ladies when she comes by.'

'I gotta have something to toast my bride with, don't I?'

Beaten at her own game, Linda looked chastened. 'In that case, we all ought to have something.' She yelled down the table to her brother, Karl, who had been eating zestfully since the food had arrived. 'Hey Karl, can you get us all something for a toast?'

Linda's brother looked up from his diminishing supply of food. 'Don't know why I should. But then, I don't know why I shouldn't, either.' He stood up a little clumsily and walked down the steps towards the bottles on the counter. Joan wondered how many times this man had ever honored a request from his younger sister. He acted now as if this were his first and last.

Everyone had finished eating; the other tables seemed to be waiting for the cake to be brought in and the toasts to begin. Joan knew there was still the cake-cutting ceremony, accompanied by picture-taking. No one spoke at the head table, which Joan found strange and awkward, so to break the silence she asked Linda the standard question, 'Where are you going on your honeymoon?'

Linda's mother looked at Joan with an eye that resembled a hawk about to snatch its daily rodent. Although it was Linda who answered Joan's question, the reply could easily have come from her mother, so closely did the woman follow the words of her daughter. 'We're not going anywhere, didn't you know? Besides, honeymoons are a waste of money, and there's no place to go this time of year. Maybe in the summer we'll go some place when the weather is nice.'

The blue-jacketed cousin, sitting across from Joan, winked at her. 'They don't have no time for honeymoons.'

When Karl returned with a tray of drinks, this time in glasses, Joan was pleased that he had remembered to include beer for his new brother-in-law. Two ladies followed him almost tripping on his heels, bearing a three-tiered wedding cake, white with silver spangles on its sides, and crowned by a bride and groom standing under what looked like a gazebo.

The bride and groom rose together, linking glasses, and repeated a kind of parody of their earlier, sanctified vows. 'I toast the bride, for better or for worse.'

'I toast the groom, for better or for best.' The diners and well-wishers laughed with approval, and Linda's father, at a nudge from his wife, rose to silently toast the bride and groom, merely nodding his head at both and smiling approvingly. After this silent recognition, a flood of toasts followed, mostly ribald and way above Joan's head. Despite her uneasiness, for she was not able to completely shed her feelings of being an outsider, Joan was enjoying herself. She had managed to drink three spiked Seven Ups, she had been greeted and welcomed by a handful of people as Bert's daughter, and she had gained the attentions of the first farmer she had ever met who was both handsome and a little bit courteous.

Karl offered to drive Joan home after the wedding feast was over and the guests were departing. Joan thought this offer more romantic than practical, since she lived only three blocks from the church, but when she saw he was driving a sedan, and not the pickup truck, she agreed. They set off in the opposite direction from her house, which did not bother Joan because she knew that a male offer of a ride home didn't necessarily mean a direct route. Karl drove slowly along the lake, past the beach that was now filled with snow. The lake had just begun to ice over, so that it was still not safe to walk on. The banks were gradually building their annual yield of fifteen or more feet of snow, enormous white craters that would remain there until the first unseasonable thaw.

Joan wasn't surprised when Karl headed for Hell's Half Acre, the traditional landing spot of most young people's routes, yet Hell's Half Acre was considered an after-dark haunt, and seemed rather inappropriate for three in the afternoon. (Later on, in late January and well into February and March, cars would get stuck in its drifts and would have to be pulled out with tractors, for neither chains nor the enormous lugs in snow tires could resist the accumulated snow that piled up without ceasing.)

Joan wasn't surprised, either, when Karl took a pint of whiskey out of the glove compartment and handed it to her without comment. She took a deep swallow – she liked to think of it as a 'long pull' – feeling proud that she could handle this liquid better than at her first attempt at the wedding dance. Although there was a definite twist of revulsion in her gut, she didn't gag, and her eyes were tearless. As she handed the bottle to Karl, she wondered what they were going to talk about.

She knew her farming small talk was not what he wanted to hear, and she wasn't sure how interested he was in hearing about his sister, either.

'How old are you?'

Joan wasn't sure about the correct response to this question. Certainly Karl could add and subtract, so he must have known that she was at least three years younger than his sister. Perhaps he wanted verification, or maybe she was expected to add a year or two to make him look more honorable.

'I'm sixteen.' Joan was not about to use fractions, and besides there was something childish about claiming fifteen and a half. Sixteen, to her, seemed more mature.

'You're jailbait!' Karl sputtered.

Joan thought of mentioning that she had always been considered old for her age. Instead, she lit a cigarette. Jailbait was a term that she had heard always used in derogatory ways, and she was astonished and hurt to hear it applied to her. 'I'm old enough to know what I'm doing, and I can take care of myself,' she replied, trying not to let her exasperation take over her voice.

Karl grinned. 'Sweet sixteen. Ever been kissed?'

Joan ignored this taunt. Kissing was something she had experienced off and on for at least three years, but never with much sense of pleasure. She thought it better to push the age question; perhaps his motives, if he had any, would then emerge.

'How old are you, then?'

'I'm twenty-three, which means I'm seven years older than you, and I've been on my own since I was sixteen when they let me quit school.'

'Didn't you want to quit school?'

'Of course I wanted to quit school. It was a drag, and about as useful as tits on a boar.'

Joan, who had always heard that education was most valuable because 'they can't take it away from you', wondered if Karl's 'they' and her own version of 'they' could possibly be related. 'Well, I don't like school much either, but I'm stuck there and sometimes it's not so bad.'

She wondered if this remark was completely honest and not totally condescending, but she was still unprepared for the fury of his response.

'Let me tell you, girlie, it isn't the same thing at all. There's not the slightest similarity between us two at all. Whatsoever. Get that?'

'What are we doing here, then? I mean, why did you bring me here?' Joan was not accustomed to male anger, and she felt shaky and afraid of what she considered an unfair attack.

'I brought you here because I wanted to see how far you would go. How far you would let yourself go with a dumb farmer who hasn't got shit next to the pile your old man has stored away.'

Joan's mind flashed back to those first moments in

church and to her discovery of the tranquil, ethereal expressions of the communicants, and of their awesome devotion and to their acceptance of the spiritual plenitude that the Catholic religion seemed to bestow upon its followers. Karl seemed like a different person from that earlier groomsman, waiting at the altar for the Host. 'I think you're being unfair. And what has my father got to do with the things I do, or choose to do?'

'I guess I'll find out for myself, then.' Before Joan had a chance to lunge toward the door handle, Karl reached over and grabbed her shoulder and began to force one hand inside her coat. She tried to push his hand away, but the superior force of his nearly twenty-three years of labor were more than enough to combat her nearly sixteen years of cautious virginity. He tore her coat open with such ease that the buttons were left intact, their threads barely twisted. 'Let's see what you've got down there,' he muttered. One hand began to root around in her panties, and although she squirmed she could not come close to pulling free of his groping paw.

'Everyone says you got a gold-plated pussy. I got to see for myself.' Although Karl had spared her coat, she felt her panties give in one, decisive rip. He pulled off her garter belt with one jerk, examined it briefly, and tossed it out of the door into the snow, all the time keeping her pinned with his right arm. Joan's terror caused a temporary spasm that relaxed her muscles, and her rigid body, tensed with the fight she knew she could never win, now became limp, almost lifeless.

'What'sa matter? You scared of me, scared that I'll force you into something you don't want?' Karl let go of her arm but kept his hand on her crotch. 'My sister says you are a hot number, that you put for everyone that looks your way.'

'Your sister is a goddamned liar. And I don't think she said anything of the kind.'

Some sense of filial decency made him amend his assertion. 'My sister said that you are just waiting for it. That all you need is a good fuck and you've been asking for it for years.'

Whereas most of Joan's conversations with Linda had usually been monitored by Mrs. Nelson and were thus restricted to the topics of clothes and domestic duties, Joan suspected that she could have said something that might have been construed as sexual longing, but since Linda was not a clever person, nor one particularly interested in other people's desires, Joan knew there was no factual basis for Karl's disclosure. She decided to concede her association with Linda, however, if only to get his hand out of her crotch.

'Look, I like your sister. She is a nice person, and I like your family, but I haven't the slightest intention of even kissing you, so will you take me home, or at least open the door so I can get there by myself? I don't really know you, but up to now I thought you were really nice – at the wedding and the way you treated your family. Now please let me go.'

Karl's defeat came as easily as his display of power. 'Okay, if that's the way you want it. I just thought that you and me could get along. My sister didn't really say all that. She just said that you were all right and could use a little fun.'

He withdrew his hand, but only after he had pinched her thigh so roughly that she flinched with pain, and then he started the car. He turned on the radio and drove to her house without speaking. At Locksley Hall he didn't bother to pull into the driveway; instead he stopped on the side of the road where she would have to walk through the snowdrifts. Joan opened the door, neither looking at Karl nor speaking to him. As she began to shove her way through the piled snow, he yelled out to her in a voice that was obviously intended for the ears of the neighbors: 'At least I had my hand in Bert Nelson's daughter's diamond twat!'

Unable to run to the house, fleeing from the reverberations of his ugly words, Joan slogged through the snow as fast as she could, but her high heels, with her nylons drooped over her ankles, reduced her pace to a crawl. Fortunately her mother wasn't at home, so her appearance went unobserved. By the time dinner was served (now by another farm girl who was not so stubborn about dinner-supper terminology, and who did not have a lot of Catholic brothers and sisters), Joan was able to describe the wedding ceremony and her place at the table of honor without crying like a baby.

Mrs. Nelson thought it unheard of that Joan was asked to preside with the wedding party. Mr. Nelson thought that it showed a gesture of respect for the whole Nelson family and the kindnesses that Linda had received. When he was pressed by his wife, though, he was hard put to explain any particular kindnesses that would entitle Joan to a favored spot. Joan would have liked to suggest that Linda's brother had blackmailed her into the whole scheme, but she didn't have any proof other than her personal struggle with Karl by the lake. She would also have liked to tell her parents something of the depths of resentment that some people seemed to possess towards them, although she was not yet aware of the extent of their resentment. But to do so would have required an explanation she was incapable of offering. Instead, she described the magnificence of the Mass in such lyrical terms that Mrs. Nelson later confessed to her husband her worst of fears – that their daughter might become attracted to Catholicism, and God only knew what else.

Chapter Ten

Virgins

Joan continued to feel weird about the wedding and Karl's treatment of her. She also felt guilty, and spent a lot of time attempting to explain to herself his reasons for assuming she was so desperate to get laid. She was not oblivious to her reputation among the people in town as the snobbish daughter of Bert Nelson, inheritor and inhabitant of Locksley Hall, a castle selected by her parents to enclose and secure their princess. That much of town gossip she could sense, but her sexual reputation was a delusion. Aside from some kissing and groping with two or three town boys, boys of her own age who seemed disinclined to proceed any further than an exchange of chewing gum, she had experienced nothing that was even remotely sexual. Or so she thought.

There was no one Joan could talk to about her own personal interpretations of sex. Her friends liked to talk about the times they were being kissed, and by whom, but kissing was the limit of their discussions. If anyone had tried Karl's strong-armed tactic on her friends, they either weren't admitting it or else they were too embarrassed to disclose anything out of the ordinary. She had read once that if a boy got fresh with you the way Karl had, you were supposed to kick him in the 'privates'. 'Nudge him sharply with your knee' the advice had stated – but her mother had dismissed that article as being unnecessary. Nice girls simply did not allow themselves to get into situations where such strong measures had to be taken.

Joan did know one town girl whose reputation was similar to Linda's, although this girl, Ruthie, was younger than Linda and a definite social cut above her. Ruthie's father worked in the bank, which classified the family as respectable, but Ruthie and her older sister always had more dates that anyone else in town (and they were real dates, too, not just pickups.) Ruthie got a lot of mail, too, from sailors and boys from towns as far away as Mankato, which was almost a hundred miles away. To have pen pals spanning a distance of more than fifty miles was exceptional for anyone, even for a senior in high school whose only visible talents were on display in cheerleading.

At first Joan thought Ruthie's voluminous correspondence might be attributed to her friendliness, and also because she belonged to the Walther League Choir, which meant traveling to a number of towns where she could easily have made friends. Ruthie loved to dance, an affection that was expressly forbidden by her church, so she did the second best thing by singing in the approved choir even though her voice was thin and reedy. At school Ruthie and Joan liked to share a Latin text and would engage in rather obvious subterfuges, like hiding the book in a locker, in order to sit together, thereby livening up the dreary sessions of the dull language and its endless tales of gods and battles.

One day, about three months after Linda's wedding, the class was attempting to wade through the story of the Rape of the Sabines, an account that held no interest for either Joan or Ruthie, in English or in Latin. Joan was fascinated, however, by the illustration to the text, which showed a group of women in diaphanous gowns being hauled away by men wearing spiky helmets who looked unusually pleased with themselves.

'I wonder what that feels like,' Joan mused, as much to herself as to Ruthie.

'If you promise not to tell, I'll tell you.' At Joan's fervent nod of assurance, she proceeded. 'We – Norm and I – we did it only once, and we really didn't do it all the way. I mean, we only partly did it, but he stuck it in and I've never felt anything so good.'

Joan didn't dispute the possibility that a person could do it and not do it at the same time. Her interest was not in Ruthie's description of herself as technically a virgin; what interested her was Ruthie's testimony to pleasure. 'Why don't you do it anymore?' Joan asked.

'We don't because we decided we'd better not or we'd be sorry, and it is wrong, you know. But we're going to get married soon, so it's not so bad. After all, we love each other.'

'Just exactly, how did it feel?' Joan ardently hoped that the Latin teacher, who had so far chosen to ignore their delinquent in-class behavior, would let them continue until Ruthie had given a full account.

'It felt like – I don't know – it felt like hot water being poured all over you and into places you've never felt before.' Despite the vagueness of her friend's description, Joan experienced a series of twitches in her crotch, and she found herself blushing as if she had been the pleasure-seeker.

'Did you ask him to do it, or anything? I mean, did you decide ahead of time?'

'Of course not. But men can't help themselves, you know, and sometimes they have to do it so bad that they develop this terrible pain that can kill them.'

Joan looked down at the Sabine warriors. They seemed joyously free from pain, as Ruthie continued her own narrative. 'You've got to watch out, though. Once you've done it you don't know how to stop, and that's why Norm and I decided not to see each other very much until we're married.'

The idea of a perpetual, unsatisfied twinge was too much for Joan. How can you prevent doing it if men are in danger of such terrible pain? And how could you stop doing it if the pain always returns? Joan toyed with the idea of telling Ruthie about Linda's reaction to sex, a reaction that seemed to occur from a completely different act, but Linda had toasted the loyalty of her friends at her wedding, which meant that Joan must preserve her secret. Instead, she stated a question in general terms, hoping that Ruthie would sense what she was driving at. 'Do all people like it that much? I mean, older people, too? And people who don't know each other so well?' Strangers; people decidedly not in love. How could she say it?

'If you love each other, yes,' Ruthie stated sententiously. 'Otherwise it's just something that animals do.'

'Why do it then when they don't love each other? I mean, they're not just animals, are they?'

'Men do it all the time. But that's because of the pain, so you have to be sure if he loves you, and I made sure before I did it with Norm that one time.'

Joan wanted to know how you determined the man's love. What kinds of tests or pledges were necessary? But she didn't like to take too much advantage of Ruthie's candor. Already the girl had gone too far in admitting her one lapse, and Joan was sure that she would later regret it, and perhaps even say one day that it was all made up, a product of her imagination – an imagination that had been stimulated by the sexy nature of the Latin text's illustration.

The Latin teacher, whose eyes had been conveniently focused elsewhere, finally zeroed in on the two chatting girls and threatened immediate suspension plus twenty extra lines of Virgil unless they both shut up. Despite the threats, however, Ruthie was able to add one bit of advice: 'Whatever you do, don't French kiss, unless you want to go all the way. That's what leads them on and drives them nuts. Norm and I don't even do that anymore.'

Joan kept her word to Ruthie, but in the long run it didn't matter, since Ruthie tended to share her delights with other friends. Eventually the story got back to her, greatly exaggerated, of course. Not knowing exactly whom to blame, she blamed all those in whom she had confided, but she was most fearful that the word would get back to her mother. Ruthie's noble experiment in temporary chastity did little for her marriage plans. Within six months of the conversation in the Latin class, Norm left town to join the military, and Ruthie was left with countless dates and pen pals, but no true love. (Three years later she married the driver of the local school bus, a man so achingly handsome that everyone wondered what she had seen in Norm.)

Joan had witnessed, during the year that she turned sixteen, an account of sexual intercourse of a romantic nature approaching the sublime (Ruthie's), as well as a gang bang so completely devoid of emotion and pleasure that it could have been frozen into *bas relief* and still have been lacking in emotional appeal (Linda's scene). She was beginning to learn of the similarities between two acts so superficially different, but making the connections between the two were beyond her understanding.

Her increasing absorption with the theoretical foundations of sex led her to Ronald Boswell, an attraction she found almost magnetic. One of the most handsome and elusive young men in town, he was the second son in a family of four sons, all of whom were less than two years apart. His father came close to claiming the title of town drunk, but apparently the pressures of his family obligations forced him into occasional, desultory employment, so he was not considered totally indigent and worthless. At times this father of four performed janitorial services for Mr. Nelson's office building; sometimes he helped out with the snow shoveling that kept highway crews busy for at least five months of the year. He was a handsome man who managed to look dignified even when totally immobilized from alcohol. Propped against a booth at the liquor store on Saturday nights, he was allowed to sleep off the effects of his double shots until one of his sons arrived to take him home. Once home he would make feeble attempts at raising hell, but by the time his sons were old enough to buy their own drinks when they came to collect him, most of his scenes were considered more amusing than frightening, pathetic attempts to create a storm that everyone knew he couldn't handle.

Mrs. Boswell had a beautiful garden and often sold vegetables to women whose gardening skills ended with the tending of gladiolas and delphiniums. A fat, placid woman without any detectable animosity at the way the world had treated her, she clearly enjoyed her four handsome sons, all of whom adored her and liked to engage in fights to protect her name.

Although she would have settled for any one of the brothers, Joan was particularly smitten with Ronald. All of them were outstanding athletes and had won athletic scholarships to colleges that they normally would never have been able to afford. They attended these colleges sporadically, often enrolling one semester but neglecting to make it to classes regularly enough to pass exams. Thus they forfeited their team eligibility and would have to drop out of college altogether, but before long they would appear at another college, ready to begin the process once more.

Joan felt that Mr. Boswell's drinking habits lent the family an air of pathos that other families lacked as well as provided a convenient explanation for the sons' lack of perseverance. She also liked Mrs. Boswell's devotion to her religion, a piety that sent her to Mass every Sunday while her men remained home. Joan preferred Ronald because he had made it clear that he liked her, and, unlike other young men in New Bonn who conveyed their affections by the oblique methods of insult and teasing, Ronald had walked up to her one night at the Korner Kafe and announced that he was taking her home. This announcement relieved Joan of having to flirt with him from afar, attempting to catch his eye or captivating him in different ways and always surrounded by a dozen or more young people. Instead, Ronald simply remained at the bar, drinking his beer, and when Joan stood up to leave, instead of appearing at her side ready to escort her through the snow and slush of New Bonn streets, he made her wait at his side at the bar while he finished his beer. Yet she didn't feel insulted by his lack of courtliness because he was so much fun to stand next to: over six-three, he towered over her by more than a foot, a spatial ratio that she thought made her look good, too, for they presented an interesting study in perspective as they stood together at the bar. Even though she had entered her sixteenth year, she still wore a junior bra and her knees were almost as large as her thighs, but her chestnut hair was long and glossy and her smile radiated a generally untroubled disposition. Ronald, gangly and dark with eyes the color of burnt oak leaves, could have played starring roles in the movies, Joan thought, but was glad his ambition fell far short of leaving New Bonn.

Ronald didn't expect to drive, even though Joan was accustomed to handing over the keys to her father's car to any boy she was with at the time. Most of the boys would automatically get behind the wheel and reach out their hands for the keys. Since Joan had unlimited use ('within reason' was her parents' formula) of one of the family's three cars, whereas most of the males of New Bonn had to rely upon the caprices of their fathers for permission to take the car for an evening, Joan had learned that this male disadvantage was a perpetual sore spot that was not easily eradicated by an evening's transferal of driving privileges.

For most males in New Bonn, taking a girl home was actually a rhetorical phrase which really designated the ways that a girl was to spend the rest of the evening. 'Going home' usually meant a cross-county trip to a more liberal village that would serve beer to minors, usually in a town where Lutherans could dance without being detected.

Joan expected Ronald to suggest a change in locale and was surprised when he said that he preferred staying in town. 'Why don't we go somewhere and park? I've had enough beer and I have to get up early tomorrow.'

Since tomorrow was Sunday, Joan wondered if he intended to make one of his rare visits to Mass. The idea of his kneeling quietly and attending to the saints thrilled her. 'Okay. I have to get up early too, and so maybe it's not such a good idea. To go somewhere, I mean.' She did have to get up fairly early to play the organ for Sunday services, but that small duty seemed childish compared to whatever noble plans he might have in mind. She also liked the idea of directly parking instead of spending time drinking beer and making conversations that never seemed to penetrate even the outer layers of whatever people were thinking. Although she was good at gossip and an excellent mime, the strain of extracting mutual interests from reluctant conversationalists, and the routine of drawing admissions from taciturn young males bored her and made her tense and edgy.

Ronald's eyes were closed but Joan doubted if he were asleep. Without opening them or looking at her, he said, 'Why don't you park by the elevators instead of the usual?' Was the 'usual' Hell's Half Acre? Joan assumed it was but wondered how she was expected to know. She had passed by the twin towers of the grain elevators almost every day she had lived in New Bonn, but she had never seen their possibilities as a haven for lovers. Now she saw their wonderful potential, for, positioned as they were, like great squatting giants, they contained between their abutting platforms a single, almost perfect space of about twelve feet, just enough to accommodate one car. 'I never thought of that!' she exclaimed as she drove into their tunnel.

Ronald looked neither pleased nor surprised at her limited knowledge of local geography. 'There are some things you don't know that I might be able to teach you.' His voice, naturally low and resonant, descended to almost a mutter, and sounded positively unctuous. Here was a man who clearly knew the ropes, Joan marveled. He was over twenty-one, occasionally attended college, and had cared for – with the cooperation of his three brothers – an irresponsible father. His mother was a credit to the martyrs, too.

As soon as Joan shut off the motor Ronald pulled her to him and began to kiss her with deep thrusts, forcing his tongue into her mouth and wiggling it around as if he were trying to choke her. At the same time his arms were clawing their way into her coat and underneath her sweater.

She remembered Ruthie's admonition about French kissing and its consequences, but Ruthie hadn't told her how physically helpless a girl is when the man is slurping with such force. He unfastened her bra with one hand while reaching with the other inside her skirt. She knew she should attempt to halt his gropings, but whenever she tried to say something he brought his mouth down upon hers with another ferocious kiss. In the moonlight his face looked like a warrior's; the cheeks seemed flattened against his thin, bony nose, and his eyes gleamed like high-powered flashlights or railroad signals. There was nothing tender or ingratiating about this man now. In fact he displayed a single-mindedness that was scary to her, but his unfamiliar nature made him stand out like a general in a field of privates. Remembering Ruthie's advice about French kissing, Joan renewed her efforts and pursed her lips while attempting to push him away. A rather gentle gesture but one that she hoped contained some authority.

'What the hell did you do that for?' He pulled his head back but still kept one hand on her breast.

'I don't think we'd better start something we can't – ah – finish.' Joan sensed the priggish sound to this explanation and tried to amend it. 'I mean, it's really dangerous, isn't it, to do this if you—'

'Oh bullshit! You want to. I want to. What's so dangerous about it?'

Joan's regard for Ronald's independence diminished. In developing strong emotions and commitments during her three-plus years' duration in New Bonn she had learned to recognize what other people were always insisting she wanted or needed, from her parents and teachers to even Linda's brother in his own warped way. 'I don't want to, and I don't care if you do, I still don't,' she responded, her voice raised to a near shout.

'What'sa matter? Why don't you want to? Is it that time of the month or something?'

Joan had never heard menstruation mentioned in mixed company. She had assumed that most men either ignored it or thought about it only when it concerned water sports or headaches. Ronald's reference embarrassed her, and it also put her in a position of denying a nonexistent condition instead of defending important moral principles. 'I don't want to, and that's that.' Let him think whatever he wanted; at least she wasn't being sucked into some kind of futile defense.

'Karl says you are one hot number.'

So Karl's rejection had been elevated into another conquest legend! Joan was curious at how far Karl had altered his sad attempts at seduction. 'What did Karl tell you about me? It isn't true, you know. I know without hearing what you're going to say that whatever he said isn't true.'

'Relax, girl.' Ronald withdrew his hand from her breast, leaving her unhooked and feeling as if she were completely disrobed. Ronald lit a cigarette for himself and then offered one to Joan. 'He didn't say much. Only that he had gotten into your blouse. Nothing else, I swear it.'

Joan was relieved that Karl's account was so mild and wondered how to explain its modest nature. 'Well, he didn't get that far, if you'd like to know, but he tried, which was something I didn't count on and I only went with him that day because his sister had just gotten married and there was sort of a party, too.'

'Yeah, I know all about it. Karl was drunk out of his mind and took you by the lake and felt your tits. Or tried to, if you say so.'

Joan had not realized that drinking episodes were treated the same way that thwarted sexual liaisons were dealt with: transformed, through some kind of crazy logic, into Herculean bouts. Now she was beginning to understand some of the community taboos against drinking for girls, for if a girl drank it was a safe bet to assume she put. 'I don't know about Karl. He wasn't drunk as far as I know. Unless he got drunk later. I wouldn't have ridden with him if he had been,' she added righteously.

'Forget Karl. He's a big liar, anyhow. I was just testing you out. Are you a cherry? Is that why you don't want to?'

That wondrous term 'cherry', which Joan had heard about in folk songs where the dirty meanings are disguised through innocent-sounding lyrics, applied now to Joan made her blush more than when Ronald had referred to menstruation. She knew that her precious possession should not be discussed between the two of them, yet she couldn't ignore it because it was absolutely central to the issue. If she weren't a virgin, she must be lusting after his flesh, or so she felt he assumed. Lusting after anyone's body, for that matter.

As a non-virgin, she would be like Linda (before she was married), a sex machine desperately seeking service, or else she would be like Ruthie, forever tempted and forever haunted by that one isolated act – an act that had condemned her forever to a route of endless desire. Whereas a virgin, which she was, could neither want it nor have it. A virgin sought her defloration through the honorable vocation of marriage. But how could she explain this, for wouldn't her theory of virginity sound like a request for a marriage proposal?

She decided to take the risk and concentrate on stating the advantages of remaining pure, hoping that her explanation wouldn't make her sound as prissy as she felt, for she did not want to be responsible for the creation of another legend – that of the frigid tease. 'Yes, I'm a virgin, but it's because I want to be. Not because anyone else has decided it for me.' She hoped that Ronald was not smart enough to attack her logic.

'A virgin! Whoopee! I've never had a virgin before!'

He proceeded to once again press his face against her and pushed his tongue into her mouth. She pushed him back so hard that his head hit the top of the car seat.

'You're not going to have me either, and let's get that understood!'

He stared at her with such surprise that she was almost sorry to have rejected him so forcefully. Had no female ever said no to him? Had he always had his way with all girls in this manner, simply by thrusting his tongue into their mouths and insisting that they were screaming for gratification? She couldn't help wondering what his mother would say, that gentle woman who tolerated so much from her men with such cheer and grace. His warrior look had faded, Joan thought, leaving him flattened by failure, thwarted by a sixteen-year-old virgin who had parked her father's car in a lovers' haven and yet still thought he deserved special treatment.

Ronald grunted and reached for a cigarette. 'You are too goddamned much. As we used to say in the army, you are too fucking much to believe for real.' Yet the idea of her virginity, of her being too much, must have fascinated him more than it angered him, for he then looked at her with an amused grin that also reflected a proprietary interest. 'Maybe you've been saving it for me, huh?'

Joan had never before been a participant in the vulgarities of a sexual argument. 'It' and 'cherry' and 'time of the month' were terms that had significance to her because of their mysterious natures. There were also words that were written on walls and were spoken among men only, words like 'fuck' and 'pussy' and 'cunt' and 'tits' and 'slut' and 'whore'. And there were those words that stated conditions that only women used, and used them obliquely, words like 'virgin' and 'intercourse' and 'impregnation' and 'menstrual flow'. She knew that both sexes had their euphemisms as well as their barbarisms for sexual experience, but she had never realized that both sexes ever used these words together in an ordinary conversation. Thus Ronald's expressions shocked her more than his unjust assumptions and his unrealistic demands upon her, and her shock produced a kind of anger that caused her to speak more firmly and more directly than she had ever thought herself capable.

'I'm not saving anything for you. I just don't want to, and I don't want to ever until I'm married.' The minute she articulated the time-honored statement she realized its basic lie, for she did want to, and she wanted to very much, so much that she felt that if he would attempt to kiss her again she would throw herself at him, for he was the sexiest man she had ever known. And the most self-confident.

Her mention of the word 'marriage' immediately mollified him. He looked at her as if he might be pondering an elopement that same evening, his gaze so eloquently tender that she instantly imagined herself the mother of four little Boswell boys and a womb quivering to contain more.

'Don't worry. I'm not going to hurt you. I won't try anything more, okay?' He put his arm around her shoulders and nestled his head into her sweater. His voice was muffled but she thought she detected an authentic pain. Tentatively she stroked his hair, luxuriant locks of such lustrous color and texture that she imagined herself swimming in deep pools of foaming water. 'I'm sorry,' he muttered. 'Really sorry. I just didn't know what you were like and what you wanted.'

She kissed the top of his head, and he looked up and smiled at her with such joy that she thought she would burst with adoration. They sat for a time enjoying each other's admiration, nuzzling each other like friendly cattle. Once his hand started to stray to her breast but she flicked it away as if it contained no more menace than a common junebug, and he placed it back on the seat without comment.

Joan saw that his watch read one-fifteen, which meant trouble for her since her curfew was supposed to be twelve. Ronald, with no one to account to for his hours, was committed only to the last Mass in the morning, if that was actually his reason for getting up early.

'I've got to get home. My dad is going to kill me. I promised to be home by twelve.'

'Tell him you were with me. I'll take the blame.' His offer seemed genuine if unclear, and she wished she could use him as an explanation, but she knew she couldn't. Instead, she would have to bury his importance to her, for she knew that neither parent would be willing to accept him as a protector of their daughter. To them he was just one of an oversized Catholic family that produced more children than it could afford. She also knew that their apprehension at her association with Catholic boys was based on the reputation that Catholic boys had earned in New Bonn: exploiters of Protestant girls, they used them until they were ready to marry; then they simply ditched them for chaste Catholic wives. The Catholic girls in New Bonn tended to confirm the reputation of the Catholic boys, for they never dated them; after a time they simply married them.

Joan felt that Ronald could very well be the exception, though, for he had already tried his seduction and seemed satisfied to accept Joan's virginity as a permanent condition, to be altered only by marriage. As Joan drove him home she was already planning and discarding plausible excuses to present to her parents for her lateness. She anticipated being deprived of a car for a designated time, but she was not panicky because she knew they could not permanently refuse her a privilege that was automatically allowed to anyone over fifteen and in reasonable possession of important faculties, as common as driving tractors to those who lived on farms.

When she dropped off Ronald at his house she was not disturbed by his quick peck on the cheek and his offhand, 'See you around,' for young people in New Bonn didn't make definite dates or construct formal arrangements, except under circumstances so extraordinary that most young people would want to avoid them, like funerals or weddings or special family occasions. She would have liked him to violate the whole custom, however, by casually suggesting a specific meeting time, but his easy acceptance of normal conduct tended to make him more malleable and more convincing as a suitor.

Joan drove home ready to accept the worst kinds of punishment for him. She found her apprehensions baseless, though, since both parents had gone to sleep before midnight and never did find out what time she came in.

Had they known that she was out defending her virginity to a Catholic boy they would have stayed up to greet her, and maybe they would have inspected her clothes – and the car – for traces of her capitulation. Tired as she was that night, she still had trouble getting to sleep. She knew her conscience should be clear, her triumph unmistakable. Why, then, did she feel like such a weakling?

Chapter Eleven

Presbyterians

Joan was fairly sure that announcing her virginity to Ronald gave her a respect, if not reverence, that all girls could use. Ronald – for some reason no one ever called him Ronnie – had the reputation of a notorious (and therefore successful) ass bandit. She knew he was bound to talk, but she was almost certain of what he would say, that here was one sharp cutie who was not going to put for anyone just because she was expected to. Or so she hoped, for she had no way of knowing what variations of the truth had contributed to his reputation. But it wasn't hard to know what the boys were saying of the girls in New Bonn: the tiny size of the community and its limited resources of communication made it impossible to escape detection. If a boy tried to unfasten a girl's bra or reach into her panties before half an hour of necking had expired, it was safe to assume that the girl already had been discussed and evaluated as an easy lay.

Among the categories of females in New Bonn, the young ones fitted conveniently into three major groups. First, there were those who were known to bestow their affections through ardent necking. (Joan supposed she belonged to this group despite her genuine indifference to most kissing and hugging.) Then there were the girls who made only token objections to having their boobs fondled. These girls were also not squeamish about French kissing.

Joan had at least two friends who belonged to this category although they never admitted to it, but she knew, from their distressed faces after long sessions of necking, just how far they had gone. Often their cheeks and shoulders would be red and sore from whisker rub, and there were usually frantic attempts, when the dome light of the car went on to signal a door opening, to pull down their skirts and to conceal their gaping breasts.

The third category of girls was beautifully simple, lacking tiresome, complicated distinctions and rules. This category consisted of girls who did *it*. Joan was certain she had no friends who fitted into this category, except for Ruthie, who didn't really count since her sole lay had been duly narrated to a number of girls. Also, Ruthie's confession had served as a kind of expiation and had the value of restoring her to the sisterhood of virginity, but in a qualified sense. That she did it but didn't really do it seemed perfectly logical and acceptable to her friends.

Of the girls who were known, without doubt, to screw, the patterns of their conduct seemed to follow a remarkable lack of discrimination on their part. They resembled a collective of Lindas, girls who put out and shut up without demonstrable emotion or feelings of rejection when their partners of a night would vanish, later to be replaced by others who were equally transitory. Most of these girls were farm girls, which suggested to Joan that farming required more primitive standards than those demanded from the village.

Yet the goals of these promiscuous farm girls didn't seem to be merely reproductory, as one might assume from being raised in an environment where everything of merit had to be fertile: testicles were sliced away because a certain kind of meat was needed; thus the lack of genitals assured a definite fate, as well as a definite product for domestic consumption. Hens were killed when they no longer dropped their minimum daily requirement of two a day, often to appear that noon on the dinner table, neatly arranged according to anatomy – the breasts, wings, and thighs fried crisp, the liver and gizzard and heart incorporated into the gravy. Corn that didn't tassel was chopped into silage; oats that didn't ripen were considered green and therefore dangerous, and were dug underground. Runts of any litter were automatically killed; without normal weight and clear eyes, even the promise of genitals was not enough to prevent their destruction.

Joan could never reconcile the farmers' emphasis on fertility – their absolute loathing and dismissal of anything that couldn't or didn't reproduce – with the passive acceptance of sex that the farm girls seemed to uphold. She could not see how sex might appear mechanical when compared to the smooth operations of the combine or the reliable movements of the disker. Now and then a farm girl would get pregnant and immediately marry, for there was never any question about marriage once a girl had become impregnated. The only question that did occur was an occasional denial of paternity, a denial that was usually answered by threats and an exchange of acres.

Joan, although belonging to the first category of affectionate girls who liked to kiss, was always aware that she might be unfairly vilified and demoted to a lower category, but it never occurred to her that she might be cast among the lower echelons – she could never imagine herself as a farm girl who screws. Her strong statement to Ronald she thought of as an attempt to establish some kind of identity, something that could ally her with one solid, definite bloc.

She felt that he could have little to gain by defaming her, and she was correct. Her virginity now became as much a burden to him as it was to her, for it served as a challenge and a conquest, but it also provided him with a dilemma, for if he gained it he would lose his sense of purpose, a purpose that for him was unprecedented in its strength and magnitude.

Despite the imminence of Ronald Boswell, Mr. and Mrs. Nelson were generally pleased with their daughter's conduct. She played the organ for Sunday services with such zest that they were often complimented upon their daughter's musical sensibilities. Mrs. Blue, long since returned from the hospital, but still looking ashy and fragile, seemed content to relinquish her role as an organist and acted as if she preferred to sit with the other members of the choir. Perhaps she liked the dignity that the black robes offered to their wearers. Perhaps she liked to participate in the processional and recessional, although anyone closely looking at her couldn't help but notice how her hands shook as if she were lugging a fifty-pound weight instead of the standard fourteen-ounce hymnal.

The choir was awful, and Joan was happy to be disassociated from them. The choir director, a bustling woman who had managed to bring in male voices previously heard from within the congregation, didn't know the first thing about music, not even the fundamentals of harmony. Unable to work from any position of strength, she compromised the entire ensemble by letting the males sing an octave below the sopranos and altos. The effect was like an augmented girls' choir, accompanied by a dozen or so lumbering male voices.

Occasionally Joan drowned out the choir, which irritated the director and necessitated the arbitration of Reverend Blue. After Joan had been warned not to undermine the efforts of those 'sincere' voices – Reverend Blue's term – she contented herself with playing arpeggios and contrasting chords, interludes and innovations that were not in the score but which served as attractive embellishments to the dreary anthems that the choir offered every week. No one objected to these diversions, and Joan thought most people didn't even notice them, yet one Sunday, after she had put the finishing touches to a series of diminished sevenths that had nicely contrasted with the stout major key of the anthem, she saw Mrs. Blue staring at her with a look so clearly hostile that she almost quit playing on the spot. Mrs. Blue had looked as if she could happily devour the organist and spit her on the keys, which made Joan wonder what kind of life was residing in that glazed exterior.

One Sunday, after feeling Mrs. Blue's glares burning holes in her back, Joan decided to duck out faster than usual. The musicians always changed robes in the church basement, but Joan decided to go home without changing her robe and then return it later when nobody would be around. She slipped out of the door to the car (she had come early to practice and was using the Starbird, her personal favorite) and made it home before her parents. She hung the robe in her bedroom closet, not because she felt especially guilty about her mild subterfuge but because she wanted to avoid explaining to her mother a simple action that could only assume complications in its telling.

She was going to the movies after their Sunday dinner – their sole concession to provincial dining hours – and she intended to drop off the robe at the church on her way, but before she could leave there was a phone call for her. It was Reverend Blue, demanding to speak to her at once.

'Joan,' he growled, 'why did you leave the church with your robe when you did?'

No preamble. No introduction. Just the implied accusation. Joan's sense of outrage at the minister's rudeness made her feel both innocent and ill-judged. 'I forgot it. I really forgot it, that I had it on till I got home. I was going to return it. In fact I was just going out of the door to bring it back.' She wondered who the hell had seen her and had told him so quickly.

'I think I had better come and talk to your parents. I'll be there in ten minutes.'

It had long been the custom of the clergy to visit homes without invitation, but Joan was not prepared for the peremptory tone of the minister. She quickly explained the purpose of the minister's visit, but her mother seemed less concerned with the episode and his intentions than she was in removing the traces of their pre-dinner highball.

Mr. Nelson joked about it. 'Maybe he's coming with the police to put Joanie in jail. Then we'll only have to see her on visiting days.'

'Hush, Bert. I don't think this is anything to laugh about.' Mrs. Nelson thought there was little material in life for jokes, and this occasion was less promising than most. 'I don't think you'd better be watching TV when he comes, either.'

Mr. Nelson went into the study and sat down in his easy chair. 'Is it all right to read the paper, then?'

Mrs. Nelson never got her chance to retaliate to her husband's mockery, for at that moment Reverend Blue knocked on the back door and then strode into the kitchen without even waiting to be admitted to the house. His pouchy face was inflamed with rage, and without even nodding to Joan's mother and father he began to scream at Joan with such uncontrollable fury that she was sure he would have a stroke on the spot.

'You told a falsehood!' he yelled. 'Young lady, you told a falsehood!'

Not since her juvenile reading of *Little Women* had Joan encountered that word. 'Do you know that your daughter deliberately lied and told a falsehood?' he addressed her parents without actually looking at them.

Joan wondered if the word seemed as strange to her parents as it did to her. She also wondered what they would do if Reverend Blue dropped dead from anger on their linoleum. At the rate he was going he could melt into the tiles and never be missed. She noticed that the four of them looked as if they were standing in a huddle, for no one had sat down after the minister had stormed into the house.

'Just a minute. What is it, exactly, that you are accusing my daughter of?' Mr. Nelson's quiet tone sounded as if he were patiently questioning an angry child.

'Your daughter deliberately walked off the premises of the church wearing a choir robe and then lied to me when I asked her why she'd done it.'

'Joan, did you lie to Mr. Blue?' Joan thought her father deliberately underlined the 'mister'.

'Well, not exactly. I told him I'd forgotten all about it, which I really had, but I was expecting to return it later.'

'You see! How can you do two things at once? How can you "not exactly" lie?'

Joan wondered why her mother didn't explode. Criticism that was only vaguely associated with morality always touched her off, pulled at her until she became an active member of a moral army. She wondered, also, how either of them could resist responding to the quaint language: falsehoods on Sundays were evidently more inflammatory than ordinary weekday lies. Yet when her father spoke his voice was gentle, with just the slightest touch of irony.

'Joan, I think you'd better apologize to Mr. Blue for what was clearly a misunderstanding on your part. I know, and your mother knows, that you didn't set out to steal the choir robe, and we both know you could easily have forgotten about it, since it's not a very important item to worry about.'

Reverend Blue sensed his defeat but was reluctant to withdraw his weapons. 'You might not think it's important, but those robes cost more than one hundred dollars apiece, and my wife and I are responsible every Sunday for checking them in and out.'

Joan imagined Reverend Blue checking off robes to Mrs. Blue the way an accountant calls off figures to his apprentice, but even this methodical process didn't explain how they had detected her lapse so soon. The robes bore neither names nor numbers; one simply grabbed whichever robe fit best and had the cleanest collar, so that one missing robe would mean a reduced number but not a definite culprit. She could only assume that the couple spied on her when she was the least aware. Perhaps they had even followed her home in their car and saw her entering her house wearing the unconventional garment.

'I'm sorry. I'm really sorry if I made you worry.' Should she add that she'd never do it again? 'I guess I'm careless. I'll try to be more careful from now on.' She was damned if she would admit to his accusation of lying, especially since she could count on her father as an ally.

Joan could tell Reverend Blue was not satisfied, but he also knew that to continue he could easily lose a substantial monthly contribution as well as a building fund figure that had been projected into the thousands. He also saw that he wasn't going to be invited to sit down, and that he had better accept what he considered an inadequate explanation for Joan's egregious act before he lost tithe, building fund, and all promises of endowments, current or posthumous. 'All right. I suppose it can happen, but it seemed unlikely to us – ah – me – when we saw you leave.' Sensing that he had been trapped into revealing more than he intended, he began to walk to the door – this time the front door.

'I suppose you have been preoccupied for a long time. You've probably lost touch with young people.' Joan detected a hint of malice in her father's comment.

'Yes. Maybe I need a vacation, or a change – I mean chance – to be with young people again.'

This last part of the dialogue mystified Joan. What on earth did her father mean by losing touch with young people? Reverend Blue had never had it in the first place, and most people had long ago given up on the possibilities of any kind of youth group, nor could they see the point in one. The Presbyterians of New Bonn had simply quit competing with the Catholics and the Lutherans for the young people. Perhaps her father was alluding to his preoccupation with Mrs. Blue, but there was hardly anything new about that.

After Reverend Blue left, the delinquent robe draped over his arm, Joan's father retreated to the TV to watch the remains of a program that he looked forward to all week. He seemed grumpy and too out of sorts to explain to his daughter his ambiguous comments. She thought of enlisting her mother's help, but Mrs. Nelson was less convinced than her husband of her daughter's one hundred percent innocence. In fact, she was so annoyed at Joan that once the minister had left in his car she hissed at Joan, 'How could you do such a stupid thing?'

Joan retorted with one of her mother's favorite expressions, 'I think he's making a mountain out of a molehill, or was trying to, anyhow. What's with him, do you know? Doesn't he have anything better to do than watch me and trail me around?'

Mrs. Nelson looked as if she would like to answer her daughter's question. Obviously she knew something that made her judge the minister's conduct in ways that differed from her usual uncompromising manner. 'Never mind. He's got a lot on his mind, that's all.' She might have said, 'poor man,' but evidently thought better of it. To her, people who had a lot on their minds were usually described as poor; sometimes they were even suffering. 'Just don't do such a thoughtless thing again,' she added.

As Joan left the room her mother said, 'We'll see that he doesn't hound you anymore.' The determination in her voice was unmistakable, which made Joan sure that the reverend and his wife would have to seek new trails upon which to snoop. Yet both parents remained close-mouthed and refused to explain any more about Reverend Blue's queer behavior. She knew that if she looked hard enough and asked enough questions she was sure to find clues and eventually answers. Her mind had by now undergone more than three years of training in New Bonn mores, which had allowed her to develop a genuine talent for asking the right questions of the right people – the only way you found out anything of importance in the town.

Although the episode with Reverend Blue had prevented Joan from meeting her friends at the movies that Sunday, it did easily lead her into an account of the incident, thereby enabling her friends to help clarify the motives and conduct of two people who had ceased being of much interest or appeal in the community. Most Presbyterians thought him bland and not especially likable, but he was accommodating enough to suit their mild requirements. He was expected to uphold the convictions of the modern Presbyterian church without flaunting any of them. He was not expected to create a virtuoso sermon performance every Sunday, and it was more important to talk about the eradication of error than it was to lament and deplore the existence of sin. The congregation did not want to be reminded of demanding spiritual dependencies, which meant that the prayers were reasonable and the requests explicit.

Joan's friend, Maryann, whose father was an elder and who thus had access to the chronicles and budget of the church, confirmed what Joan had surmised, stated in the form of a direct quotation from her father: 'Presbyterians aren't supposed to make damned fools of themselves. We leave that to the Catholics and the Lutherans.'

Joan also learned from Maryann that before Reverend Blue, who had been in New Bonn only seven years, there had been a kindly old widower who had quietly gone off his rocker one Sunday morning and had to be quickly replaced. The nearest Presbyterian college and seminary, Macalaster in St. Paul, had sent Reverend Blue as an interim replacement, on approval until a permanent replacement could be obtained. Reverend Blue had just graduated from the seminary and had been stranded without a regular appointment – during the summer he would fill in for vacationing clergy – until the call from New Bonn summoned him to an interlude of rural service.

Although he looked like a farmer, with his broad shoulders and thick legs and icy eyes that often looked as if they were studying cornfields or judging bean yields, he was really from Chicago and had spent all his life in large cities. As if to compensate for his lack of rural familiarity, he announced that his wife was 'fresh off the farm' – a description that did not sit kindly upon the ears of his first congregation. At first his sermons had been boring to the point of being unbearable; people slept openly while others fanned themselves and yawned. Then Maryann's father, whose openness combined with insouciance produced a kind of extraordinary charm, suggested privately to him that he might liven up his sermons with an occasional joke. Reverend Blue's eager reaction to this advice was almost as bad as his early tedious talks, for he then adapted the habit of prefacing each sermon with a joke taken from the latest *Reader's Digest*, repeating jokes that were neither funny nor novel. Maybe someone told him that he was overdoing that practice, too, because he eventually dropped the *Reader's Digest* format from his sermons in favor of lame anecdotes that could, at best, produce a few snickers.

By the time Mrs. Blue arrived in New Bonn, the townspeople had constructed from their imaginations a pious but lusty farm woman, ready to take on the duties of hostess as well as spiritual mistress to the congregation. Their disappointment was immediate; so frail that she had to be practically carried from the car to the parsonage, she continued to be tended constantly by her husband and the Ladies' Aid. So after seven years at New Bonn, the assignment of Reverend Blue was still considered temporary by the church officials.

It was sadly true that although the wealthiest and most influential members of the community were pillars of the Presbyterian church, it was also true that its budget was the lowest, its parsonage the shabbiest, and the church building itself was the architectural monstrosity of the community. All the money that could be considered surplus was being invested, by the elders, into a building fund, which meant that there was very little left to maintain the preacher and his wife. The church was actually a converted barn to which some skilled artisan had added a bell tower and had arranged the interior to correspond with the pitch of the roof. Instead of stained-glass windows there were windows of colored glass with Biblical scenes superimposed upon them. The basement had been dug and finished long after the church had been operating, which gave it the look of a school cafeteria.

The Presbyterians were not stingy; they gave to their building fund with the high hopes that its investments would yield quick and profitable returns, but they were unwilling to extend themselves to the point of luxury. While entertaining plans for the next, they were determined to get what they could out of the present building. Joan felt that there was a direct correlation between the church building fund and the tenure of Reverend Blue. She saw him as being good enough for the time being, but his days were definitely numbered, inextricably joined with the progress of the budget. He must have been aware of his tenuous situation, but his sermons had not become sour as a consequence. Lacking much life to begin with, they maintained their same pace, piddling around with familiar authorities but not in threatening ways, asking God's help for occasions that seemed judicious and beyond reproach. Ministers' wives were expected to do certain things, but since these things were basically so unimportant it didn't matter who did them as long as they were accomplished by someone, or so it was explained to Joan by her friend, Maryann, who was subject to privileged Presbyterian knowledge and gossip because of her father's position in the organization. Joan thought Mrs. Blue's ailments had something to do with female organs, since so little was openly said about the woman's fragile nature.

Never reluctant to discuss hernias or piles or goiters, the people of New Bonn never openly discussed complaints that had sexual origins. At first Joan thought Mrs. Blue might be sterile and her frequent hospitalizations a result of tests. She had heard of one exam where they blew colored dye into your ovaries and then you had to wait for days in the hospital to find out if you were all right. To Joan, the possibility of Reverend and Mrs. Blue engaging in sexual relations was as extraordinary as having tainted ovaries. She had read *Jane Eyre* and thought that Mrs. Blue probably had incipient TB. She would have been content with her picture of Mrs. Blue quietly spitting into her hankie until the final hemorrhage took her out of the provincial life forever, when one day Maryann confided to her that actually Mrs. Blue was a secret drinker and that her visits to the hospital had really been visits to a private sanitarium for drunks. That was what was getting to Reverend Blue, for the sanitarium was expensive and the minister was afraid he couldn't manage her expenses much longer. Furthermore, the elders had denied him a raise and he was desperate for money, so desperate he had gone to the bank for a loan and had spilled out his troubles to the president. A regrettable confession, indeed, because the president's wife was always included in the bank's confidential negotiations. Maryann's mother, a close friend of the bank president's wife, was her daughter's informant, and she had sworn her daughter to secrecy.

'If she drinks, why doesn't she act drunk?' Joan asked. 'And furthermore, why can't we smell it?' Joan, who always relied upon Sen-Sen, knew about some methods of furtive drinkers.

'She doesn't act drunk because she's always that way. You just aren't used to her any other way. I don't know why she doesn't smell. Maybe she has some magic formula or something, but just take a look at her eyes some day.'

Joan had always thought that Mrs. Blue's eyes were no different from those of other high-minded Presbyterian ladies. She saw little to distinguish her from the others except for her fragility, her flimsiness. She wore the same kinds of loud floral print dresses and sensible shoes as the others, and her wispy hair was usually tucked into a straw hat, if it was summer, or a velours hat if the time was past Labor Day. Her eyes seemed no glassier, no more smirking and vapid than her Ladies' Aid counterparts, and there was no tell-tale network of red lines wavering across their surface.

Joan decided to try her mother for more information. She knew her mother shared some of her sense of outrage at Reverend Blue's unfair attack, so one day she asked her mother what she knew about the mysterious illness of Mrs. Blue. Her mother looked only slightly surprised at her daughter's point-blank question. 'What illness? What do you know about it?'

Joan mentioned that she had heard that Mrs. Blue's illness was actually a cover-up for her perpetual intoxication.

'How did you find out about it?' Mrs. Nelson looked at her daughter with some admiration.

'Oh around. I just heard about it and thought maybe you knew if this was true.'

'Yes, it's true. Honestly, is nothing secret in this town?'

Joan murmured her assent, and then added, 'How does he, her husband, put up with it? I mean, isn't a minister supposed to set an example and not put up with that sort of thing?'

'I don't know how he puts up with it. Dr. Richardson is there half the time, and he must spend everything he makes on doctor bills.'

'Does Dr. Richardson give her the booze?' Mrs. Nelson realized that she had been trapped into revealing more than she had intended, but she was far more eager to discuss the secret vice of Mrs. Blue than others Joan had questioned her about, like Lorraine and her string of small-town businessmen, or the Peacock Lady's trio of neglected bastards.

'Dr. Richardson gives it to her just the way a doctor gives a patient medicine. He gives her only enough to keep her going and he also gives her injections to calm her nerves.'

Mrs. Nelson then went on to explain that the injections caused the shaking, not the booze itself, and that they were responsible for the occasional episodes, usually during the processionals, when she looked as if she wanted to fly away, to soar above the ugly roof of the church and straight through the bell tower, where she would be borne aloft and sustained by the flapping sleeves of her choir robe.

'Why does she have to go to the hospital, then, if Dr. Richardson takes care of her so much?' (Dr. Richardson was almost a town joke; a notorious quack who never washed his instruments and had been known to see patients in his underwear and socks, most people steered away from him. They preferred the hour's drive to Worthington and the clinic there, where their chances of medical competence were vastly improved.)

'He can't treat her all the time because her system changes and then the injections don't work. Then she has to go to the hospital where they change the medicine and she's all right for a while.' Mrs. Nelson sighed, perhaps as a lament for her own father, whose medical specialties had also been sadly limited.

'If this has been going on all this time and so many people know about it – I mean, it's not exactly news to you, for example – then why was he so mad at me for forgetting and wearing that stupid choir robe out of the church? He treated the whole thing like a terrible sin, as if I had done something unspeakable.'

Mrs. Nelson sighed again. 'I know he did, and that's why it seemed so unfair, but I think he's often out of his mind with worry and half the time he doesn't know what he's doing.'

Joan thought this queer behavior for a pastor, whose primary function, she understood, was to guard and save souls.

'I really think he was beside himself that day and didn't know what he was saying once he got started.'

'Okay. One more question. Why does she hate me so much? Don't look so shocked. I know she hates me. I can tell by the way she looks at me that she hates my guts.'

'I don't think she hates you.' Mrs. Nelson's explanation sounded to Joan almost like an apology. 'She probably doesn't even know you very well, but she must feel bad because you're playing the organ and she isn't. You know that he made her quit playing.'

Joan was suffused with disgust. Clearly she had been duped by the most important local representative of the Presbyterian church, a man who had first taken advantage of her musical intelligence, and then had played on her own desire for public recognition. All at the expense of his wife, whose function as helpmate and faithful subordinate had been reduced to the level of second soprano, third row, on Sundays.

'Next he'll expect me to sleep with him.'

'Joan! What a terrible thing to say. The poor man has troubles enough of his own without you slandering him that way.'

'Okay. Okay. I take it back. But I don't think it was very nice of him to take away her job of organist. It's not that much of a job to begin with.'

Joan's mother glared at her daughter, her patience evidently drained. 'They certainly couldn't let her play the way she was. What would have happened it she spoiled the service some day?'

Joan privately felt that there was not much to spoil. Yet her view of alcoholism tended to correspond with the community's, which equated the sin of drinking with the sin of idleness, a demonic combination, and one far removed from the effete so-called 'scientific' equation of illness and disease. Even though there were a few people who sympathized with Mrs. Blue – themselves secret nippers who sneaked slugs out of bottles hidden in china closets or pressure cookers, no one openly protested at the way she was treated. So long as she was protected by her husband she was not regarded as a victim of anything other than her own weaknesses.

Joan felt no anguish for either of the couple. She refused to see Reverend Blue as a martyred husband living out his days administering to the wanton miseries of his weak-willed wife, as some people had suggested. Mrs. Blue she found gutless and incapable of anything more interesting than her perpetual helplessness. Joan could see why priests never married and why they left the squabble of the parish to their parishioners.

As a result of her feelings towards the minister and his

wife, Joan began to take less pleasure from her Sunday meanderings upon the organ keys, and her desire for invention decreased as her contempt for Reverend Blue increased. One Sunday she called him half an hour before services were scheduled to begin, informing him that her sore throat, which she felt was almost certainly a strep infection, would prohibit her from playing that morning. Unable to protest that she was leaving the congregation high and dry, that their carefully rehearsed anthem would have to be shelved for another week, or even longer if she didn't soon recover, he would only state his concern over her illness and assured her that she would be included in the morning prayers.

Her father, although worried about a daughter who was susceptible to strep infections, smiled with amusement as she hung up the phone. 'Better go back to bed and we'll bring you some breakfast. Take the funnies with you,' he added. As he handed her the Sunday papers, she wondered how much he knew of her own feelings towards the authority of the church they had selected for her. She longed to ask him why he had ever gotten mixed up with such a bunch of lousy hypocrites. But of course she couldn't. She was not yet ready to ask the question, nor was she prepared to accept its answer.

Instead she returned to bed, smoked two cigarettes before breakfast (which infuriated her mother), and read most of the paper before she fell asleep. By Tuesday she had acquired an authentic strep infection, one so obvious that even Dr. Richardson could see the white spots.

Chapter Twelve

Laughter in the Dark

By the early spring of Joan's senior year in high school, she had engaged in a number of mild skirmishes with Ronald, whose attempts to deflower her persisted despite the desultory nature of their encounters. The more she protested, the stronger he insisted, until their evenings together formed a predictable, dreary pattern, with the same arguments reiterated, the same proclamations of her virginity being stated by her only to be argued against by him.

Joan thought she was successful in concealing Ronald's importance to her from her parents. Since he never called her – he relied upon running into her in one of the local joints or else he found her by the lake – she didn't have to worry about explaining phone calls. Nor did he come to her house, which was not unusual; most New Bonn girls found their escorts away from home. Just as there were three kinds of females in New Bonn, there were two kinds of males: boys and men. The boys were those who went to school, regardless of their age. Their commitments were yet unknown, for they were still operating under the authority of some school system. The men were simply all those who weren't in school. That these men could be chronological boys was unimportant to the distinction; thus a farm boy who had quit school at sixteen was considered a man. Ronald was definitely a man; although he did occasionally attend a nearby junior college, his commitments were not directed towards any kind of school system. He had also been in the army, which was enough to qualify him for manhood.

Joan knew that her parents would consider him unsavory. He had little ambition, his father was an acknowledged loser, and he was a Catholic. Any one of these details was enough to condemn him in the eyes of the Nelsons. Had they known he was actively engaged upon a campaign to rid their daughter of her virginity, they would have packed her off to boarding school.

Since Joan was so close to graduating from high school, perhaps her parents felt that their daughter was safe until she could enter college, where she was bound to meet a number of honorable young men who would recognize her worth and protect her accordingly.

Joan met Ronald by the lake more than she encountered him in uptown spots. Some evenings he would be sitting on the grass, hidden from her so well that she would be startled when he yelled at her. Occasionally she would ask what purpose he served hidden from view. 'Why do you always hide down here?' she would ask. Was he ashamed to be seen with her in public? she wondered, or was he also protecting himself from the indignation of the Nelsons, especially her father?

'I'm not hiding,' he would insist. 'It's just more fun here when you know no one can see you.'

At times when he said this Joan imagined his teeth turning into fangs, her precious hymen dangling from his jaws, fragile and bloody. She did appreciate his indifference towards material possessions, though, for he never seemed to care whether or not she was driving or walking, and although her parents were usually generous with their cars and saw that she had one to drive whenever she asked for transportation, she did sometimes feel that she was taking advantage of their generosity in using one of their cars for the series of sexual stalemates that the evenings with Ronald produced.

Often, when she had a car, he would not get in, preferring instead to sit on the lake bank where the grass was tall and the cattails high and dense enough for concealment. 'How much longer is this going to go on?' he would invariably ask.

Rather than responding with another defense of virginity – a defense so stale that it often seemed to Joan like a recital from a prepared text – she would instead sigh, 'I don't know.'

This admission held little relief to Ronald, who would immediately press for information. 'What are we waiting for? Just what the hell is it that you want?'

Joan could scarcely say that she wanted at least an engagement ring, or even a class ring, and she knew that she didn't want to get married right now, for she was too young. Yet she wouldn't have minded being engaged; that way she could still go to college and have Ronald. She was sure, though, that an engagement relied upon her relinquishing her virginity. If Ronald sensed her dilemma he never expressed any understanding of it. His comments were always more specific, dedicated to his pain, to his burning passion that she refused to oblige.

'Don't you think it's as hard for me as it is for you?' she sometimes asked him, thinking that a paraphrase of Ruthie's advice might check his passions, or at least soothe him a little.

'Jesus! Where'd you hear that one? And just feel this, if you think that's true, that what you feel is hard for you.' He would guide her hand to the bulge in his pants, a knotted mass that meant nothing to her except it was supposed to be the source of all his insufferable pain. He would then push her back on the grass and kiss her so hard that she felt she was being ground into the earth. Then his eyes would shine like polished agates and the muscles in his arms would stand out like ropes.

One night, after a particularly ferocious attempt to wrangle out of her what she refused to freely give, he became uncharacteristically tender. 'Look, I respect you, see, and that's why it's so hard for me.' He began to caress her breasts, a liberty that she had but recently allowed him, hoping that this kind of concession would stall him indefinitely. 'I really love you, you know.'

Joan was astonished at Ronald's admission. She had never heard it said before and had read about it only in very romantic sources, so that now it was hard to believe it applied to her. She also felt that there was a good chance that a statement of love could protect her from any more futile plundering.

'Goddamn it! Why are you holding out on me?' The hands that just a minute before had been tenderly playing with her breasts were now tugging and kneading as if she were bread dough, then being tweaked and punched the way a masseur works over a client. With a notion so quick that he caught her completely off guard, he stuck his middle finger into her vagina and began to probe with rapid, jerking moves. 'There it is!' he exclaimed. 'There's that precious thing you've been sitting on!' He was hurting her, but there was a stimulation to the pain that she had never felt before.

'Feel good?' The pain had diminished while the pleasure increased until she felt a kind of liquid warmth, a tingling that began from within and spread throughout her body, sending tremors of sensation that seemed to radiate and spread everywhere. Her first realization of being manipulated occurred as a question: What's he doing to me? and then she wondered how she could ever stop him.

She wondered, also, how much this happened to other girls, and what they did about it. Was there any solution other than to submit, and if she did give in what would happen? What would he think of her afterwards? In the dark she couldn't see his full face, only its outline with a profile that now looked to her like Hiawatha about to mount his maiden, prepared for enemy attack as well as mating rite.

'I am going to take you. I won't hurt you. I'm going to take you now.' Murmuring these words, almost like a litany, he began to pull off his pants.

In retrospect Joan thought that it was this chant-like refrain that spoiled the mood he had taken such pains to create. Had he said 'screw' or even 'fuck' Joan would never have felt so self-conscious, but there was something so stagy and contrived about his using the word 'take'. It reminded her of summers spent in reading trashy novels where the hero is always ready to 'take' or 'have' the heroine, which forced her to giggle, a response that quickly turned into hysterical laughter. Her struggle to control her spasms of laughter made her pitch higher and more shrill.

'Goddamn bitch! Goddamn slut!' She thought he would smash her face and grind it up until it matched the soil they had been floundering on, but her laughter continued, a lone sound that seemed to echo across the lake, rather like a northern loon, nocturnal in habit, who signals its bizarre needs to its mate in the rushes.

'At least shut up. Shut up.' He didn't have to add 'or I'll slug you' because she knew that he would. Yet she couldn't stop laughing. It was mirthless and unsatisfying, not the kind that released emotions. This was laughter that substituted for emotions that she was terrified to let go. She knew that she could just as easily cry as laugh, and that crying would certainly be more acceptable but she couldn't accomplish the transformation. Although the tears were running down her face, she continued to laugh in noisy gulps.

'For God's sake, shut up and get a hold of yourself.'

She wondered what would happen if she didn't soon gain control of herself. Would he go away, or would he call for help and she'd be carted away to some loony bin? She knew that she had humiliated him to the point where he could never forgive her. No one likes to be laughed at – especially me – and she knew that he interpreted her laughter as an indictment of him. And just what the hell was she laughing at? She could no more account for her hysteria than she could justify the great challenge of her virginity.

Ronald stood up and kicked the grass where she was sitting, missing her sprawled form by a few inches. She couldn't look at him, nor could she speak to tell him she was sorry. Although her noisy spurts continued, the tears continued to stream. He began to walk up the bank; his shirt was sprinkled with grass and a few fox-tails clung to the folds of the cloth. She remained on the edge of the lake, struggling for control, but whenever she thought she had finished laughing another unwilled chortle would emerge, almost like bubbles that appear on a lake when the fish are beginning to rise to the surface for their evening's feed.

She stayed on that spot for at least half an hour. The gulps and the streaming tears finally dissipated to slight chuckles until the quiet tears – those she had so longed for when Ronald had been with her – finally appeared. She brushed the grass and twigs from her dress, fastened her bra, and started up the same path that her suitor had used for his solitary exit. Her car was parked away from the path, at least a quarter of a mile from the site of their skirmish. She knew that she looked terrible. She had no purse and neither comb nor Kleenex, but she hoped to find something in the car to help patch her together, at least temporarily.

The car was located just down the street from the house of the Goldust Twins, a short distance which she could easily run. At this time of night there was little chance of detection, and there was only one streetlight burning, the others having been shot out earlier by someone with a BB gun.

Joan was so absorbed in her sprint that she didn't notice the porch light glowing and the Goldust Twins standing on their front lower step, looking like twin sentinels without guns. One of them called out to her, 'It's Joan, isn't it?'

Joan was startled. Was she expected to stop and talk to them, or could she ignore them and act as if she hadn't heard?

'Joan, is that you? Come here, Joan. Joan?'

Joan moved towards their house, trying to keep out of the light.

'We thought it was you. You're out awfully late, aren't you?'

So are you, Joan muttered to herself, and just what in hell were the old bags doing up at this hour? And just how much had they seen? How much did they know? She felt it best to cultivate their good will – a futile endeavor even under the best of circumstances – and be as well-mannered as possible. 'I didn't realize the time,' she replied. 'I guess I'd better hurry home.'

One of them, probably Sarah, stepped down from the porch and onto the grass. (It was hard enough to tell them apart in the daytime, and tonight they were wearing identical chenille robes and curlers in their hair, which made them even more identical.) 'Come here, Joan.' Fragile as they both looked, the voice had a steely, commanding tone that Joan could not ignore. She walked closer to the lighted porch, still trying to keep in the shadows, and wondering if there were still twigs and briars in her hair, and also wondering why these women, who refused to answer their telephone or accept gifts from well-meaning townsfolk, were now choosing to make a public appearance. 'Come here where we can see you.'

To Joan the voice and the commands sounded so much like the refrain from the Big Bad Wolf that she almost burst into laughter again, the same kind of laughter that she didn't want and was sure she couldn't manage. 'Who's afraid of the Big Bad Wolf?' traveled through her mind, banging against her ears like a relentless snare drum. She stepped to within ten feet of the witch who was standing on the fringe of lawn by the sidewalk.

'Joan, have you been drinking? Have you been with a boy?'

The old hag's deliberate pronunciation of the word 'drinking' reminded Joan of Ronald's earlier 'take', a word so unmistakably sexual in connotation that it would have been intelligible to the village idiot whose habitat was the lake. For a minute Joan was tempted to confess that she had almost been *taken*, and clearly she had been fingered, but she could honestly be indignant about the accusation of drinking, for she was cold sober. 'No, I haven't been drinking.' She hoped her assertion was strong enough to dismiss the sexual question. 'I haven't been drinking, and now I'm going home because it's late.'

She wondered if the hags were contemplating seizing her and dragging her into their house for a breath examination. What was the purpose of this inquisition, anyhow, from two snoopy old bitches who had previously reserved their business to cheating at cards and taking advantage of the town's most vulnerable streaks of sentimentality? Never had these women been known to display any interest in the characters of the village youth, male or female. She could imagine herself a captive in the musty house of the Goldust

Twins, prevented from escape by their mysterious cunning, a secret faculty unknown to the townspeople. Perhaps their cistern was full of virgin bodies that they had discarded after ordeals of unimaginable torture.

The same stern voice interrupted Joan's contemplation of atrocities. 'You run along home now, Joan. We thought you had been drinking because you were laughing so hard down there by the lake. And we thought someone must be with you, too, the way you were laughing.'

Joan was mystified that anyone could mistake her mirthless sounds for joviality; how could hysteria sound anything like joy? Yet she was relieved at the abrupt dismissal, and she ran to her car and drove until she was a block from home, where she stopped to comb her hair and give her aching gut a chance to rest. She felt it was useless to prettify a face that was so ineradicably changed.

She arrived home to find her parents sitting in the library, watching TV, which gave her a chance to slip past them. Her arrival diverted them but a few seconds from *The Lucy Show*, and although her father seemed a bit too preoccupied with a program he normally ridiculed, she didn't notice any shocked reaction at her face, which she feared could convey everything at first glance.

Joan was concerned with her own close call, and she was also concerned with her loss of Ronald's affections. If she were ever to regain any of his one-time regard for her, she knew that first there would have to be some kind of discussion of their terms: romance? courtship? Whatever the hell it was, they would need to do something to define the terms. She considered such a discussion highly unlikely, though. It simply wasn't his nature to want to talk about anything other than her motives at keeping him at bay.

She was concerned, too, with the presence of the two old women whose actions that night seemed more and more supernatural as time went on. Were they secret guardians of tempted virgins, secular saints disguised as unapproachable hags? She never told anyone else about her encounter, which left her to wonder alone why they hadn't rescued her from her temptation, thus sparing him the ignominy of humiliation. And what about her own bizarre laughter? Why hadn't they spared her if they had the power? Sometimes Joan thought they must possess magical unfathomable powers, while other times Joan dismissed them as women who were more morbidly snoopy than anyone else in the community knew of or supposed.

Since there was no one in whom she could confide her fears and imaginings, she kept quiet about the entire episode. She could not confide even a small part of the evening, for were she to tell even one part of the story she would have to admit her own close call – that she had been manipulated to the point where her will had vanished, that her moral code she had once considered inviolable was actually flimsy, so vulnerable that a few moments of finger fucking could send it forever flying. For many days she felt listless and had trouble breathing. Her mother thought she was not getting enough sleep and was run down, and prescribed early hours and a terrible-tasting tonic that Joan swallowed without protest. She didn't see Ronald and she tried to avoid those places where they normally would have met, but the size of the town prevented her from feeling safe – a chance encounter was always possible.

It didn't occur to her that he might be hiding too, for she considered herself the loser in a battle that she had never wanted but must have inspired. Her loss of control that one night gradually receded from her consciousness, but it persisted in her dreams. She continued to dream that she was lying on a raft, being nuzzled and cheerfully fondled by a small boy with a blank, anonymous face. He would be stroking her gently and then he would start to paw at her genitals, his face changing into that of a snarling chow dog, who would then try to bite her. Whenever she tried to struggle she would fall off the raft into water whose slime created a thick screen of green scum that hid the depths of the water. Falling through the scum her hair would get caught on reeds that seemed to be sticking up through the mud although their stems were invisible. She would gasp for air, the tendrils of the reeds tugging and pulling at her, and she would try to cry for help even though she was swallowing water in gulps that she knew were sure to drown her. Sometimes this dream produced audible cries for help. Often Joan's father would appear by her bed and wake her up, reassuring her that the dream was over and that she was safe. Joan knew better. The dream, and its horrible variations, she knew would persist. They were now a part of her self, a self that she had just begun to meet, and which she plainly despised. Yet despicable as she felt herself to be, she knew that she must attempt to conceal that knowledge from others.

Chapter Thirteen

Hoedown

One night, three or four weeks after the laughing episode, Joan got a phone call from Linda. She was surprised to hear from her, since she didn't consider herself a real friend of Linda's, and she had also assumed that once girls married they no longer try to see unmarried acquaintances. Once a girl married she automatically devoted herself to the cultivation of her husband's pleasures, which would exclusively involve his circle of friends. But since Linda's husband was old, there would probably be few friends for Linda to entertain.

Linda wanted to know why Joan hadn't been to see her; she was irritated at Joan's negligence and let Joan know it. 'I honestly didn't know you wanted me to visit you,' Joan explained. 'I mean it, or I would have come before.' Joan had rarely thought of Linda since the wedding, and she scarcely thought of Karl once the humiliation of his crude overtures had worn off.

'Why don't you come over tomorrow night? We're having a party.'

'I'll have to see about getting the car.' Joan thought this might take some haggling since her mother was not likely to relinquish a car for an occasion that she was sure to disapprove of, and her father's feelings towards Linda and her family were still not clear. 'I think I can come. I'll see, and if I can't I'll call you back. Is – ah – Karl coming?'

Linda sputtered a short, mirthless laugh. 'No. You don't have to worry about him. He never comes to see us anyhow. It's just going to be some people around here. You might know two or three of them, but I doubt it.'

Normally Joan would have rejected Linda's invitation by inventing some excuse that would satisfy neither of them, but she was still at the stage where she needed to make herself scarce. Going to Linda's farm near Chandler would only subject her to more farmers, she knew, and they would be no different from their New Bonn counterparts, maybe even worse since they were bound to be older. Yet farmers seldom gave parties, and the novelty of the occasion appealed to Joan who had been to her share of family gatherings, where the farmers liked to hold gatherings that often bring together three, sometimes four, generations into one steaming kitchen, creating a mob scene distinguished by its super-abundance of food and its ratio of squalling brats to senile grandparents. The elders liked to sit for hours at a kitchen table that seemed to engulf the entire room, breaking their chicken into small pieces that their toothless mouths could contain. Staring into space and saying nothing, they moved only to propel their forks and to swat at occasional flies. Noisy babies and bustling cooks never seemed to distract them. When the old people had finished eating they would simply vanish into the parlor or a bedroom and lie down until they were ready to be driven home.

In New Bonn the only people who gave parties regularly were those women who entertained their clubs, and these occasions were usually reserved for afternoons devoted to special days – a St. Patrick's Day bridge party was one Joan remembered well because she had to drive the twenty-five miles and back to Worthington in order to buy green nut cups. Adults didn't give evening parties where couples would dance and drink and talk about politics and local economics, and the young people of Joan's age had so many prohibitions attached to them that parties were out of the question: the Lutherans weren't supposed to dance; the Catholics weren't supposed to dance or mingle with Protestants; and the Presbyterians were considered stuck up and unapproachable by both Catholics and Lutherans.

Joan liked the idea of a party, regardless of its host or hostess, and she told herself that she would stay only for a while to see what kinds of people Linda hung around with. It was no problem getting a car for the evening, either. Her father was delighted that Linda had called. 'She was a nice girl. It's too bad we can't see more of her,' he stated, leaving Joan to wonder why he hadn't defended her more when she was their servant.

Her mother didn't share her father's enthusiasm, although she was less hostile than Joan had expected. 'Just don't stay too late,' she instructed. 'And drive carefully, especially on those country roads.'

Lately Mrs. Nelson had been leaving magazine articles about teenage drinking scattered about the house in places so conspicuous that Joan felt insulted by her mother's lack of ingenuity. Baffled at her mother's easily-won permission, it never occurred to Joan that she was lately so miserable to be around, her moods so dark, that simply getting her out of the house was a relief to both parents.

Mrs. Nelson was interested in what Joan intended to wear, a sure sign that her mother's curiosity was more than casual. 'It wouldn't be right for you to show up the best dressed of the guests,' her mother had warned her, which Joan considered remarkably unhelpful advice since neither of them knew anything of the others invited. Mrs. Nelson thought a dress was in order, but not one that had been purchased in Minneapolis. With her mother's guidance, Joan selected a princess-style dress of pique, a garment that had been listlessly hanging on the racks at Gertie's Gown

Shop for months. Joan hated the dress, with its red piping running loose on the hem and finally landing in a double loop at the skirt just below the right knee, but it was, as her mother remarked, 'inexpensive and modest-looking without looking cheap.' Joan would have preferred to wear her riding clothes. Perhaps Linda had a horse or two that her groom had preserved from his early years, although this was unlikely, since no one she knew rode horses for pleasure. Her own days of riding were now so few that her horse was overweight and wild from his unattended days at pasture, munching on succulent spring grass.

Mr. and Mrs. Nelson were more pleased that their daughter had been invited to a party than they were at the nature of the party. After living so long in Minneapolis, the customs of rural Minnesota were often difficult for them to uphold. Occasionally they would spend weekends in Minneapolis, usually staying with relatives or close friends, but sometimes indulging themselves by staying at a downtown hotel, where they would rent a large double room and spend their days shopping and visiting. In the evenings they would dine at restaurants where drinks were openly served and where food appeared on individual plates and serving dishes, not in communal bowls. These weekends, pleasurable as they were, did not compensate for what they considered Joan's deprivation of civilized pleasures. They were glad that their daughter would soon be departing for college, although they secretly wondered if she would be considered too much of a hick for acceptance into the worldly society of sororities and fraternities. Consequently they encouraged Joan to keep her horse even though she rarely rode him, for they contemplated sending him along with her daughter to college to board at a convenient stable. Mrs. Nelson thought that the horse might add the touch of distinction Joan might need after living in New Bonn for four years.

To the Nelsons, a party meant dancing, moderate drinking, and conversation interesting and intelligent enough to accommodate spans of location and time. They knew that Linda's efforts could scarcely resemble their own social ideals, but they applauded their former servant's pluck in attempting a local novelty. They also had become weary of their daughter's moods – her mealtime silences were especially tiresome, silences so impenetrable that no amount of Mr. Nelson's joking could remove their pall.

Of course they knew about Ronald, or at least a little about him. They knew that their daughter had been seeing him, but they weren't sure how closely her present behavior was connected to his attentions. They didn't approve of him, but they could hardly forbid their daughter from seeing him, especially since their meetings seemed to have stopped. They disliked him on principle: he was too old for her; he had little promise – off the basketball court he loped like a gorilla. Worst of all, he was a Catholic.

'I just know he's not sincere,' Mrs. Nelson often commented to her husband, which meant that his intentions were less than honorable toward their daughter. Both parents knew that Catholic men habitually seduced Protestant girls on principle, and they were also aware of the confessional favors that the priest always bestowed upon the successful seducers of hapless Protestant girls. The offending Catholic males, it was known, were scolded for their violation of the Sixth Commandment while at the same time being praised for having spared Catholic females their sins. They knew that the Catholic church presented no great obstacle to all those young Catholic males who were so eager to get at the Presbyterian daughters, so the Nelsons were relieved when their daughter appeared to have escaped the clutches of the pernicious Ronald, even though she had made herself miserable as a result. They hoped that Joan's disappointment, or moodiness, or whatever it was that bothered her, would pass with time. Consequently, when Joan accepted Linda's invitation she did so with the anxious approval of both parents. They were happy to see her leave the house, safe for once from a prearranged tryst with Ronald that could easily be ruinous to them all.

Joan left for the party wearing the odious pique dress. At the last minute her father gave her a brown paper bag containing a fifth of whiskey. 'Give this to the newlyweds. It's for them. And have a good time,' he advised.

Joan thought her father's contribution reflected a trust in his daughter he was unable to express directly. 'He trusts me!' she kept muttering to herself on the twenty-mile drive to the farm. 'He trusts me enough to give me the car and some whiskey for people who mean nothing to him.' She had never before felt so awesomely responsible. Her spirits rose as she drove along, and for the first time she made a genuine effort to eradicate her feelings for Ronald, to stop thinking about what he might be doing now that she was out of the picture. She would create a new picture – the metaphor appealed to her – a new picture that would not include young men who were dedicated solely to conquest and to the abuse of naïve young virgins.

Linda's farm – or rather the Schultz farm – was hard to find. It was at the end of a dirt road, but it was easy to miss the turnoff. Although Linda had warned Joan and had given her careful directions, Joan did miss the turnoff, partly because she was preoccupied with her new resolutions, and partly because she never listened to directions (she wasn't any good at giving them either). When she did arrive the yard was full of pickups and cars. The farmhouse, itself, was a squat, one-storied white building, L-shaped, with an attached shed. It didn't look like the home of a prosperous farmer, but by now Joan had become accustomed to rural Minnesota building customs, where the wealth was usually invested in the barn and other outbuildings. The few farmhouses that were more than conveniences were usually old brick buildings that had been constructed at least two generations ago by Old World men who had grown exhausted at the complaints of their wives,

At the ages of seventy, or even seventy-five or eighty, those farmers, not yet completely Americanized, would construct houses that reminded them of grand places on the Rhine – places they knew of mostly from paintings and legends – but modified for American use, and considerably plainer. If a current farmer had been lucky enough to inherit one of these brick buildings he usually had enough sense to let it stand, making only the most necessary improvements, like the addition of running water and flush toilets, converting from kerosene to electricity, and altering wood-burning stoves into natural gas furnaces. But most people started from scratch, and those who did erected the kind of L-shaped farmhouse that is a permanent feature of rural Midwestern architecture.

The L-shape was convenient, too, for it allowed an almost endless number of rooms to be added on, often times in arbitrary or whimsical fashion. It was not unusual to find the only bathroom connected to a bedroom, with the passage to the bathroom contingent upon the arrangement of the bedroom furniture. The central room was always the kitchen; then there was usually a parlor leading off from the kitchen, and one or two bedrooms, sometimes attached to the parlor, but often next to a shed or sometimes attached to the kitchen. The cellars contained a minimum of a full year's supply of canned vegetables and fruit stacked upon the shelves in neat rows and arranged according to the dates they were put up. Frequently there was a washing machine, and clotheslines that ran back and forth across the room, but many women still used the one-hundred-gallon galvanized tubs their own mothers had used. There was always a dark area, off to one side, that served to protect the potatoes and winter apples from the light.

Joan was glad to see that there was no privy. She didn't think Linda would have put up with one, but she wasn't sure how much influence Linda had brought to their marriage, and the existence of a privy seemed a valid test. A few chickens picked around in the gravel and scattered when Joan's car lights shone on their wretched, stringy bodies. Joan recognized the chickens as a bad sign, for they meant that Linda was careless of the chickens and indifferent about the appearance of her yard. Chickens, themselves, Joan considered a dead giveaway, for she had yet to meet a farmer's wife who didn't depend upon her egg money for personal luxuries, like permanents, cosmetics, and clothes that were not homemade. (The allowances that farmers gave their wives were not intended for commodities that couldn't be produced at home. Since it was considered frivolous for a man to bother with chickens, the farmers' wives were the ones responsible for the keep and care of the chickens. The most a farmer would even consider was to help with the construction of a brooder house, and this he did reluctantly, often postponing construction until the slackest season when the crops were all in and the ground completely fallow.)

To Joan those chickens meant that Linda was following the narrow paths of rural living that represented the trap she had hoped Linda might somehow avoid. Not that she had really considered Linda exceptional, but she had hoped for something better for her.

As Joan stepped out of the car, Linda appeared on the porch, waving a bottle of Grain Belt beer. She looked nice, with her hair swept back from her face and piled high on her head, giving her a slightly regal air, and she had on a red dress that looked like silk, very low cut to show off her cleavage, and pulled tight at the waist by a wide sash. She teetered on the spike heels of red satin pumps. Joan wondered if this were a trousseau dress, and decided that Linda could not be pregnant yet, for no one who is pregnant wears three-inch heels and wasp waists.

'Hiya, Joan. Glad you could come.' Linda's cordial welcome was genuine, her smile authentic. 'Come on in and see my old man, and I'll show you around.'

Since Joan had already met Linda's husband, she accepted this greeting as a display of pride on Linda's part. She decided to wait until she had talked to both husband and wife before she produced her father's gift. Linda put her arm through Joan's and squeezed her elbow.

'Let me look at you. Long time, no see.' Linda's beery breath suggested pickles and homemade bread; for the first time in weeks Joan realized that she was ravenously hungry.

Inside the farmhouse the two females were met by a chorus of greetings that came from a circle of men sitting around the kitchen table. At first Joan thought there were at least a dozen men sitting at the table, dressed in T-shirts and khaki pants, standard evening wear for almost all Minnesota males. They were all drinking beer from bottles and none of them seemed at all drunk. In fact they sat so quietly that they could easily have been mourning some recently departed friend or relative. Joan was not acquainted with any of them, but they all appeared to be much younger than Linda's husband – Karl's age, perhaps, or even Linda's. There was no sight of another female, and for one horrible moment Joan remembered the night of the wedding dance and feared that she might have been invited as Linda's accomplice to a prolonged orgy. Yet the group of men and their innocent appearance discouraged such a sordid assumption, for they looked like nothing more than young neighbors who had been invited for poker, although there were no cards on the table.

Linda had told Joan that she was giving a party, yet this gathering resembled no party that Joan had ever imagined. The various men greeted Joan politely, but as soon as this formality was over they resumed their conversations and continued to drink their beer. No one suggested that either of the two females sit down at the table, and Joan wondered how long she was expected to stand there before she could decently suggest joining the group.

'C'mon, Joan. Let me show you the house.' Linda pulled Joan away from the kitchen without offering her a beer, although she continued to hang onto her own half-empty bottle.

'This is the living room.' Linda led Joan into a room about the size of the kitchen. It was dominated by a couch that had recently been upholstered in a velvety material in shades of green so vivid that the thing looked as if it sparkled in the sunlight. Linda pointed to it. 'Like it? It's a new kind of material, sixty percent nylon and forty percent wool, and it's supposed to be washable.' There were two matching chairs on either side of the couch and arranged so that anyone lying there could have a visitor at both head and feet if desired. Across the room was an enormous TV console that contained both radio and phonograph, and next to it was a record cabinet that prominently displayed albums of Patti Page and Hank Snow.

Joan recognized wedding gifts carefully arranged on end tables and knickknack shelves: ash trays of silver and china; an outsized cigarette lighter residing in the middle of a ruby-colored glass bowl; and a peach-colored porcelain vase containing a bunch of wilted sweet peas. There were no religious pictures on the walls but there was a holy-water font nailed to the lintel of a door separating the parlor from the kitchen. There were no curtains on the windows, which surprised Joan, but there were shades, which had been pulled down to their ledges, revealing their advanced age by the cracks and splits and brown spots on their crinkly surfaces.

Before Joan could comment upon the décor of the room, Linda directed her to the next room, whose door was directly behind the couch so that they had to side-step around it before they could proceed. 'This can be hell if you're three sheets to the wind and it's dark,' Linda giggled. Then she turned on the lights and announced 'Ta-da. The Master Bedroom!'

Linda had outdone herself in this room, which explained the lack of curtains in the living room and the unattended flowers in their vase. In the center of the room was a double bed, covered by an enormous bedspread of quilted pink satin and hemmed by a good six inches of white organdy flounces. Occupying an entire wall was a dressing table with a three-way mirror. On it was something that looked like a spice rack and was full of lipsticks, nail polish, eyelash curlers, mascara pencils, and manicure equipment. Linda pointed to the arrangement. 'Joe made that for me. He was sick of my stuff spilling all over and rolling on the floor, and he was always stepping on it.' Linda smiled at herself in one of the three-way mirrors as if in congratulation for her feminine triumph. 'Joe has also built more closets. Actually he extended the ones he already had. You shoulda seen this place when we moved in. The worst was the bedroom. That's how I've been spending all my time, fixing it up so's it looks fit for decent people.' As a kind of afterthought she added, 'Of course he didn't spend much time in here before, so it looked like some hermit's den.' Pride in the transformation from a masculine to a feminine bedroom was reflected in the way she pointed to a chair resting against the wall. 'See that? Well he didn't have a chair of any kind and nothing besides a bed. I made him buy me the entire suite the day after we got married.' The chair, constructed of the same pine as the dressing table, was painted in the same white gloss, with gold scrolls worked into its legs and back. The seat was tufted with pink satin that harmonized, but didn't completely match, the colors of the bedspread. The one window was adorned with flimsy gauze curtains, also of pink.

My God, Joan thought, all this pink looks like a nursery. Yet on the walls there were framed nudes, themselves very pink, that looked as if they had been clipped from the pages of some nudie magazine. Linda noticed Joan staring at the representations of female flesh. 'I got them for the old man. Helps to get it up, he says.' Her tone was flippant, but Joan thought there was real concern in Linda's voice. 'Do you think they're all right? I mean, not too out of place? Of course we take them down whenever the old folks visit,' and to confirm her strategy, Linda extracted from a dresser drawer a matching pair of Madonnas – His and Hers, Joan surmised, just like towels.

They inspected a bathroom decorated with His and Hers towels of graduated sizes, almost certainly a wedding present, and then a cubicle of a room that looked as if it had once been a closet or some kind of storage area. Now it was big enough for a sewing machine and an ironing board; without windows it seemed more like a cell than an area devoted to production. Finally, they came to a room that was set off from the rest, obviously recently built, for in order to get there the girls had to walk through a door that was so new that it still lacked a doorknob. Linda turned on the lights to a space that was completely empty; the floors had been sanded and varnished but the wood still smelled like freshly cut pine. There was no paint on the walls, only the raw, gray stucco. 'Joe added this after we got married.' Linda looked defiant. 'It's supposed to be a baby's room, but I don't give a shit what it's supposed to be, we have no use for it now.' She quickly extinguished the lights and backed out of the door. 'Let's go see what they're up to.'

Joan followed Linda's mincing walk. The ridiculous spike heels gave her stride a fragility that she didn't deserve, and Joan noticed that her earlier tipsiness had vanished as soon as the guided tour was underway. She would have liked to ask about the rest of the guests at the party – who the hell were they? – but instead she inquired of Linda's family.

'They're okay, I guess. We don't see them much, only when we go to Mass in New Bonn.' Her look took in Joan's girlish dress. 'Including Karl,' she added.

By the time the two girls returned to the kitchen the noise level had increased. Someone had added a bowl of potato chips to the table, which added to the litter of beer bottles and brimming ashtrays. As far as Joan could tell, the topic of conversation hadn't changed – still crops and rainfall but now noisier and more animated. Linda's husband pointed to a tub full of iced beer. 'Help yourself, girls.'

Joan decided that this was a good time to present them with her father's gift, and she brought it out of her catchall purse. 'Here, my dad sent this.'

Joe Schultz looked at the brown bag with a smile, then quickly peeled off the wrapper. 'Hell, it's Old Crow. He didn't have to do that.' He examined the label as if it were written in a foreign language, then gave the bottle a paternal pat and placed it on the top shelf over the sink. 'That's sippin' whiskey. Can't mix it with beer. Too good for this crowd, too.' He winked at Joan, a conspiratorial gesture that was clearly intended for the whole group. 'Come on, drink up. There's beer, beer, and more beer, and plenty of it.'

Joan continued to stand by the table. No one had offered either female a chair, and Linda was busy rummaging after something in the refrigerator, her back turned to the table. Joe leaned over from his chair and ran his hand up the inside of his wife's leg, past her thigh, until his hand settled, on one buttock. 'See here what I caught!' he whooped. 'Ain't this a prize good enough for the Murray County Fair!'

Linda whirled around and slapped his hand, but the blow was so faint only a slight sound was heard. 'Cut that out, you son-of-a-bitch. Don't you ever get enough?' The men at the table guffawed. It was clear that they were not embarrassed by this public display, and Joan suspected that they would have been disappointed without it. Joan, however, was embarrassed. She stared at her beer bottle as if it contained a secret message. Finally a man who had been sitting next to Joe Schultz got up from his chair and came over to her.

'Are you going to eat it or drink it?'

Joan's repertoire of snappy comebacks, never very large, contained nothing for which she and her friends had practiced for this occasion. Instead of responding with words, she put the bottle to her mouth and drank off a good half of its contents.

'Well, look here, Joe. This little girl is a regular lush.'

Joan examined the wag who seemed to be setting up himself as her judge. Like the others he was a farmer, but his T-shirt was blue, not white like the others. He had enormous brown eyes that immediately reminded Joan of Bambi, and his round, apple cheeks seemed like an artistic frame for his lovely eyes. There was a little curl on his forehead, separated from the rest of his short hair, that looked like the spit curls that beauty magazines of the 1930s recommended to flappers. He was swaying slightly as he stood next to Joan, but this movement, like his isolated curl, seemed to Joan artificial and melodramatic. 'Why don't we go into the other room and dance?'

Although the man didn't appeal to Joan, she felt dancing with him was preferable to standing around in a room containing only farmers discussing annual crop yields. He put his arm around her waist and propelled her into the living room, and as they were walking away one of the men at the table yelled, 'Hey John, take it easy! Remember, she's jailbait.'

His name, then, was John, and it wasn't hard for Joan to get more details out of him. He lived on a farm near Clayton and had graduated from high school six years ago. The fact that he had graduated from high school should have separated him from the other farmers, who usually quit school at sixteen, when the state permitted them to leave, but he must have enough in common with the rest to be included in this rural gathering. Like the other farmers Joan had known, this one was a wonderful dancer. Joan had never stopped being amazed at the grace and ease that men, who looked as if they only belonged behind a plow, accomplished miracles on the dance floor. Joan, who tended to be stiff and tense when she was dancing, was immediately at ease with her new partner, who dipped and glided with the agility of an ice skater.

She wished they had something better than Patti Page to dance to, but John didn't seem to mind. His hand rested casually on her back, a touch so neutral that Joan felt he might have been patting a pet dog.

'You're awful stiff, little girl. Why don't you relax?'

Such advice rarely put her at ease, but John sounded as if he were making an observation rather than a judgment, so she tried to cooperate by giving him a bright smile.

When the music stopped he escorted her to a place on the front porch that she had overlooked when she drove in, a small area where there was an outdoor glider and some wicker chairs. They both sat down on the glider, which sprang into action with a pleasant motion more rhythmical than its rusty springs suggested. John leaned his head back and looked up at a sky that was full of bright starts and tiny, rainless clouds. 'This is the life,' he announced, with an enthusiasm so genuine that Joan thought she must be hearing things. How could simplicity like this ever be deemed *life*?

'Yes, it's nice here, but it must be awfully lonely.' Joan was thinking of Linda, whose attempts at life so far had been restricted right now to decorating rooms and trying to please a husband whose needs seemed less interesting than her own. Unless the chickens counted: they were as close to 'life' as Joan had seen. 'Doesn't Linda, don't they have animals or anything? I mean a dog or a cat?'

'I expect Joe has a dog. He always used to, but he's probably sleeping it in the barn.'

Joan knew her question had been a stupid one; farmers, whenever they did have pets, always relegated them to the outbuildings where they would skulk around waiting to be fed along with the livestock. Cats were almost never kept as pets; they were considered too important to the barn to be allowed house space, and they usually nestled in special heaps of straw near the cows' stalls where they could be assured of milk twice a day. Furthermore, Linda had never demonstrated the slightest interest in the Nelson's cocker spaniel. Although she had never been seen mistreating him, Joan suspected that she kicked him around when the family was not present because the dog always ran the other way whenever he sensed Linda approaching him.

'They have the finest herd of Guernseys in the county, though.' John's admiration for the Schultzes' cows seemed natural and without envy.

'Do you like – I mean – do you have lots of cows, too?'

John grinned. 'You're awfully cute when you try to play farmer, you know that?' He gave her knee a friendly pat. 'No, we only raise beef. Steers, you know.'

Joan wanted to object to his implications of her ignorance, but she was too embarrassed to defend herself by means of a discussion of steers, which she felt John was goading her towards. Instead, she launched into a recital of information that she had acquired mainly from her father, then stopped in mid-sentence when she noticed that John wasn't bothering to listen to her. 'Have you known Linda long?' she inquired, knowing that a direct question regarding his own experience would interest him.

'Not her. I've known Joe a long time, though. I've helped him with threshing sometimes.'

'Are the other men, the others here, Joe's friends, too?' John's responding grin suggested lewd, private knowledge.

'Of course. You don't think they're her friends, do you?'

Joan would have liked to ask him what he thought of the marriage, for she felt that he probably knew as much about it as anyone around, and he didn't seem like the kind of person who would coyly withhold information just to tease her. Yet she felt it would be less than honorable to question him here, in the newlyweds' house, where they had been dancing in full view of their brilliant pink bed.

'Do you want to go back and dance some more, or shall we have another beer?'

Neither choice appealed to Joan, yet dancing to music she ordinarily scorned seemed more palatable than joining a group of men whose interests excluded her. She wanted to get away from the atrocious music and the farm talk, yet there seemed to be no way she could accomplish either while still in this house.

When they returned to the kitchen, Linda had moved to her husband's lap, and she was tickling his ear with a toothpick. 'Why don't you go outside and look at the moon?' She smiled brightly at Joan, revealing smeared lipstick and eyes slightly crossed. It's the beer, Joan thought. It's the beer that's making her look loopy and floppy, as if she's being held together with glue.

The others were now eating from large platters of ham and sausage, and there were two bowls of potato salad and pickled beets and sliced tomatoes crowded together with no special arrangement that Joan could see. Someone had emptied the ashtrays, and the beer bottles had been pushed to one side and arranged into a triangle – no doubt the result of someone's nervous hands that had been relieved to discover a definite chore. On a sideboard there were two cakes, as yet uncut. Joan's hunger had decreased upon her arrival at the farm, but now when she saw the cakes, with their thick chocolate twirls, she remembered how hungry she had been when she first walked in the door and saw all those men occupying places they were not going to relinquish to her. John must have noticed her wistful look, for he said to her reassuringly, 'Don't worry. We'll just drink our beer and be right back. They'll save some for us. There's plenty.'

So far as Joan could tell, none of the men except John had left their chairs, and she marveled at the capacity of their bladders. As they walked out of the door, Linda yelled after them, 'If you gotta pee, go behind a tree. The septic tank is on the blink again.'

John laughed. 'Aren't they always?'

John's pleasure in his own joke was revealed in his wide grin that brilliantly displayed a gold filling that covered at least a third of a front tooth. His gold tooth was another indication to Joan that here was no ordinary farmer; he had to be a cut above the rest since most farmers visited dentists only for extractions. (Joan had known many farm kids who had entered the ninth grade without ever having visited a dentist.)

'You're pretty smart for a town girl,' John remarked.

'Aren't town girls supposed to be smart?' Oh my God, Joan thought, in a minute he's going to suggest a trip to the barn to see the baby animals.

'I'd like to see you again. Would you like me to call you sometime?'

'Sure. Why not?' The prospect of a farmer as a suitor – even an extraordinary one – was something she knew she'd have to deal with later. First of all she would have to fabricate some story to make him more appealing, unless her father knew the family. Then any efforts at white-washing him would be futile. But maybe he didn't need to be improved; he certainly appeared respectable enough, although his association with the Schultz family could cast some doubt upon his character. She would have to investigate his family before her mother beat her to it with the facts, a prospect she didn't relish but knew was important.

'Let's get something to eat.' John's suggestion seemed so natural and unselfish that Joan felt she could have made it herself.

There was still a lot of food by the time the couple returned to the kitchen – enough to feed an army, Linda had said – and Joan's turbulent, but unreliable, appetite was quickly satisfied by a ham sandwich and a piece of chocolate cake. The men seemed to have finished eating and were now sitting around the table in a kind of stupor. Occasionally a man would belch, and someone would walk outside for a minute to pee against the nearest tree – judging by the amount of time he took, the existence of a tree was not important. One man lurched against the steps as he was returning to the house, and he simply sat down and remained there with his head folded into his arms. From the arrangement of bottles on the table and those that had appeared on the floor, Joan saw that enormous quantities of beer had been consumed, yet no one was boisterous, and the talk was more like a murmur than a conversation.

The men looked more tired than drunk. Fine red webbings threaded their eyes, and one or two were playing with their bottles – tipping them on end, making chugging noises into their necks – in such desultory ways that Joan wondered how they managed to stay awake. Linda was not in the kitchen, but her husband still sat in his original chair; evidently he possessed a gut and bladder of cast iron. His grin seemed to be more foolish than it had been on the day of his marriage, and his eyes, though a little bleary, focused sharply on Joan. 'Linda says to tell you goodnight. She couldn't take it no longer and went to bed.'

Joan was relieved at being given an excuse for leaving, for surely she could no longer remain now that she was the only conscious female on the premises. 'Well, I've got to get home, too. Time to call it a day. Or night. And thanks very much for the nice party. Please tell Linda goodbye for me.'

Linda's husband nodded. No one offered to walk Joan to her car, not even John, who had earlier implied that this was not to be their last meeting. The most he offered was a flip of his arm in a casual wave.

As Joan walked down the path to her car she noticed a man sitting on the running board of a pickup truck, his shoulders hunched over and his head between his legs. From his miserable pose Joan thought he must be sick, and she was considering offering some help – how she wasn't sure, perhaps a drink of water – but as she started his way he lifted his head and asked her, in a hearty, booming voice, 'Going so soon? The party's just getting started.'

Chapter Fourteen

Unnatural Feelings

Mrs. Nelson had not heard of John, but Mr. Nelson knew the Lambert family by reputation. Frank Lambert had operated an implement store in Clayton before he had made the move to the farm. The family's motives for changing vocations were suspect, for although they hadn't exactly prospered in the implement business, they hadn't gone broke either. Many people felt that the father had bought the farm in order to prevent his son from being drafted – an un-American act that was condoned by no one in the county. The war and its effects seemed to be part of Frank Lambert's identity; he was always tied up with it one way or another, which made people suspicious. Before the war he had run a Ford agency in Sioux Falls, but he had sold his franchise when the promise of war decreased his allotment of new cars. In Clayton his farm implement business was more secure than the earlier car sales because farm machinery continued to be manufactured. During the war years tractors and combines were not sacrificed for tanks and airplanes the way new cars were.

In addition to machinery, Frank Lambert managed a feed business on the side, and he was always eager to reduce his prices for the grateful farmers who had been repelled by the advancing rates of the big-name outfits. Most people in the community didn't resent Frank's cut-rate operations – John's draft dodging was another matter, though. What no one could forgive was his taking over the run-down farm of a family who had farmed for at least two generations, a family with four sons, one of whom had been crippled for life at the Battle of the Bulge.

This family, a Polish Catholic combination, had farmed over a section of land when the first generation arrived to homestead the land. They had stubbornly clung to their original Polish name, full of consonants and containing but a single vowel, until a second-generation male adolescent, mortified at the continuous obtuseness of his teachers and peers, had insisted that the family modify the consonants with workable vowels. Those who remembered the history of the family claimed that their decline in fortune was a direct result of this capitulation.

Regardless of cause, the family did deteriorate: more girls were produced than boys; one daughter died in childbirth; a brother and sister disappeared at the same time, never to be heard from again. Eventually the land, which had lain fallow and ignored for years, was sold off piece by piece, until there was only a quarter section remaining, left to be cultivated and cared for by an elderly father and three surly, resentful sons, plus the one useless son confined for life to a wheelchair.

Frank Lambert had little trouble raising the cash for a payment on the land, and most people admitted that his price to the Polacks was fair, if not more generous than necessary. The sons, once released from their farm duties, quickly vanished from the country to the city, where they must have been absorbed without much difficulty since they never returned to Clayton, not even to visit relatives or friends. The old man bought a little cottage on the fringes of town and spent his days puttering in his dusty garden, swearing at his few chickens. (Few remembered his wife. She had either disappeared with the earlier offspring or died in her own country, a version favored by the more charitable.) Everyone referred to him as the Old Polack, and his cottage was called the Polack's Place, but so was the Lambert farm, which Joan found confusing.

Thus the people in the community disapproved of Frank Lambert for taking over a situation that they thought might have worked itself out if the Poles had only been given a chance. They also disapproved of the Lambert family because Frank dressed more like a country squire than a real farmer. Instead of bib overalls, he preferred khaki pants and denim jackets, and Millie Lambert was even worse, for she always wore men's jeans and low-cut boots, refusing to honor the traditional housedress attire, even for visitors.

Millie Lambert was at least twenty years younger than her husband, yet she always treated him like a lover rather than a respected spouse. They liked to drink and to carouse in nightclubs, and some evenings they would begin a drinking session in Clayton only to end it in some town in Iowa or South Dakota – and these bouts might last for days. While they were gone John was expected to maintain the farm, but many times he would do nothing but the chores – a couple hours of work at the most – and then he would head for the local taverns to complete the day. Sometimes he would hang around the gas stations where he would pass the time of day and occasionally pump gas or help with oil changes. He had barely managed to graduate from high school; his grades were low and he was often truant, yet one of the first complaints Joan heard from him was the grief at not being allowed to attend college had wrought him.

John was sure that his father kept him enslaved. He had always wanted to attend Notre Dame, he told Joan, but the old man had kept him home by refusing to fork over any money. Joan was touched by John's account of human bondage, although she did wonder why he hadn't at least attended one of the local junior colleges since they took so little effort and even provided one with the label of college student. She thought Notre Dame a curious aspiration for John, for the Lamberts were not Catholics, although Frank was said to possess some early strains of Catholicism that he had abandoned after meeting his wife.

Millie Lambert had been a beautician when she met Frank, which gave her a community ranking closer to whore than housewife. Her one approved feature was her loyalty to her invalid mother, a woman who had been born in England and who had come to America in her early teens. Now the old lady was confined to a wheelchair but her gentle nature and her superior manners enlisted the sympathy of the community.

When people visited the Lambert family it was usually to see the old lady, who would preside from her wheelchair, an afghan tucked around her useless legs. She would drink cups of tea and deliver non-stop comments on country ways, comments that offended no one since their source was considered so quaint. The old lady considered her son-in-law too uncouth to take seriously, but she doted on her grandson, and she spent a good part of her days wheeling around the kitchen making him pies and tarts.

At Christmas she insisted on making plum pudding, 'the English way', a project that lasted for days. It never bothered her that she got in people's way, nor did she consider her confections to be at cross purposes to the standard fare of meat and potatoes that was served at least twice a day.

John encouraged his grandmother in her efforts to please him, not because of a great appetite for her productions – he secretly considered most of them awful – but because he enjoyed seeing his father subordinated to the old lady. 'Now Frank,' she would say, 'if you'll just hand me the molasses there – it's on the top shelf – I'll be out of your way in no time.' Frank had to oblige, knowing full well that 'no time' meant hours and hours. John liked to be on hand at those times to witness his father's attempts to inhibit his rage.

Until she met John, Joan had never known anyone who so openly and fervently expressed paternal loathing. One of the first things he told her when he arrived at her house two weeks after Linda's party was that his father had taken over his life until he had no hope of ever escaping his dominance. Perhaps to compensate, John drove his father's car at high speeds and so recklessly that Joan was more scared than impressed. Yet he always saw to it that Joan left no traces of cigarettes nor any objects that might reveal female origin.

'Are you afraid of him or something?' Joan asked one night, her exasperation at John's pickiness causing her to be more bold than usual. Since John's smoking and drinking were scarcely a secret, she wondered what he was trying to conceal. (His drinking exploits were so well known that they were often paired with those of his parents.) 'Does he beat you?' Although farmers beat their sons as regularly and habitually as they planted and sowed their crops, they usually abandoned the practice when the boys became old enough and strong enough to create their own physical threats.

'He's never laid a hand on me. The only time anyone ever touched me was once my mother spanked me when I was in the third grade. The old man gave her hell afterwards and wouldn't speak to her for a week.'

Joan considered her own fears, which seemed so different from John's. She was always afraid of detection but not its consequences, whereas John seemed so open about things and yet was so afraid of the reactions of his father, a man whom she had been told (by her own father, but in milder language) didn't really give a shit about anything or anyone except himself.

She was not especially attracted to John. His bovine eyes in some ways made him too girlish, and he had a pronounced stutter that had at first seemed interesting but which later embarrassed her to the point that whenever he got stuck on a sentence she would practically have to bite her tongue to prevent herself from finishing it for him. Yet she was grateful to him for calling her and for proposing legitimate dates – movies and picnics and baseball games – events that involved phone calls and being picked up properly at home.

He was also a respite from her tumultuous feelings towards Ronald. He did no more than kiss her briefly and fraternally at the end of an evening, and he gave no indication that he expected more. She felt safe with John, for she knew that he was incapable of inspiring in her the kinds of physical upheavals that Ronald provoked just at the mention of his name. And she was content with him; he made no demands on her body and few on her intelligence, for despite his talk of frustrated college ambitions, he was not a reader, and his ideas were as aimless and limited as the dullest of people she knew. Unlike Ronald, whose political opinions were inaccurate and badly informed but still were passionately wrongheaded and full of misguided zeal, John's interests were concentrated upon personal, past injustices all delivered by his father.

He was not interested in sports, which made him suspect in a Midwestern environment that seemed to base its seasonal development on the changes of official games: baseball in spring, football in autumn, and basketball in winter. One night, however, he did take her to a baseball game where they saw Ronald make a spectacular play, a fielder's choice of such purity and grace that Joan's heart stopped.

Because John's expectations of Joan were as limited as they were for himself, Joan could enjoy drifting along in his company. She was neither bored nor stimulated. Instead, a queer equanimity settled in that she could respond to with relief, to the point where she thought she could let things stand indefinitely. Her feelings, she supposed, were being suspended for a while, put on ice and stored away until the time would come when she'd need them. Her only problem was with her father, who openly, and without inhibition, hated John.

His first reaction to his daughter seeing John had been contemptuous. He had threatened to get himself appointed to the draft board so that he could send him off to be a man. The farther the better, he claimed. 'I'll get him sent to Korea,' he promised Joan's mother, 'to the loneliest, most remote hill in the farthest countryside, with nothing there but pigs and water buffalo.'

Joan could not understand her father's contempt and knew his judgment was unfair, and in a burst of righteous indignation she told him so. 'You don't know he's a draft-dodger. He happens to be running a farm almost single-handed, and you've never criticized other farmers for doing the same thing.'

Sensing an indiscretion that could only work against him, Mr. Nelson modified his attack, concentrating more upon the Lambert family in general while including the son mostly by association. Since Joan had yet to meet the family, she had no effective ammunition to defend against her father's assault, but she did attempt to point out that a son did not have to be a carbon copy of his father.

Mr. Nelson, while approving his daughter's theory, pointed out that in practice this was not, unfortunately, the case.

'There is not one damned bit of difference between the old man and the kid. Except their age,' he insisted.

'They have different first names.'

Joan's sarcasm infuriated both parents, but perhaps they

were afraid of arbitrarily violating their own policy of fair play and open-mindedness, for they allowed her to see him provided that he conform to the house rules. The rules were easy, though, so simple that John had no trouble meeting them, for all they amounted to was that dates had to be specified: an evening had to be proposed with its purposes stated. Thus no vague 'driving around'; instead, a specific destination was required. Joan made sure that she arrived home at the designated hour, that they attend every event they had mentioned, and that there were no loopholes from which they could allow themselves any latitude.

Since the Nelsons couldn't help but be relieved that their daughter's infatuation with Ronald seemed to be over, they decided it would serve no purpose to alienate their daughter from John for Ronald's appeal could never be underestimated. 'As long as that guy is alive he's a threat,' Mr. Nelson remarked to his wife one evening as they were once again engaged in a discussion of what to do about their daughter and her misfit suitors. 'Let's just bide our time. She'll be leaving for college in the fall. We might be in for some long months, but at least she'll be definitely going away. Right now I feel we're between the devil and the deep blue sea. Why can't she find some *normal* guy for the summer?' he asked, not really expecting an answer. 'We're taking an awful chance with this one.'

Mrs. Nelson had acquired some of her husband's contempt for the Lambert family, but she did not see John as its obnoxious mutant in quite the same ways as her husband. Like her husband, she was worried about Ronald's latent powers, yet she felt that the actuality of John was preferable to the possibility of Ronald. 'What do you expect her to do?' she asked her husband. 'Certainly you wouldn't have her staying home every night.' To Mrs. Nelson the idea of an uncirculating daughter was more appalling than a daughter temporarily involved in dubious company.

'I'm going to have a talk with her and see where she stands,' Mr. Nelson announced.

'I should think that would do more harm than good.'

Despite the courteous diction, his wife's tone irritated Mr. Nelson. 'I don't understand you sometimes,' he replied. 'I really don't. Here she is, going out with a bum, the worst damned bum in the county, and you say that's better than staying at home.'

'I don't know that he's such a bum. He seems honest enough. He gets her home on time, and they go places that are perfectly decent.' She didn't add that their daughter no longer came in with red eyes and whisker burns because she preferred to keep that memory to herself.

'I wish to hell I knew what he's after.' Mr. Nelson waved his arms around the library with a sweeping motion that suggested that John might be armed and was preparing to take over the books.

'I suspect he's not after anything. Joan is an attractive girl, you know, and maybe he just likes her company.'

Mr. Nelson's defeat was complete. 'Attractive' was a term he wouldn't have used, but his wife's description of his own daughter made him feel guilty for having imposed such ulterior motives upon anyone happening to be lucky enough to gain his daughter's attention. As a result of his shame, he agreed to hold off with his interrogation. He couldn't promise to be nicer to John, though, a suggestion of his wife's which she thought might make their daughter more comfortable, and perhaps more open, with them. Instead, he made arrangements for an August vacation, something he usually did not permit himself since the crops and the farmers' demands were most visible at that time.

'Maybe we'll take the whole month off and go somewhere interesting, like Colorado or Lake Louise, or maybe somewhere more remote, like Mexico.'

Mrs. Nelson was not misled by her husband's plans, nor

did she expect Joan to be, but she didn't anticipate any objections from Joan. They all loved to travel, and the novelty of a month's vacation in August would be a sure relief from a situation that she could see was becoming more volatile every day.

Although Mr. Nelson never permitted himself to ask John about his intentions towards his daughter, Joan, herself, often contemplated the very question. What was the basis of her appeal to a man who appeared so indifferent to most things? She wondered if he might be enjoying vicariously the college experience she was about to begin, but that possibility seemed remote and far-fetched. And how could he enjoy something that hadn't yet occurred to her? Given his capacity for enjoyment of anything (which was comparable to that of an energetic slug) she dismissed this explanation as completely unreasonable. It also occurred to her that Frank Lambert might be involved in some way, that he could have sent his son upon some kind of family revenge errand, but her father's business associations never coincided with those of Frank Lambert's, even indirectly.

Sex was definitely out. Their goodnight kisses remained their only means of physical exchange other than neutral hand-holding at the movies. Joan's musical interests were not part of John's world, either; although he loved to dance, he cared little about what kinds of music accompanied him, and he rarely took notice of what was being played or by whom. She knew he liked to drink – his reputation suggested that drinking was his controlling vice – but when they were together he limited himself to two beers at most.

Usually they talked about people they knew – his acquaintance with Ronald was limited to an occasional nod – and what would become of them. John liked to imagine unlimited poverty for everyone but himself. His favorite topic of conversation was his father, and eventually Joan recognized a pattern. Frank Lambert would occur in every imaginable subject that involved, or even implied, a grievance, and any privation or display of inequity would eventually evoke the specter of Frank Lambert. Once she recognized this pattern, Joan realized that John was totally obsessed – actually demented – upon the concept of paternal authority.

The only time John ever became obscene and foul-mouthed was when he landed upon the personality of his father. (Joan first heard the word 'cocksucker' during one of his tirades.) Then his fawnlike eyes would change so radically that they appeared to be spewing out sparks, his voice would become tremulous, and he would stutter on every consonant. During those transformations Joan was sure that he had selected her, for mysterious, inexplicable reasons, to be an active conspirator in a plot to destroy his father. She was slightly afraid of her admission to his confidence, but she also considered herself a benign ear, an innocent party whose presence allowed him to let off steam, which had to be healthy. She felt that if his hatred ever came to real measures she would be opposed, but she doubted that he would ever suggest concrete actions. She was prepared to refuse, though, and even to tell her father if she had to.

The depths of his loathing fascinated her. She had never known anyone who so openly and consistently despised, and who had committed his life to unmitigated hatred. Almost eighteen, still a virgin, she had read little and absorbed even less.

Chapter Fifteen

Salutatorian

High school graduation in New Bonn always took place before Memorial Day. (American schools traditionally have based their schedules on crop times, and New Bonn was no exception.) Officially, school would begin in the fall, the day after Labor Day, but few farm kids would show up until sometime in October, when the last bean was threshed and the final bales of hay were stored away to wait for winter prices. In the spring, once the ground had finally thawed, absences became more and more frequent, yet there was nothing the administration wanted to do to combat the desultory attendance of the farm kids: either they had them for a few months or they didn't get them at all.

So long as the school district received its state-allotted funds, no one complained about the extended bouts of excused colds that the farm kids claimed, but it was always hard to plan and to schedule school events. Instruction would end the last week in May, but this was merely a bureaucratic date, for practically no one would have been around for the last two weeks. There was no senior prom because of the Lutheran prohibition of dancing. Some years back there had been a Junior-Senior banquet, but this event had been so indifferently attended that the practice was dropped without protest. No one resented the short academic year, but a high school graduation in May presented problems that residents of Minnesota uniquely felt, for one day there might be clear, strong sunshine, while the next day might produce a hailstorm of such magnitude that crops and outbuildings would be pummeled and trampled to ruin. The girls felt they suffered the most from this early spring event, for they were obliged to wear long summer formals – not the traditional caps and gowns – and, unlike their male peers, they could not rely upon coats, or even shirts.

In a school where home economics was obligatory for four consecutive years, most of the senior girls chose to spend their entire final year working on their dresses. There were few rules governing the dresses; they were merely supposed to be in good taste, which meant that strapless or low-cut necklines were not acceptable, and all the dresses were supposed to be in pastel colors. The Home Ec. teacher, who looked a little like a Quaker in her muted grays and browns, kept a careful eye on her charges, making sure they didn't sneak in a flaming red or try to get by with showing more arm than was considered proper. The girls found their fabric choices were limited to organdy, dotted Swiss, or starched pique. Silk was considered winter material and fit only for the finery of old ladies. The colors tended towards variations of pink and blue, with an occasional lavender selected by someone who mistook lavender for a shade of pink. Yellow, the only other pastel color that the girls considered, was found to be terribly unflattering under the florescent lights of the gymnasium's auditorium. White was reserved for weddings, and even pale green was discouraged, for it seemed to reflect a slightly sophisticated association. 'Not pastel enough,' was the way the Home Ec. teacher put it.

Joan, whose attempts at sewing were as pathetic as her attempts to liberally interpret Euclidean geometry, chose to rely on her mother to supply the dress. Mrs. Nelson didn't sew, either, and although she would have liked to have been able to boast at having sewn her daughter's graduation dress, she was practical enough to foresee the difficulties inevitable in homemade construction. Joan and her mother spent one long, futile day in Sioux Falls looking for appropriate dresses, but none of the stores had anything that was at all suitable to New Bonn standards. Either the necks plunged too far or the pastel colors blended into other, more outspoken colors, or the fabrics were not summery enough. There was one Mrs. Nelson liked but her daughter couldn't stand it, a baby-blue dotted Swiss with puffed sleeves and tiny white ribbons attached to its bodice and hem. Joan held out, and rejected it with such fervor that her mother conceded with only a few, carefully timed martyr's sighs. 'We could always cut the ribbons off, you know,' she suggested halfheartedly.

'It's not only the ribbons. The whole thing is awful. It makes me look like a stupid little girl going to a birthday party.'

Mrs. Nelson thought the dress brought out the best in her daughter – her girlish mien was enhanced by the swirls of puffy skirts – but she knew that if Joan didn't like the dress she would be careless with it, perhaps even burning a hole in a place conspicuous enough to prevent her wearing it. Since Joan was the salutatorian, which meant that she had to give a five-minute speech, Mrs. Nelson wanted her daughter to look her happiest during her public appearance.

There were a number of women in town who did occasional sewing (although no one called herself a dressmaker), and it was to one of these women that Mrs. Nelson went to negotiate the creation of her daughter's graduation dress. Mrs. Nelson had lived in New Bonn long enough to know that a person did not simply approach another and request a piece of work. First the material had to be bought, the pattern selected; then the mother and daughter were expected to present the ingredients to the prospective seamstress for her approval. If she liked the project she would agree to work on it, but if she thought the colors wrong or the pattern too complicated or indecent, she would refuse.

The first woman they visited had already promised to do Maryann's dress, but she didn't inform them of her earlier commitment until they had already spread the material on the floor and shown her the pattern. Their second choice, Mrs. Stoner, reluctantly agreed when Mrs. Nelson told her, despite Joan's shocked look, that she could go ahead and change the princess style to something whose skirt was looser and more flared. The material was organdy of such a transparent quality that a full-length underskirt had to be made in order to conceal Joan's waist and thighs.

The only thing Joan liked about the dress was its color, a blue so pale that it was almost silver. The senior class had already voted on acceptable jewelry, and their verdict left as little latitude as the kinds of dresses allowed. Pearls were all right as long as they were the small seed kind and not the big, ropy strands older women wore to church. Lockets and gold necklaces were approved without objections as long as the necklaces didn't have large stones. Everyone expected to wear a graduation watch, so the issue of bracelets never came up. Ankle bracelets were pronounced taboo, but only after a long, heated protest from the farm girls, a protest that Joan joined simply for the hell of it, for she considered them inexcusably vulgar, objects that only farm girls would want to wear. Her protest was based on the disgust she felt for the whole series of stupid rules that seemed important only to those in the position of creating them, but she and her farm peers were loudly and derisively shouted down.

The graduation program was simple, one that had been established years before and from which no one ever felt obliged to deviate, so brief and painless was its simplicity.

First there was the procession. Each pastel girl would enter on the arm of a properly jacketed boy to the music of 'Pomp and Circumstance'. Then a clergyman would address the audience with a brief, introductory prayer. (The Presbyterian and Catholic clergy alternated every year – the Lutheran pastor never appeared on a public platform with other kinds of clergy.)

After the prayer there would be two or three musical selections, gleefully rendered by juniors and below who were at last admitted to the ranks of first chair, and then the valedictorian and salutatorian. Their speeches were usually focused on what high school had meant to them, their words composed of personal, but vague, testimony, sprinkled modestly with quotations from Shakespeare that an English teacher had helped to locate and insert. Then the superintendent of schools would speak a few encouraging words about the character and disposition of the current class, indulging in a few mild jokes directed at the athletic prowess of a few boys. He would then take his place at the lectern and withdraw from a carton at his side the individual diplomas. Each person, when summoned, was supposed to shake his hand and quickly smile, until the stage was filled with cheerful graduates clutching their official documents.

After a selection from the band, one of a serious nature like an isolated movement from an opera work or a symphonic reduction, the alternating cleric would pronounce the benediction and the graduates would file out, accompanied now by some Russian or Polish march instead of the earlier Elgar. After the ceremony, the parents and relatives would reward their graduating offspring with multi-generation family gatherings – elderly grandparents often traveled hundreds of miles for the event. These events were always rich in their abundant presentations of food – tables bearing all kinds of food – but no booze.

If the graduates could escape the family parties after a decent contribution of their time, they met at prearranged places before they set out on their climactic drinking binge, for most people in New Bonn accepted graduation night as the one legitimate juvenile drinking night. Mothers who normally patrolled their children's paths conceded this one evening, allowed their offspring the privilege of staying out as late as they pleased, and turned a blind eye to the disreputable conditions of their return. Not all parents felt this way, of course, but enough did to make the occasion relatively free from parental snooping.

Joan's plans for the evening were more vague than most of her friends. Since the Nelsons were really from Minneapolis and were living in New Bonn more like visitors than permanent residents, there were no local relatives to invite and no family friends interested enough in Joan's graduation to drive the two hundred miles from Minneapolis. No nearby relatives, either, other than an elderly aunt of her father's who lived in a nursing home near St. Paul.

Joan didn't care that she was being deprived of a traditional family gathering, but her parents felt obliged to compensate with alternative plans: a weekend at one of the northern lakes; an excursion to the Black Hills; even a trip to Chicago to visit Uncle Sid. All of these possibilities were intended to cheer her and to prevent her from feeling too deprived of tradition. Joan accepted none of her parents' offers even though she approved of them and understood them as attempts to relieve a temporary pain that did not, in actuality, exist.

Consequently, her graduation watch was almost embarrassingly elaborate; unlike the modest Bulovas and Elgins and Hamiltons of her friends, hers was a foreign-looking object encrusted with diamonds. Diamond watches, she had often heard her mother say, were only worn by 'pushy women' – aka Jewish women – who lunched at the Standard Club in Minneapolis and who played noisy bridge games afterwards, and then returned home to berate their Scandinavian maids and their brilliant, scholarly children who spent all their time studying and who never went outside to enjoy the fresh air.

Joan thought she detected an apprehensive look on her mother's face when she opened her watch, but her father was so obviously beaming and enjoying the surprise that she decided that this was one object that hadn't been seriously disputed. Joan also received a copy of Sullivan's book on Beethoven from Mr. Schlage, an elaborate, leather-bound edition that was easily the price of four lessons, and from Reverend and Mrs. Blue she received a subscription to *Etude*, a magazine she had detested since puberty.

In an uncharacteristic moment of whimsy, Joan had titled her graduation speech 'Where Do We Go From Here?' although its contents bore little resemblance to the title. She had really wanted to talk about the advantages of a classical education – Mr. Schlage had often spoken with great wistfulness of his days at a Heidelberg gymnasium – and she thought the German education sounded magnificent, but her English teacher had warned her of post-war hostility. America, now embroiled in a remote war against an Asian people who meant nothing to most people, was still riding high on its World War II victories, helped along by the refresher course in patriotism that Senator McCarthy was administering to a credulous nation. Also, as her teacher had pointed out, she would be arguing foolishly for something she had never possessed. After all, her teacher had reasoned, 'Your education got you to where you are right now, or otherwise you wouldn't be giving the salutatorian's address.'

Since Joan had been nudged out of top place by three-tenths of a percentage point by a young drudge whose strong suit was math, she conceded the argument.

'Think about your future, Joan, your future, and talk about that. Things that are closest to you.'

It was this suggestion that had prompted the title of her speech. From the title the rest was easy; given the assumption that most people aren't going to go anywhere, but like to be told they are, she had no trouble weaving clichés into an intelligible strand of acceptable bullshit. The theme was neither useful nor original: 'We are both coming and going and only time will tell,' was what it amounted to, with the final message residing in the affirmation that somewhere along the line: 'We will have settled down and also have learned valuable lessons that our children will cherish.'

The only unusual quality of the speech lay in its choice of quotations. Deliberately ignoring Shakespeare, Joan instead had added words from Tolstoy, lines from Donne, even an epigram from Pope, and she had used them in such a manner that it was almost impossible to distinguish the wisdom of serious men from the insipid statements of the graduating senior.

Yet she thought her speech was as good as the valedictorian's, whom she had heard rehearsing his declamation one day in the band room when he thought no one was around. She thought it sounded like something they had once struggled with in Latin class, and when she confronted him with her observation he blushed and admitted to a free translation from Livy's commentaries on Old Age.

'Why don't you give them a little Ovid, instead?' Joan joked, attempting to reduce his embarrassment.

Tim, whose immediate destination was a small Catholic college, which his scholarship secured, and eventually the priesthood, either didn't understand her allusion or pretended not to.

'Why don't you jolt them a little, read them some sexy poetry. The kind that you have to take Latin IV to translate.'

Joan was ashamed to be goading a nice boy in such a mean way, but she was more ashamed because her hostility was not really aimed at him but instead at her position of second place. Yet she couldn't resist pursuing what she saw as a weakness in his character, a weakness that in later years could turn into a harmful liability if he weren't careful. 'Why are you going to bore everyone with outdated ideas on old age when people have come to see young people? Aren't they more interested in what youth has to say than about age?' Lamely stated, she knew her argument made little sense, and that it also sounded selfish and small-minded – qualities she had hoped she would never possess, yet her present conduct seemed to be inclined towards them.

'I'll talk about youth, too. Don't worry, but sometimes you have to tell people a little bit of what they don't want to hear.'

Joan's astonishment grew as she stared into the earnest eyes of this young aspirant. She could almost hear the bells announcing Mass, the choir beginning its sequence of litanies, and her repressed love affair with the Catholic church lurched awake after its slumber of almost two years. 'Sorry, Tim. I didn't mean it that way. I really didn't. I know you'll say good things. I'm only sore because I'm stuck, I guess.'

'That's okay. I'm upset, too. It's not important.'

For a moment Joan wondered whose choice the priesthood had been for this quiet, serious boy. How could he possibly listen to daily accounts of suffering and pain without becoming immersed in some terrible struggle himself? Or did the vocation of the church require a kind of formidable compassion? The terrifying thought that maybe he was thinking of atoning for her, too, reduced her to a humility she never thought she knew. 'Maybe you could help me out with some of the rough spots in mine, like the parts that need more explanation.'

'I'm afraid I can't do that, Joan. Then it wouldn't be yours.'

God damned conceited cheater! Joan would have given anything to have yelled this at his retreating back, but her sense of propriety – after all, they were on school property – yielded instead the milder 'Creep!' which he couldn't help but hear. It gave her little satisfaction, though, for it had slight correspondence to the feelings that churned away inside her: rage, for having made the mistake of feeling lesser than he, and fury for having revived the pain of Catholicism, a religious inclination that had strong overtones of her futile love for Ronald.

On the night of graduation Mr. Nelson poured champagne with generous splashes into wine glasses that the family ordinarily used for water.

'This is nice. We should do this more often.' Mrs. Nelson's stern face appeared more relaxed and less tense than usual.

'Yes, we'll do it every time our daughter graduates from high school.'

Joan's approving giggle was accompanied by her mother's exasperated sigh – she could never successfully accept her husband's humor. 'I mean, we should have wine more often, not just on special, unique occasions.'

'Do you know the trouble I had getting this bottle of champagne? First I had to go to Worthington – you should have seen the shocked faces when I asked at the local liquor store – but they told me they were out of champagne. In Worthington, that is, although it's unlikely they've had any in stock there since before the war. Then someone offered to call the warehouse in Sioux Falls and they said they had some but it was American – Virginia Dare or some such stuff.' Mr. Nelson looked at the green bottle that was nestled against a chunk of ice in the ice bucket, a magnum bottle so green and continental-looking that Joan could almost hear it murmuring '*Alors*!' or '*Voila*!' or whatever it was the French wine spoke.

'None of this American stuff for me, I told the proprietor, who by then had become interested in my problem, and so the two of us made some calls to distributors until he found one who was due to leave Minneapolis the next day and he promised to bring a case of the French stuff, the real McCoy.'

'Why Burt, you didn't buy the whole case, I hope?'

'No. The man was glad to buy a case. Said that it was good to keep on hand, that maybe we were starting a trend. I didn't have to buy a case, but I would have if it meant not getting the real thing.'

Joan was sorry that New Bonn's only undisguised liquor cabinet did not boast a case of French champagne. She sensed her father was also disappointed in not having to buy out the whole supply. 'I'm really glad you got it, Daddy, but was it worth all that trouble?'

'Only for you.' Mr. Nelson glanced at his wife, who was either tipsy or sad at the prospect of her daughter's departure from the state of schoolgirl. Her eyes were blurry and her mouth was set in a line that suggested she couldn't take much more emotion. 'I bought some for your mother, too, when we had our twenty-fifth anniversary,' he added.

Mrs. Nelson seemed cheered by her husband's acknowledgment of another important event, but little could be done about the general mood that now descended upon them once the wine had been drunk. There are few things sadder than the letdown that inevitably follows from the boisterous guzzling of champagne, when, after the cork has been popped and the first glasses filled, accompanied by the approving murmurs of the drinkers, the wine begins to go flat, its effervescence mixing with saliva and stale cigarette smoke, until the last drops are finally bolted down with regrets, glass stems idly twirled by nervous hands, and laughter evolving to queasy belches. So the Nelsons, were happy to leave the house for the graduation ceremonies, their empty bottle the sole testimony to the evening's tastes, which were far too exotic for New Bonn and the program for the evening.

'Are you all right to drive?' Mrs. Nelson asked this question to both husband and daughter, since they were taking two cars to the event. (J oan was allowed a car for the evening for her own personal binge, although no one referred to it in those terms.)

'Sure, I'm fine. Can't feel a thing.' Joan wondered if this were true. She did feel slightly giddy, but more like she needed sleep or the rest of the dinner she was unable to finish.

'You look fine, just fine. Remember to speak clearly and not read too fast.' Her mother's admonition was appropriate, for Joan did have a tendency to race through whatever she was reading, knowing full well she was being gazed upon rather than listened to. Clutching her speech, which her father had wrapped into a tube and tied with a piece of purple yarn so that it resembled a royal diploma, Joan thought she looked like nothing more than a seedy Alice in Wonderland, in her ice-blue pastel gown and her hair held back by a blue satin band.

True to Minnesota May weather, the evening had turned cold, which produced goose bumps on her unprotected arms. The wind had whipped up to a force that could become a genuine gale. Decidedly not good for the crops, Joan thought, as she made her way to the girls locker room, her long skirts pushing against her legs as if they were attempting to fly loose.

Inside the locker room the graduating seniors were clustered at the mirrors – combing their hair, applying lipstick, and congratulating one another on the success of their gowns.

'Oh Joan, you look marvelous, you really do.' Maryann, who usually wasn't given to flattery, smiled beatifically at Joan; perhaps with a twinge of guilt, too, since she had aced the Nelsons out of the town's best dressmaker. The number one rank of the dressmaker showed in her product, too, for Maryann, who ordinarily looked as if she had left a part of her at home, tonight looked as if she had been assembled by many hands. She looked perfectly integrated. The color of her dress, although labeled pastel by the garment industry, was just strong enough to suggest a firmer conviction. Not exactly pink, it was more like the shades found in the nicest hybrid roses, and the neckline plunged to a level conspicuously lower than those displayed by the other girls.

'My God! How did you get by with that?' Joan's envious eyes traced the plunge and stopped at the cleavage.

'The old bat is practically blind. I just told her to cut more and she never even noticed.'

'Didn't your mother have a fit?' It was not like Mrs. Handslip to leave unsupervised any action of her daughter, and it was inconceivable that she hadn't inspected each stage of the gown's creation, from the first basting stitches to the pinning of the hemline.

'Of course she did, but by the time she noticed it was too late. I couldn't very well show up with nothing on. That's what I told her, anyhow.' Maryann's pleasure at having outwitted both mother and dressmaker was so contagious that Joan's envy was charged with admiration.

'Well, more power to you, I say.'

'I'll catch hell when it's over, but it was worth it,' Maryann stated.

Joan and Maryann had made plans with three other girls

to cruise the county in Joan's car, and Joan was now afraid that the dress might somehow alter their plans. 'We're still going out afterwards, aren't we?' For a minute Joan imagined her friends stuck with irrevocable family plans involving hordes and relatives and loyal friends of the family, plans that were sure to leave her shut out high and dry.

'Sure. It's still on as far as I'm concerned. I only have to put in an appearance for a few minutes – my dad promised me – and you can come too he said.'

Joan was flattered by her friend's invitation, pleased that the family had, for once, managed to countermand the domination of its mother. There were few people who Joan liked less than Mrs. Handslip, who always made her feel uneasy and guilty. Even though she tried to get along with the mothers of her friends even harder than she attempted to get along with her own mother, Mrs. Handslip remained obdurate, totally unmoved by Joan's attempts to please or charm. She was a woman who persisted in reproaching her daughter for acts not yet committed, a woman who warned of dangers to come and slyly hinted at secret knowledge of contemplated sins. She made Joan feel as if she had snuck into the house despite its locked doors. If she looked at Joan in church, Joan would become rattled; once she had lost her place during a hymn which put her a full two measures behind the congregation. She had to wait for the refrain to catch up.

'Where's the juice?' The girls always referred to alcohol as juice, an expression they thought clever although they knew it had long ago lost any powers to deceive.

'It's where I said it would be, in the culvert.' That afternoon, Joan had given Brian Boswell, the oldest brother of the beloved Ronald, enough money to buy two pints of Old Crow. The five girls had pooled their money and had insisted that the occasion of graduation demanded Old

Crow. Joan had driven to an isolated spot four blocks from Locksley Hall and had hidden the bottles in an old culvert that had once buttressed a driveway. 'It's safe, perfectly safe,' Joan whispered, 'unless there's a flash flood, so don't pray for rain.'

Mrs. Flauntzer, the most elderly of the English teachers, jingled her tiny brass bell and called out 'Girls! Girls! It's time to line up now. Take your places.' She had served as chaperone and guide for at least two generations of senior graduates, and she clearly enjoyed her job. 'You look lovely, all of you. You must never forget this night and its importance for all of you.' She beamed upon each graduate as if she had managed the process, and perhaps she was correct in taking credit, for the kinds of things she had taught them – the significant dates of Western culture, for example – would later recur for Joan, unsummoned and unprovoked. Twenty years later Joan could still produce one of Mrs. Flauntzer's elaborate outlines of literary events, devoid completely of context or content, but its capital letters and Roman numerals and lesser Arabic and lower case letters still preserved.

'You look so pretty standing here, like petals on a bouquet of fresh, spring flowers.' Maryann groaned while Joan suppressed a snicker, scoffing not at Mrs. Flauntzer's lack of originality, but rather marveling at the number of years she had managed to bring off this observation without altering syntax or diction.

The band sounded tinnier than ever, depleted as it now was of the first-chair seniors, and not yet having had the opportunity to establish its own younger sound. As the senior girls entered, escorted by the senior boys wearing their sensible jackets and clean white shirts and Sunday ties, Joan noticed that no one was trying to keep step as they had practiced in rehearsal. Escorted by the valedictorian future priest, Joan was the last to arrive on stage, where she was guided to a center seat by the superintendent of schools.

The auditorium was darkened but it was not difficult for Joan to pick out her mother and father, sitting in uncomfortable straight chairs that had been known to collapse without warning. Her father looked cheery as usual, but her mother appeared strained; the champagne had obviously lost its kick and the familiar tense lines that characterized her face had returned. She was scowling, looking as if she were about to hear a disagreeable sermon from a source that lacked authority. Joan also spotted Reverend Blue, who had donned a gown for the occasion, but who was without his wife – no surprise there; she rarely appeared in public except for the obligatory church attendance. After Father Sturm's brief invocation, during which he conspicuously crossed himself three times – compelling the other Catholics to imitate him – the program followed without a hitch, until it was time for Joan's speech.

As Joan walked to the lectern to take her place, she realized that she had only hastily prepared for what a salutatorian's speech promised. Never quite convinced of the seriousness of the situation, she had always thought that somehow she would be spared. (Had she believed in divine intervention, or had even studied it a little so that she could recognize its possibilities and signs, she might have explained her lack of preparation on those grounds. Instead, her belief was based on a very practical assumption that her words were inconsequential, so completely unimportant that their very lack of value would keep her from speaking.)

Taking her place at the lectern, she realized that what she had put together was a phony oration consisting of a string of clichés strung together like a necklace of babies' beads. She unrumpled her speech and placed it in front of her, rubbing her hands across it to smooth it down, as if this gesture, itself, would allow any holdout magic genie to finally appear and rescue her. Glancing at the wrinkles as if they might be ignited into flames, she began to read fast and in a lower voice than she had pitched in rehearsal, where she had been warned against racing the clock.

She glanced up from the second page and saw that the audience could not hear her, but they seemed to be tolerantly sitting there waiting for her to finish her charade. She had only one page, plus one paragraph, to go, and although she didn't look at her watch, she knew that she had used up, at most, a couple of minutes. She was tempted to improvise, to elaborate upon one of the previous clichés, and she had just about decided to expand upon the 'time-is-knowledge' theme when she saw a woman in one of the back rows nudge her male partner with a kick to the shin so quick and sharp that the man was almost jolted out of his chair. Joan smiled towards this victim and addressed herself to his discomfort: 'And now I would like to refer to the title of my speech.'

There was a rustling of programs as the audience attempted to check the printed title against the drivel that Joan had been holding them captive with for the past two minutes.

'You don't have to look. It's called "Where Do We Go From Here?" A catchy title, you probably thought when you saw it. A slangy modern one, and therefore a good one since it shows an interest in things we have always wondered.' Joan refused to look at her parents, who would know that she was digressing. Instead she kept her gaze upon the man whom she was depriving of sleep. Looking at him, then at the woman sitting next to him, she smiled reassuringly. 'Actually, I think it's sort of silly for any of us to suggest that we can know where we are going, especially since most of us haven't even thought about it at all, let alone asked the question.

'I guess we really aren't going anywhere, and that those of us who think we are getting somewhere or are going to do something important are just kidding ourselves. We'll probably be the same kinds of people and do the same things that last year's class did, and the class of ten years ago, and maybe even the class of fifty years ago.'

Joan saw Reverend Blue shift in his seat as if someone had placed a rock under one of his buns. She noticed, also, a slight movement in the audience, as if they now sensed that she was deviating from her prepared material and were now getting ready to see her go out on a limb or hang herself from the nearest ideological rope. 'I guess that there is no difference between the way we look at the music that has been played or the things we say and do from the class of last year. The only difference that I can see is that I'm telling you things that you already knew yourselves.'

Joan thought she saw some confirming nods among those faces that had become more alive than when she was reading from her text, but she was now at a loss to complete the challenge of her words. Could she now go on to tell them that they had produced and spawned an environment that was so hopelessly dull and enervating that the best any of them could manage would be to flee somewhere else, where they could then set up their own equally uninspired realms? Did she dare to suggest that their massed dullness had only served to perpetuate its own kind of unimaginative complacency? Or should she instead sympathize with their staunch, resolute narrow-mindedness, applauding them for having succeeded at modest tasks for which they had long ago set modest limits?

All of these possibilities seemed to fit the occasion, yet she knew she couldn't make any statement of the kind, not because of her own lack of confidence but because of the nature of her father's regard, for she realized that it was her father's regard – really more like a friendship between two people who respected and helped each other without imposing impossible demands or expecting unreasonable responses – that contained her, that prevented her from testing this mass of people at the expense of their feelings. Refusing to disgrace her heritage at the expense of becoming a community legend, despite its momentary attractions, Joan continued her declamation. 'I know that I might sound conceited or selfish when I speak for the rest of my class, but I don't mean to. I only mean that I am *satisfied* that we're not going anywhere – away – to do impossible things and then be disappointed when we failed at them. I'm content to know that my class isn't that much different from others and so we don't have to make a big splash in order to prove ourselves.

'We are all pretty decent people and we intend to continue that way, to be credits to all of you, but in ways that aren't big or important. Instead, in ways that are really ordinary. But I think that's enough.'

There was a smattering of applause, but no tumultuous roar, as Joan had for one minute crazily hoped for. The audience must have felt let down, disappointed at the climax to a speech that had promised more than it had delivered. Surely they were not to blame for being unaroused at such an overwhelming endorsement of mediocrity, and Joan's combination of brazen honesty and public humility was not the right compound to stir their admiration. Her father looked relieved, though, as well as grateful, for he knew what she was capable of when she was inspired. Her mother looked resentful; any deviations from set courses always caused her terrible anxieties, but she also looked a bit disappointed, as if she, too, had been left at the dock after the boat had sailed. Joan's classmates smiled their approval, perhaps relieved at having been spared the familiar closing lines – another quotation – and by the time the valedictorian had concluded his oration the events of the program had returned to their normal course.

After the ceremonies Joan saw her father talking to Reverend Blue and two Presbyterian elders, and several days later he told her that they had congratulated him for his daughter's silver tongue and her ability to extricate herself from difficult situations. 'She'll go far, Bert,' they insisted, which only contradicted her own assertions for herself and her peers.

'I wish I would have had the guts to tell them all to go to hell,' she had confided in her father.

'That's exactly what I was afraid you were going to do,' he replied, giving her a pat on the shoulder. She was never able to satisfy herself that he was completely relieved that she hadn't, though. The night of graduation he had given her a twenty-dollar bill, one so fresh and crisp-looking that it seemed to have been manufactured especially for the occasion. 'Here,' he had said, 'buy yourself a celebration drink in a town that will serve you.'

Chapter Sixteen
Aftermath

Joan's friends were waiting for her on Main Street, and when she arrived they were noticeably out of sorts. Each of them had been obliged to make up her own personal excuse for departing from family and fold on graduation night, and they were all incensed with Joan for making them cool their heels.

'Where the hell have you been?' Joan had spent less than half an hour at the home of the valedictorian, Timmy Getzel, whose mother had insisted she visit the family after the ceremony. Most of that time had been spent praising the miniature altar that Timmy and his father had constructed and placed in a bedroom that was also designed and made by father and son. But not wanting to begin a narrative that could only sound more complicated than it really was, Joan said, 'Get in. I'll tell you later,' and then she realized that she had forgotten to retrieve the booze – her responsibility. Her oversight made her friends angrier, but their common search gave them all something to do, uniting them in their sinful purpose until their ill will gradually evaporated.

After they had uncovered the bottles they discovered they had brought neither mix nor cups. 'So what. We'll drink it straight, then, at least until we can get to Clayton.' Maryann's suggestion made them all feel unusually brazen. 'Why not?' she continued. 'I've heard it's better for you that way. Not to mix it with a lot of sugary stuff. That's what makes you sick, you know.' True, they knew, but still it was hard to take more than a small swallow without gagging, wondering if the hastily downed graduation food wasn't going to come up in one great gush, thereby ruining their carefully acquired graduation dresses.

Their original plan had been to drive to Clayton – only fifteen miles – and cruise any joints showing promise of action. Since it was easier to buy setups than beer, even in towns like Clayton where they fancied themselves practically unknown, the girls considered their greatest challenge lay in the attractions of Clayton's bars. There were sure to be other New Bonn male graduates at Clayton, but those familiar products were not what anyone wanted nor had in mind. Graduation night demands new faces, preferably mature ones, they all agreed. For one long painful moment, Joan thought of Ronald with such intensity that her gut performed its customary plunge whenever she thought of him.

It was unlikely that she would encounter him, though, since he rarely left New Bonn, even for his heavy drinking. She had no idea of what she might do if she did meet him. It was clear that she couldn't trust her reactions for these days tears came as easily as smiles.

Maryann claimed that she had heard of a bunch of guys from Pipestone who were supposed to be in Clayton that night, and this tiny string of a rumor – no one even dared to ask her its source – was enough to provide the girls with an immediate goal.

'It's Pipestone we're after. How I'd love one of their letter sweaters!' Carol roared. Joan smiled indulgently. Carol, whose brains were mostly in her butt, liked to imagine one prolonged first date where the boy obligingly handed over his class ring, letter sweater, and an eternal pledge of fidelity in return for one chaste kiss and a wink which promised more to come after their engagement. So far Carol had managed nothing, but she was never discouraged. A believer in Prince Charming, she was too naïve to question her continuous lack of success.

When she had first started to drive, Joan's father had instructed his daughter to always drive slower than the speed limit, for he knew the dim view that the highway patrol takes of teenage drivers, and because they were passing the bottle back and forth – taking small sips that sent them into fits of coughing, Joan was more cautious than usual. Two carloads of New Bonn boys passed them on the highway, honking and waving, and one car appeared so loaded down with passengers that the rear end sagged, dragging the car almost to the pavement. The second car slowed down and waited until Joan was almost on top of it before the driver sped into the left lane. One of the passengers yelled, 'Race ya!' and lobbed a beer bottle at the Nelson car, but when Joan refused to accelerate the driver bore down and raced ahead, evidently deciding to play games with the first car.

'Those boys are damned fools and they are going to get hurt very bad if they keep it up. Who are they, anyhow?' Joan felt more horrified than angry at the taunting shout and the flung object.

Both Carol and Marjorie thought they recognized three members of the New Bonn graduating class, but they were not sure of the rest. 'Farmers,' they announced. 'Farmers, they're all farmers and they drive as if they're still in the fields.'

The quickly vanishing taillight of the speeding car made the girls feel uneasy, but they also felt rather prim about their respectable speed, and by the time they arrived in Clayton both of the earlier cars had disappeared.

'They're probably in Mankato by now, the rate they were going.'

'You mean they're probably in hell by now.'

Joan thought Carol's remark rather insensitive, for she could see too much similarity among revelers, including them; reckless drivers were just another kind. 'There, but for the grace of God, go I,' she muttered, not sure if anyone could hear her. Despite their consumed whiskey, she knew the girls preferred to think of themselves as cruising innocents, and besides, two pints for five people didn't amount to much at all.

When they arrived, the girls spotted several familiar cars parked on Main Street near the entrance to the Silver Star – the favorite joint of minors as well as those of legal age – from towns as far away as Worthington and Pipestone. One reason for the popularity of the Silver Star lay in the democratic ideas the owner-proprietor held towards community drinking. 'If they're old enough to want it, they're old enough to have it,' was his stated position, and he operated on this principle. Joan had never known anyone who had been refused beer at the Star, as everyone fondly called it.

The owner, a huge, chunky Irishman named O'Connell, was a native of the county and somewhat of a legend himself. Some people said that he had acquired the tavern in a poker game, while others insisted his father had bought it for him to keep him out of trouble. The truth resided somewhere in between, for O'Connell had bought the place some years back from a gambling friend whose indifference and laziness about everything other than his nightly stakes had allowed the tavern to decline. Content to run a place that accommodated only a continuous poker game, the original owner had neglected his domain to the point where he was threatened with expensive repairs and changes by the health department, an official agency that ordinarily maintained a laissez-faire policy of unsurpassed aloofness. Old timers claimed that the tavern was so filthy you had to compete for space with the rats. O'Connell, whose previous business experience had been limited to four years of quartermaster service in the army, came up with enough cash to buy the place and to install new floors in the johns. He also abandoned the poker game, which forced the regulars to the barbershop, and he began to encourage new blood by staying open after hours and creating a tiny dance floor where packing cases had originally stood.

The police surveillance he managed easily, for the chief of the three-man police force was his brother-in-law, whose simple tastes were quietly satisfied by regular donations of booze and an occasional visit to a Sioux Falls whorehouse. The deputies fell in line. Men past the age of retirement, they were content with generous Christmas gifts and an occasional side of beef from the locker co-op in which O'Connell shared an interest.

A better explanation for the popularity of the joint lay in its peculiar seediness. It was located in the basement of a former dry goods store, so no windows spoiled its illusion of perpetual nighttime. The wooden steps were scarred and bumpy, and there was only one fifty-watt light bulb at the bottom, which meant that there were at least two or three falls a week, but there had never been any serious injuries resulting from the falls. Most who fell were usually too drunk to notice the pain, and those sober people who did succumb were outsiders, anyhow, those who hadn't been warned, who literally tumbled into the place. They either took their lumps in good grace – for there was always a crowd at the bar to guffaw over the latest accident – or they left in outrage, threatening suits that never reached litigation, and returning to their safer saloons in their own villages.

The walls had been painted a dingy rust color years ago and they had never been so much as touched up. The few lights were mostly focused around the bar, which gave it a kind of halo effect, while the booths that lined the walls were left in almost total darkness. The johns were of the most unusual arrangement Joan had ever seen. Adjacent to each other, the male populace had years ago drilled holes through the thin wallboard so that they could be on-the-spot witnesses to female elimination. For a while O'Connell had attempted to patch up the holes, but the tin strips that he placed upon the holes had a life expectancy of no more than two evenings. Finally he quit altogether, so the holes remained, but in order to thwart the males from their continuous peek show he removed the light from the women's john, which meant that the females peed in the dark while the men peered through the holes in exasperation, seeing only the hazy outlines of squatting women, more like silhouettes instead of the full-fleshed figures they were after. There was also an odor that seemed to hover there, unlike anything Joan had ever encountered (including her visit to the Chicago stockyards with her parents years ago), a stench so strong, and representing so many different elements, that it was impossible to assign it to any one major cause. It was so powerful that it made the back of Joan's throat ache.

Joan secretly hated the Star and its unique filth, but she was loath to admit her feelings to anyone. She also realized that its unique sordid nature kept it absolutely safe from even the most zealous of parents. All of Joan's friends had been forbidden to go there, and Joan was no exception, yet no parents had ever dared to personally see if the daughter had honored the parental ultimatum. Once Maryann's mother had been inspired to call there for her daughter, but had gotten nowhere since O'Connell had merely answered the phone, said that he would ask if she was there, and had never returned to the phone, leaving Mrs. Handslip sputtering with indignation after half an hour's wait.

There were more people than usual on this weekday night. All the booths were full and there were people three-deep at the bar. Some seemed to be waiting for booths, while others were attempting to introduce more bodies into a constant amount of space by sharing stools and standing sideways instead of full face. There were several New Bonn graduates who had gotten a head start on Joan and her friends; one girl was staring at a brown stain that began at the bodice of her coral-pink dress and continued towards it hem. Another girl stood near the juke box with a drink in one hand, weeping with great noisy gulps over some secret sorrow that no one seemed interested in learning. The two carloads of New Bonn boys who had passed Joan's car with such flamboyance were nowhere to be seen, but there were other young male graduates, still wearing their coats and ties although they looked rumpled and hot. One boy, an angular lad whose father operated the feed lot, removed the carnation from his buttonhole and attempted to stuff it down the front of Maryann's provocative dress, but his eyes were so glazed and his coordination so inaccurate that when Maryann jerked away he ended up making loopy circles with his flower, his arm traveling in wider and wider arcs until he knocked the glass from the hand of the boy standing next to him, another graduate who giggled loudly at his friend's unaccustomed boldness.

Joan and her friends had already decided to waste no time with local products. Their sights were set on those from at least Pipestone, although they were resigned to settle for others so long as they weren't their wretchedly familiar classmates. Clustered into a tiny space near the bar, Joan and her friends stared into the dark space away from the bar, hoping to spot at least two or three prospects. The May evening, which earlier had given them goose bumps and icy fingertips, receded into the peculiar climate of the Star. Hot and clammy with sweat, the girls began visibly to wilt. Two dark patches began to appear under Carol's sleeves, and Marjorie's nose was collecting so much sweat the Joan reached over and wiped it off with her linen hankie.

Joan was carrying one of the pints of whiskey in her purse; the other had been consumed on the drive, and she wondered if they reflected its disappearance. Maryann's low-cut gown, which had earlier looked so sensational, now resembled the clothes that adorned the calendar girl behind the bar – at least in color and cut – making her look like a growing girl experimenting in adult disguises. There was a continuous level of deafening sound; the shouts of the customers, the music of the juke box, and the clink of bottles and glasses all contributed to a sustained, unintelligible noise. Conversation was impossible, but so was listening to the music. Two couples were attempting to dance, a testimony to their drunkenness, or perhaps they were trying it on a dare, because there was no room for them even to sway. Stumbling into one another and occasionally spilling over into a nearby booth, they continued to mark time to the unheard music until one of the girls finally tripped and collapsed onto the floor.

'For God's sake, let's go. We're never going to get a booth here.' Joan's suggestion, so indisputably practical, could not be dismissed, but it proved irksome since it implied there were other places to go.

'Let's not. We haven't seen who all is here.' Marjorie and Carol, whose fantasies of Pipestone boys persisted despite contrary evidence, wanted to stay for at least another ten minutes. 'Anyway, where'll we go? There's no other place here, and it's too early to go home.'

The idea of returning home like defeated warriors inspired them to search for alternatives. 'Look, we've still got most of a pint left. Let's just get out of here for a few minutes, at least until the mob has gone, and then we can always come back,' Joan suggested. 'We can even get some mix and take it with us, but please let's leave for a little while. I'm ready to pass out from the noise.'

Joan's friends tended to dismiss her intellect and her practical suggestions even more readily than her own parents, but they did react to her descriptions of her physical condition. Known as the possessor of a notoriously weak bladder, she was also regarded as the owner of a precarious stomach. She could vomit practically by suggestion, and there had been many times when an evening of relatively mild drinking had been brought to an abrupt halt by her unreliable gut.

It took them a few minutes to buy their mixes, which gave Marjorie an opportunity to carefully search out the joint for prospects – if they *had* to leave they could at least satisfy themselves that they weren't leaving anything important – but they were too late for the Pipestone boys. Maryann had been correct; there were six boys from Pipestone visible in their purple letter sweaters – a perfect number, with even one to spare – but they had been appropriated by some Clayton girls who evidently had been on hand earlier than anyone else.

Jim, the boy who had tried to donate his carnation to Maryann's bosom, was standing by the door as the girls left. 'Leaving so soon? Where'ya going?'

Joan had never felt kindly towards this foolish boy, and she felt less generous now that he was making himself an obstacle to a departure she felt responsible for engineering. 'Just a minute. We'll be back in a minute,' she muttered. His glazed eyes had settled in a permanently crossed position, which made him look even more like his oafish father, a man used to wearing bib overalls over his plaid shirts. 'You'd better go home. You look like you've had enough.' Joan's advice, while accurate, sounded spiteful.

'You wanna take me?' His leer was so unmistakably

amateurish that Joan considered taking him up on his offer. She also wondered who he was with and how capable any of them were of driving. She lingered on the bottom of the stairs until her friends had reached the top, where they yelled down at her to hurry. 'It was your idea to leave, you know,' Carol reminded her.

Joan looked at the lumpish obstacle once again and added, in a more kindly tone, 'Look, we'll be back. Why don't you take it easy till we get back?'

'That's okay, don't worry about me. I'm okay. I'm with Howie; there're some other guys down at the park. Was s'posed to meet 'em. They'll be around.'

Joan was tempted to ask him what others he was referring to, but she knew that an attempt to give specific names would be too complicated for him, and this would make her friends even more impatient. Without saying anything more, she squeezed past him and made her way up the stairs. After she had joined her friends she mentioned what he had told her. 'Why don't we take a quick drive down there and see what he was talking about? Maybe there's another load of Pipestone guys there, or at least maybe some more Clayton boys.'

Carol and Marjorie, and even the quiet Louise, who rarely broke her silence except to giggle, had been noticeably sullen and resentful towards Joan for a strategy they considered unfavorable to all of them. Here was now a chance to locate other boys at a location they had not foreseen, and although they usually considered any park an exclusive haunt of infants and toddling juveniles, the novelty of a park containing available males held an immediate appeal.

Even though there were two parks in Clayton, only one saw any use. The one adjacent to the county buildings was almost always unpopulated; although there were benches, few people congregated there. Occasionally in nice weather a lawyer would pause for a minute with his client to rehearse their plea, but more people ignored the benches and garden as they passed to and fro among the cluster of county buildings. Since the purpose of the park was display only – KEEP OFF THE GRASS! signs appeared at regular intervals – there were no swings or sandpiles, nothing that would suggest a child's pleasure. It was simply a well-maintained plot of land, conveniently located for those on county business, otherwise ignored by most people who resided in town.

The other park had neither name nor official description. Sometime early in the 1930s a retired banker and real estate developer had donated ten acres of land to the city, stipulating that it was to be used for a children's park. His motives remained a puzzle, for as a bachelor and the last survivor of a respectable family of merchants and tradesmen, he seemed like the last person to be interested in the physical activities of children.

Although the land was in the nicest part of town, complete with a creek and cheerful-looking meadows extending from its banks, the place had been neglected and run down as long as Joan could remember. Playground equipment had vanished, although there were still some remains of the chain swing. The outhouses had been tipped over and had finally settled into the ground. In the winter they were submerged in snow where they lay buried like Indian mounds. The creek no longer flowed. It had been diverted to a more productive area where it now fed into another, larger stream. The park now was mainly used as an auxiliary town dump, strictly illegal, and there was always someone prowling around at night, in search of the perfect place for lovers perhaps, yet most people who were not familiar with the terrain avoided it, not wanting to explain to curious parents the existence of grass stains or dog shit on their clothes. Yet, like the Silver Star, the park had its appeal, an appeal based on similar qualities: so dirty and run down and badly lit – no city council wanted to continue replacing lights that were shot out by BB guns as soon as they were installed – few parents patrolled it, while the village police would drive around its periphery only once or twice a night.

When Joan and her friends arrived at the park they saw the two cars containing the New Bonn graduates who had tried to play games with them on the road, but there was no sign of any occupants. 'Probably passed out on the grass,' Carol suggested.

'What grass?'

Joan giggled. For some reason the idea of smooth manicured lawns amused her. 'If I had this land I'd turn it all into quack grass, every inch of it, until it choked out the weeds and cans and the ass-wipe that everyone is always depositing here and all the other crap that would take carloads to haul away. I'd cultivate quack grass – "that botanical nuisance" – she was quoting her father's term now – and see how it gets along.' She wondered if the whiskey was producing this kind of nonsense, for surely she had never before considered possessing land, let alone plan for its functions.

Marjorie, loyal to anyone's suggestions, especially if they coincided with her own strong feelings towards romance, announced her own modified plan. 'If I owned this park I'd convert it into one big lovers' lane. Every inch of it.'

The idea of a personal oasis affected them all, and there was a long silent pause while each one imagined ordering her own personalized Starbird convertible with matching leather upholstery. Joan slowly drove around the perimeter of the park. In addition to the two familiar cars belonging to the New Bonn grads, they now saw several others parked at the curb, but no indications of human activity. Each car was either abandoned, or else its occupants were hiding.

'Where on earth *is* everybody?'

'Maybe they're all having a wiener roast. Or toasting marshmallows.'

Joan knew that their attempts at humor were disguised ways of hiding their disappointment as well as covering up their anxiety, for there was something spooky about the deserted cars within the dumpy atmosphere of the park.

'Hold on! I see someone over there by the water fountain.' Someone, of course, meant a boy of some kind, so Joan obligingly slowed the car in case he could be identified, for certainly if there was one boy there had to be others.

They never did identify the boy. Later on he was remembered as the figure responsible for their stopping. Yet their slow-moving car had attracted a voice who yelled out, 'Hey! Wait! Come over here.'

Although 'here' was an insufficient direction, the girls thought it practical to park and track down the voice, a decidedly male voice that sounded robust, if not bossy. They decided that if there had been a real emergency there would have been distinct cries for help. Joan parked at the end of the land, away from the other cars, vehicles that could have been inhabited by ghosts, so devoid of life was the whole scene.

The girls got out of the car, intending to bisect the park. They told themselves that it was not that large, that if there were people around they were bound to detect them. Curious, Joan thought; what had once begun as a quest for eligible boys had now turned into a kind of scavenger hunt, until here they were, searching for the source of one voice, rather like tracking down chattering squirrels in the woods.

The girls had walked almost a block from the Nelson car when they heard another noise, this time a muffled laugh of such undisguised glee that they spun around as if to face an accuser.

'Ha! Ha! Ha! Fooled you this time. Fucking snobs!'

The Nelson car, which until a few minutes ago had been parked next to no one, was now being maneuvered down the street with terrible grinding noises emerging from its transmission and harsh squeals from its brakes. Joan, whose panic almost immediately gave way to rage, shouted furiously at the departing headlights, 'Come back! You can't do this! It's not your car!' before she realized the absurdity of her commands. She felt in her purse for her keys and found them next to her billfold. Secretly proud of never having conceded to the New Bonn tradition of leaving keys in the ignition, she now wondered what difference it made. All the local boys she had known had been just as capable of handling engines of all sizes and complexities – which included the simple task of hot-wiring a car – as they had been at home with anything that contained wheels connected to a single piston apparatus.

'Who was it?' As if in answer to her dumb question, Maryann added, 'Don't worry, they'll be back.'

Joan knew they would be back, not because of any deep sense of loyalty to her peers nor of school spirit, but because the felony of theft, even among acquaintances, was too much of a threat for them to allow more than a few minutes escape. None of them could be sure about the exact identities of the thieves, but they guessed (and correctly, as it turned out) that they were the same New Bonn boys, or at least part of the crowd, whose two cars were now quietly resting in their parallel positions next to the curb.

'What should we do now? Should we go for help?'

The idea of adding the police into a strictly private caper was unacceptable, especially since there was an empty whiskey bottle lying prominently on the back shelf of the Nelson car, a punishable offense that no one dared overlook.

'We'll be better off waiting for them here. God, how I wish there was someone to help us.' Joan thought of calling John, enlisting him to pursue the fleeing thieves – this was, after all, his home town and territory. She decided, though, that chasing around on back roads was just the sort of thing he might like to do but would be rotten at accomplishing. Also, it would give him too easy an occasion to sound off about girls and drinking, especially unescorted girls, a combination he frequently pronounced lethal. 'You're just asking for it,' he was fond of saying, 'whenever you see a girl drinking by herself you know she's just asking for it.'

Joan regretted her own stubbornness at refusing to learn simple mechanics. All those opportunities she had ignored when she saw boys and men tinkering with their engines now reappeared to her. Here were two abandoned cars in what looked like impeccable working order, and naïve females, all of whom had just been presented with a high school diploma, and not one of them knew the first thing about hot-wiring a car, a job so simple that not even a screw driver was essential.

In frustration, the girls arranged themselves at the curb, for the grass looked dusty and parched, and the last picnic table had long ago been vandalized into shreds. They discussed plans to repossess the car, but more as a way of killing time than as an actual strategy. None of their proposals had much merit, for they all involved splitting up and scouting the streets, activities they considered both risky and futile. Other than expressing their own disgust at not being able to perform the child's task of hot-wiring a car, there were no suggestions of vengeance, although Joan privately thought it would be a simple matter to let the air out of the tires of both cars – no tools necessary, just a simple hair pin – but she knew that such a move could easily prolong their misery, for surely if an owner were to spot two cars with all the tires deflated there would follow an endless series of pranks, undoubtedly becoming malicious as they took hold. Also, they were not sure about the identities of the culprits although they could determine that Jim Hansen was the owner of the blue Chevy whose front fender Maryann was sporadically kicking. They were pretty sure the other car belonged to Duane Hillsdorf, a mild-mannered farm boy with seven older brothers – this impressive sequence of male sons had allowed him the time needed to attend and complete high school. Perhaps it was Duane and his seven brothers who now rode around in the Nelson car.

Yet how could eight boys – or eight girls, for that matter? – fit into one medium-sized Buick sedan? And if there were two carloads, wouldn't that make at least thirteen or fourteen? Or had they commandeered another car? The prospect of these unknown louts combing the streets, seeking other carloads of unsuspecting girls in order to heist their cars, made Joan feel better. Misery, even discomfort, was always easier for her to bear when she knew that she was sharing it with someone. It didn't really matter much who her fellow victims were so long as she was aware that they were around. She noticed that her friends were also miserable; huddled there on the curb in their pastel graduation dresses and useless, spike-heeled satin shoes, they looked chilled, almost lifeless in their misery.

Mostly they were miserable because their evening had turned out so badly, for all of them had deserted family gatherings, with their enormous spreads of meats and potato salads and nonalcoholic punch and chocolate cakes and apple pies, so that they could force down their gullets scorching swigs of raw-tasting whiskey in preparation for a chance encounter with hypothetical carloads of Pipestone boys, or other kinds of unfamiliar boys, whose own subterfuge and defections had undoubtedly been similar to theirs.

Joan, in her misery, also felt guilty, as if she had forced their defections, as if it were her fault that they were all sitting there in the middle of the night on a dirty curb, all in a line, like eager and obedient chickens awaiting their evening feed, when they could still be at their homes, enjoying their bountiful suppers, maybe even opening presents from relatives who had traveled from as far away as Sioux City, Iowa, to share their good fortune. Joan, who was usually so cautious about weeping in public, now began to sob.

'Cheer up, Joan, they'll be back soon. The car is all right. They wouldn't have the guts to do anything to the car.' Maryann, always loyal, patted Joan's shoulder, who was at least relieved that her friends considered her tears appropriate, but she still sensed their resentment, although no one was bold enough to mention blame.

'I wish I were back at Timmie's house.' Somehow this kind of blubbering made sense. 'He has the most beautiful altar in his house. I've never seen anything like it. If you haven't seen it you've got to sometime.'

The girls were curious. Years before, when the family had first begun construction of the altar, there had been a lot of talk about it, even among non-Catholics, and for a while people had gone out of their way to present the Getzel family with souvenir saints or Virgins that they had picked up while traveling. After the collection was complete, though, the curiosity had diminished, so now Joan's mentioning it was like the introduction of a novel topic. Joan was describing the waxy quality of the tiny plastic flowers when a police car drove up, shining its lights full blast into the startled faces of the girls. For a minute no one could see the car or the driver, the lights were so powerful, and by the time the cop had approached them it was too late to whisper any kind of fabricated story to account for their situation.

The policeman, who Joan recognized as the chief, sauntered to the curb, his gun and billy club sagging from his belt (like the genitals on an enormous bull, Joan would much later recall). 'You Joan Nelson?' His stare covered them all.

'I'm Joan.'

'If you're Joan Nelson, we've got your old man's car. If you want it you'd better come with me.'

'What happened? Where is it? Is it all right?'

'You wanna see it, you better come with me.' Joan rose from the curb and looked at her four friends, who now resembled cringing children about to be struck. They seemed to have contracted together, shrunk as if to fit a newer, smaller, space.

'I – that is, is it all right to leave everybody here?

'Sure, leave 'em here. You got here, didn't you?'

Although it would have been possible to fit the five girls into the roomy patrol car, Joan didn't dare suggest it. Neither did she suggest that she would be right back. For all she knew, she might be taken to jail, although for what she wasn't sure. Joan let herself into the patrol car and sat down. She would have liked to have waved to her friends to reassure them, but she was afraid that any gesture of hers would be misinterpreted by this ill-mannered, taciturn cop. Remembering the whiskey they had all drunk, she was glad of the Sen-Sen in her purse, but as she furtively reached into its depths, hoping to pop a few grains into her mouth before the cop rolled up the window, he reached across the seat and grabbed her purse.

'I'll take that,' he announced, and tossed it into the back seat.

Why is he doing this to me? *Does he think I have a gun*?

Joan felt panic, yet she could no more ask him for an explanation for having seized her purse than she could inquire where they were going. She decided to keep quiet.

She was the one who needed information, and she realized that she would not get anything by initiating questions.

Chapter Seventeen

Crimes and Criminals

'So your old man is Bert Nelson.'

'Yes, that's right. Do you know him?' Joan hoped that her father's name and exemplary reputation might provide the kind of leverage she needed.

'Do I know your father! Doesn't everybody?'

Despite the sheriff's announcement of her father's popularity, Joan was not convinced that he personally knew her father. Clearly, he was not the right kind of person to exchange familiar anecdotes with her father, and she suspected that they had few, if any, friends in common.

She couldn't figure out where they were going. They seemed to be driving down a street that she had never seen, and they were traveling slowly, as if the sheriff were savoring every minute of the mysterious trip. There were no landmarks she could anchor upon, so she could only wait to hear the man's further comments on her family's reputation, hoping that her genes were in some way important to the location and disposition of the car.

'He bought the Buick for you, did he?'

Joan didn't like the sheriff's tone. It sounded as if he were suppressing glee, holding back until he had deposited her at the mutilated corpse of her father's sedan. 'Oh no, that's not mine. He only let me use it for the night, to – ah – celebrate graduation.' Surely it could not harm her case to remind this upholder of the law that this was a special evening – just a look at her dress and absurd shoes would verify that – and so a night which permitted its revelers conduct that was normally scorned.

'Yeah. I know. You people had your graduation tonight. I've been picking up the pieces ever since. We had ours night before last. What a night that was.' Joan detected a sneer in his choice of 'you' and 'we'. He's acting as if we're the invaders, here to conquer their precious territory, she thought. But who'd want it? She wondered if she should say something nice about Clayton, that it was famous for its county buildings or prize-winning basketball team. She was afraid that whatever she said would sound phony and condescending, like a queen admiring the children of her serfs.

Sensing that they were crawling, she glanced at the speedometer and was not surprised that they were going under twenty miles an hour. She would have preferred a hundred-mile-per-hour dash, with sirens blaring and red lights twirling, to this tortuous crawl. Other than to needle her about her family's respectability, what was he trying to prove in keeping her from her father's car?

The sheriff glided the car to a quiet stop on a country lane that was full of ruts and boulders. He turned off the ignition and opened his door. 'C'mon. We have to walk from here.'

Joan pushed her door open and stepped out, landing, in her silver pumps, on a surface of sharp pebbles and sticky sand. The sheriff strode ahead, leaving Joan to grope alone in her silly shoes, but she felt that if she were to remove them she would be admitting some weakness. Anyone else, she knew, would have helped her along, or at least waited for her to pick her way through the ruts, yet here he was striding ahead, holding his flashlight as if it were an avenging sword. He had traveled so far ahead of her that she feared she had lost both him and her bearings, and she was just about ready to yell out for help when she saw his beam of light focused upon something huge in a deep ditch. The Buick lay on its side, looking like a beached whale. One of its wheels was still slowly revolving, adding pathos to its helpless position.

'Oh my God, was anyone hurt?' Joan's wrath at the unknown felons evaporated. The image of an emergency hospital ward, crammed with male graduates bleeding from enormous gaping head wounds, cluttered with stray arms and legs strewn on the floor, and attended by white-faced doctors in blood-specked smocks with masks only partially concealing their grim, teary eyes caused Joan to retch. Her stomach convulsed once and then her nerves took over, settling in her hands and legs which shook without control. The sheriff concentrated his light on the driver's side of the car, and she saw that both doors on that side were slightly open.

'Sprung,' he said. 'The jolt sprung both of 'em so's you couldn't shut 'em if you wanted to.'

Joan forced herself to look, since his description of the car seemed to be paralleling the fate of its occupants.

'Windshield didn't shatter, though. This safety glass is great stuff. The bastards musta been doing fifty at least.'

Joan thought this judgment must be a good sign, for surely no one, not even the most callused or irreverent of men – and she considered the sheriff a top candidate in both categories – would dare refer to the dead or the dying – even the seriously crippled – as 'bastards'.

'Then they're all right?' She hoped he would verify her assumptions as well as reveal the identity of the 'bastards'.

'Course they're all right. They were so drunk they didn't know what hit 'em. Only cuts and bruises, although one of them might have a broken nose.'

'Where are they?'

'I hope they're right now home and in bed, but they

might still be waiting for their moms at the hospital.' His scorn for 'moms' was unmistakable. Irresponsible 'bastards' should not have mothers available to bail them out of hospitals and jails. 'I had to show you this so's you can tell me what to do with it. We can't just drive it outta here like it was leaving the showroom. Your old man is insured so the damage won't be too bad, but the repair job will keep you walking for some time to come. C'mon, let's go back. I gotta call your father.' He reached into the front seat through an open window and honked the horn. 'Still works,' he announced, and then he extracted three empty whiskey bottles, quart-sized, from the front ledge. 'Evidence,' he gloated. 'Found 'em rolling around in the back, practically still warm. They say you gave it to them.'

Joan stared at the bottles. Four Roses, quart-sized, clearly a cheap drink. Joan felt absurdly righteous. Four Roses was the beverage of farmers, or else it was purchased by minors from unscrupulous boors who took advantage of their legal age by foisting rot gut into the vulnerable stomachs of inexperienced drinkers. 'How can you accuse me of giving them booze? I don't even know who the people are who stole the car.'

'Oh come now, you don't expect me to believe that, do you?'

The sheriff clicked the bottles as if he was issuing a command. 'You don't usually go around loaning your car to strangers, do you? Or rather, your *father's* car!'

Why must people become sarcastic when they were goading you and have all the advantages as well? Joan couldn't decide how much of the boys' stupid sob story had been bought by this stupid man, how much he was taunting her just for the hell of it, and how much he really wanted to believe a fabricated tale narrated by a collective of drunken, scared adolescents. Her shakiness returned, and she knew that it would be merely a matter of seconds before she broke down crying. Attempting to force the sobs from the back of her throat into the safer recesses of her intestines – for so she viewed anatomy – she responded with a slight tremor in her voice. 'Yes, I do expect you to believe it. You saw me – that is, us – by the park. Somebody had swiped the car and we were waiting there for whoever had taken it to bring it back. I still don't know why they took it, but if I ever get my hands on them—'

'Atta girl. Knew I'd get your goat sometime. I don't know if I believe you or not, but it's your old man who'll have to pay. After all, it's his car, like you say.'

A stern, Lutheran bishop couldn't have sounded more convincing than this secular law enforcer. Here was a voice that carried all the allegations of filial ingratitude and personal wickedness that she had always suspected she possessed. Many times they had been implied by other authorities – in church, at school, even at home by parents and parents of friends – but now they appeared to her in the form of a judgment in khaki. You are playing with *fire*, girl! roared in her Presbyterian ears.

The sheriff drove Joan to his own house. 'We can call from my house. No sense driving all the way to the station.' Then he said nothing more while they were driving, but he looked at her often. Perhaps he was checking the position of the lock on the door; perhaps he was routinely inspecting her face for signs of an imminent confession. During the drive Joan resolutely tried to plan the time when it would be safe for her to cry, but when they arrived at his house she decided this was still not the time for tears. Although she expected his house to display foreboding signs, she was not surprised to find it no different from the other houses on the block. A light was burning on the porch, giving it its only distinction. Otherwise it was just one of many ordinary houses on the block, certainly without signs of a fortress. 'You wait here while I call your old man,' he commanded as he slid out from the steering wheel and opened the door.

Joan knew it was useless to give him the phone number. All he had to do was ask for the New Bonn operator and he would be plugged into the community monitoring system. Within five minutes of the call at least half of the non-sleeping members of the community would be aware of the wreck, if they weren't already, and by morning everyone would know. Yet there must have been previous calls to New Bonn because of the boys' role in the incident. Didn't he say that moms had been called from the hospital? Joan wondered if her father had been alerted yet, and she hoped now that the sheriff would not feel obliged to mention her own role as a suspected whiskey profiteer.

Waiting in the car, Joan could see no signs of life in the sheriff's house. The windows remained dark and she could hear nothing. She would have liked to confront the sheriff's wife, for what kind of woman would put up with a man whose sole purpose in life appeared to be aimlessly driving young girls around the countryside, at low speeds, trying to badger them into confessions for uncommitted crimes? Joan imagined her in a blue chenille bathrobe with curlers in her hair and cold cream masking her face, staring at her spouse with terrified, cow eyes, until he shoved her back to her bed with a slight heave of one massive shoulder. If there were children she saw them chained to their beds, with Papa the sole possessor of the master key that unlocked them every morning just in time for quick bowls of cold cereal before they were released for school.

Or perhaps they were kept in the cellar with the canned fruit and sauerkraut. Joan saw a line of rusty cots; concealing the frail bodies of a half-dozen bruised children were dun-colored army blankets. There were no pillowcases to cover the pillows. Poor little sad mites, she thought. To be confined until they were old enough to shoot their way out was the sad fate she had imagined for them.

When the sheriff returned he was humming a song that Joan despised, 'The Girl That I Marry', and wearing a half-smile on his face that made him look a little like Dick Tracy in one of his more relaxed moments. Joan was not going to give him the satisfaction of parrying questions that she fed to him, so she kept quiet while he settled himself into the car and started off. Although he appeared pleased with himself, he kept the source of his pleasure to himself, but she refused to risk another question in order to hear his extended, oblique explanation, an explanation that was sure to carry another rebuke to her character.

As an animal lover and person inclined to fanciful musings, Joan tended to classify people according to their resemblance to domestic animals. Clearly this man was neither bull nor bear, descriptions she usually applied to big men. Rather, he looked like a salamander or newt – Joan could never remember which was which – with his leathery cop's hardware and his dun-khaki uniform. It was not difficult to imagine lidless eyes popping and darting from his forehead either, although in the dark there was little else to see of him other than his enormous bulk, a shape that she sensed contained horrible life of its own, writhing and seething beneath its scaly surface.

Joan reminded herself to get a grip or she'd end up thinking everyone changed their skin and is ready to pop out like a forest of night creatures. Forcing herself to stare straight ahead, she gazed at a road without landmarks or familiarity of any kind. I could use a strong dose of faith right now, she thought. Certainly Catholics would have the proper prayer to the proper saint for this occasion, which at least spares them from hideous morbid thoughts. And where were they going? They had already seen her father's car, lying pathetically on its side in the ditch; she had been informed of her role in contributing to the delinquency of minors (who were yet to be named); and her father must have been called. Was he, then, taking her to jail? The idea of a holding room, a booking officer, and a crowded cell full of county drunks appealed to Joan's already over-stimulated imagination, yet she knew that physical incarceration was not the custom of the county. She had never yet heard of anyone being jailed in Murray County, not even the most belligerent of drunks, for the community took pride in being able to handle its own.

The sheriff turned onto a road that Joan at last recognized. It was the old county highway and it ran parallel to the main road. As a thoroughfare it was relatively unknown except to those natives whose residences dated back to the days before the construction of the new road. Full of ruts and potholes, and not well-maintained because so little traffic didn't warrant any kind of full-time work crew, the old road was ideal for lovers. Joan had been here with John a few times, and each time she felt as if she were entering a dark nightclub or drive-in movie – it was that popular a place.

The sheriff's silence was broken with his announcement, 'Thought I might as well flush out a few on the way.'

So that's what he's up to, killing a number of helpless birds with one stone, Joan realized, as the sheriff turned off his lights. Joan knew the tactic, for John had shown her how parking spots were selected in this choice area. First you turned off your lights so as not to disturb the other occupants, who could become easily startled – and sometimes enraged – whenever high-beam lights shone into the rear windows of their vehicles. Like all nocturnal creatures, they spooked at the first blinding glare, and they became quickly rattled, unsure of their moves. Should they duck out of sight, or should they first grab the assortment of garments that usually littered the floors of the back seats? After finding the right spot, which was achieved by gliding with the motor shut off, the site was honored by remaining in the car, although some males would occasionally stumble through weeds to the nearest bush to pee. It was all right to play the radio, but this was often a risk since the ignition had to be kept on. Unlike Hell's Half Acre in New Bonn, which was mostly like an after-hours joint or an open-air club with its patrons yelling at one another and frequently passing around the booze, the Old Road was strictly a spot for serious lovers. It was inhabited almost exclusively by couples, for it was rare to find a car with more than two people in it, and the usual couple almost never occupied the front seat.

The sheriff tonight would have a field day – field night? – Joan mused, but she was scared of the consequences of his mission. She wished there were some way she could warn the potential prey, and she wondered, too, what crimes they were supposed to be committing. Indecent exposure, perhaps, and probably drinking in public. How many people does this man arrest on nights like this, and how do they settle their legal accounts? She had never heard of any court dealings that mentioned the multitude of infractions that were committed nightly on a lover's lane.

'Maybe we'll find your boyfriend. I think I saw him headed this way earlier,' the sheriff announced, as if they were engaged in a treasure hunt.

Joan wisely refrained from asking him which boyfriend he was referring to. Not wanting to sound like a coquette, yet proud of her acquaintance with residents of the county seat, she was tempted to respond to his remark, yet she knew that at least part of their present detour was designed to force some sort of admission from her.

The police car crawled along at a pace that would have humiliated a novice sprinter. Joan shifted in her seat until she was almost parallel with the dashboard; at least she would not be associated with this man's rapacious hunting.

'No need to scrunch down like that. No one can see you and they won't see me either till it's too late.' His tone suggested a similar distaste for her; she was quite sure that he didn't want her associated with him as his accomplice.

'Should I duck down on the floor, then?' She thought this an advantage worth pressing.

'No need. I said they can't see you.'

As soon as the words snapped out of his jaw he swerved towards a parked car that Joan could see only when they were practically on top of it. The sheriff turned on his floodlight, revealing a vacant front seat and the scared face of a man in the back seat whose mouth seemed to be permanently frozen into an enormous O. Only his head was visible, but it was not hard to imagine the frantic groping and fidgeting that the rest of his body was experiencing while he was in the spotlight. Evidently his partner was on the floor. The sheriff chuckled, blinked the spotlight twice, and quickly shifted into first gear, so that the police car roared and spun its wheels, casting off showers of gravel in quick spurts like the movements of a shy, startled horse.

They continued to drive without lights, which Joan felt was a good sign. She knew there were other cars parked along the road, for she could feel them the same way that a person can sense occupants in a room that is supposed to be unoccupied, yet the sheriff appeared content to drive slowly on, perhaps resting on the laurels of his single, token exposure. According to the time they had spent along the road, Joan thought they were almost at the end of the course, ready, at last, to swing back onto the main highway to town, and the sudden increase of speed increased her hope. The sheriff shifted into second, indicating their farewell to the area, but then he slammed on the brakes, jolting her forward so abruptly that her nose banged on the dashboard.

'Sorry.' He didn't look at her. Instead, he switched on the spotlight and jumped out of the car, leaving the engine idling until it gave a short gasp and then quit. Joan refused to help by turning off the ignition. Let him do his own dirty work, she thought; let the battery wear out and let him walk to town for help. Her nose was bleeding from the bump, an appropriate response, she felt, to the mortifications of the evening. More out of anger than curiosity she looked out of the window to see what prey he had landed this time, and was astonished to see John standing by the side of his father's pickup and arguing with the sheriff. She was even more astonished to see Linda standing next to him. She almost yelled out, 'Linda! What are *you* doing here?' but the answer was obvious. She was playing around with someone other than her husband, putting horns on his head no doubt.

In the glare of the official light John looked more angry than scared, whereas Linda looked drunk. Her various kinds of makeup had blended together into several large streaks that crossed the surface of her face in crazy angles: powder, rouge, lipstick, mascara and dirt all mingled in lumpy designs. Her hair had fallen out of its beehive and rested now in clumps on her bare shoulders. She was wearing either a combination of flesh-colored bra and panties or a summery halter and shorts outfit in skin tones – Joan couldn't tell and felt the difference was unimportant. Linda clung to John with both arms in the same way that Joan had seen farm women attaching themselves to runaway calves, grasping at whatever part of the body they could find at the time and hanging on till they could fell the rebels.

Although the windows were down in the police car, Joan was unable to hear their conversation, but she did pick up a few terms that she recognized as familiar to John's language: 'pig's ass' and 'flying fuck' were ones she heard repeated. She wondered how he managed to work them into a conversation when he was supposed to be the culprit.

She watched John extricate himself from Linda's grasp. He merely shrugged her off in one brisk, twirling gesture, so that she sank to the ground like a slow-moving puppet, even like a freshly baked cake that begins its slow descent once it is removed from the oven. Joan thought she looked quite comfortable sitting there on the ground, and certainly more independent than when she was clinging to John's arms and shoulders. As soon as John was free of his burden the two men stepped away a few paces and lit cigarettes.

Joan pitied Linda the hangover she was bound to feel in a matter of hours, and she wondered again what on earth she was doing in such a notorious spot with a man who had little to offer her other than a ride home and a few reminiscent laughs. When John and the sheriff returned to the pickup, Linda made no attempt to get up, and when John opened the door on the passenger's side Joan was afraid that one of the men was going to prod Linda with a boot. Instead, John reached down, and with both arms grabbed her armpits, yanking her backwards so that her bare heels scraped the dirt as she was being tugged to the door.

'I can make it myself. What d'ya think I am, helpless or somethin'?'

Her outrage was drowned by the guffaws of the two men. John then said something to the sheriff and climbed into the driver's seat and started the motor, but he sat there with his engine idling and not moving until the sheriff opened his door to the police car. As the sheriff slid into the seat he looked at Joan with such satisfaction that Joan imagined that the whole evening had somehow been staged as a preparation for this event: the smashed car, the juvenile thieves, the criminal whiskey – could they all have been contrived to secure this final scene?

As if in response, Joan's nose began to bleed again;

small, regular blobs steadily dripped onto the bodice of her dress, assuring her that the graduation dress would never be resurrected, never altered into something less pretentious and less festive that could serve for non-ceremonial occasions. She did not bother to ask the sheriff for permission to get at her purse. She simply reached into the back seat and recovered it from its place next to the evidence of consumed whiskey, and although she would have liked to stop the steady flow of blood, there was something gratifying about its persistence. The sheriff couldn't very well ignore it since the dripping was audible and it would be visible soon, for she was spilling onto the floor.

The sheriff drove to the Silver Star, announcing that Joan's father should be waiting for her there. 'That's where you started, that's where you'll end,' he proclaimed.

Although the legal time for selling alcohol had passed hours before, the crowd seemed to have become even more dense than it was when Joan and her friends had attempted to initiate their evening's quest. Looking at the same faces, now more lunatic in their drunkenness, Joan marveled at how everyone else seemed to be engaged in the same dance. The only difference that Joan could see was that those few who had been drinking beer during the legal beer-selling hours were now drinking hard liquor. It made no difference to O'Connell, who was legally entitled to sell mixes at any time, and it was certainly up to the customer how he wanted to drink his own Seven Up.

Joan was glad to see her father, but she was distressed at having to meet him at this dive. She knew that he must be appalled by the place, and there was nothing about it that could help her – everything he saw would only confirm its reputation and verify the scandals that were always circulating about the dump. She still didn't know where her friends were, and she hadn't asked the sheriff. Having felt the one advantage her wounded nose gave her, she didn't feel like pushing it towards another rebuke.

The whereabouts of her friends seemed like a good introduction. Genuinely concerned about them, she didn't feel as if she was exploiting them by mentioning them first, and she was happy to hear her father's assurance that they were long safely home, and, he hoped, in bed.

'John Handslip drove over after them. They called from someone's house after you drove off with the sheriff and it looked as if you weren't going to come back for a while.' Mr. Nelson nodded in the direction of the sheriff, who was now standing behind the bar talking to O'Connell, his brother-in-law.

'Did you see the car, Daddy?' Joan's eyes began to mist, and she couldn't stop the wavering in her voice.

'No, I didn't see it, and I don't want to now. There's plenty of time to see it tomorrow. I don't think it'll go away.'

Joan knew that his attempt at humor represented an effort to cheer her, but she couldn't help noticing how forced his words sounded. 'What did the sheriff tell you? Did he tell you who the guys were?' She didn't want to mention her part in the whiskey story until she could hear his account of the sheriff's story.

'I don't think there's any secret who the scoundrels were. They're the Hillsdorf lot. Didn't you know that?'

One of the abandoned cars at the park had belonged to Joel Hillsdorf, but Joan wasn't sure how many of this notorious hell-raising clan were involved. Besides the one who had graduated with her, plus his seven brothers, there were at least two more cousins among the graduating class. Her father then said that somehow the boys had managed to pack nine of their number into the car, so that it was overloaded and bursting at the seams, and then they had roared down Main Street and through the town, honking and yelling at anyone they could see, so that by the time they had spent five minutes in the stolen car half the town had known about it.

'The other half didn't give a damn, then.' Joan remembered with resentment the time she and her friends had spent agonizing at the curb, thinking up senseless strategies to capture the thieves who had practically deposited their calling cards on Main Street.

'They were going damned fast,' her father continued, 'so fast and they were so weighed down that by the time they hit that country road they simply rolled and landed end-up in the ditch. They spilled out like sardines from the can, that's how tight they were packed in there.'

Joan sensed that he was relieved that everyone was safe, insulated from serious injury by a simple mass of bodies, their own stupidity, and perhaps protected by their cheap booze. Her father studied her for a minute as if he was considering telling her more, then he looked at her again and exclaimed, 'My God, what happened to you? You look as if you got the worst of it and you weren't even in a wreck.'

Joan hoped that she looked as wounded as she felt, but the only objects remotely resembling mirrors were the metal napkin holders that were placed on some booths, and their booth didn't have one. When she rubbed her nose an immediate shock wave of pain resounded in her face and down to her shoulders. 'Don't touch it!' her father warned. 'You'll only make it worse!'

So it was swollen. Did she look as if she had been beaten up? Tentatively she scratched at a place near her cheek and felt a thin crust of blood. How much was smeared on her face, and was it possible there were cuts somewhere that she hadn't felt, that were now open and dripping on their own? 'I had a collision with a dashboard. The sheriff's.'

Mr. Nelson handed his daughter his hankie, the kind that Joan had always loved, with its smooth texture and embossed initials. 'Here. Try to clean up a little. You look a mess.'

Joan was grateful that he hadn't suggested a trip to the ladies' room – how much did he actually know of this place? – and she liked the way he aided her by pouring some soda water into a corner of the hankie. 'The only thing this guy stocks is sweet stuff – Coke, Squirt, Seven Up. I had to go through hell and high water to get this,' he stated as he poured a little more soda into the folds of the cloth.

Joan welcomed this diversion. An account of her father's success at finding soda water in a community of unschooled drinkers could easily restore them back to the earlier, happy part of the evening, when her father had so zestfully recounted his triumphant purchase of the champagne. But Mr. Nelson seemed reluctant to discuss it; what had seemed to Joan like a victory was by now a lesser achievement for her father. 'Clean that speck off, over there by your eye – he placed a gentle finger on her right cheek – and then let's go. I have to see the sheriff for a minute. He wants to know what kind of charges I'm going to press. I have in mind hanging, except that's too good for them.'

Joan waited in the booth while her father talked to the sheriff, who by now was sitting in a booth with a man who was idly toying with a cribbage board. Her nose felt puffy and sore, her dress was muddy and dotted with blood, and she noticed two vertical tears that began somewhere near the waist and ended just below the knee. Linda came to her mind. I wonder how much I look like Linda now? she wondered. Except for her bareness, I bet I look like her, ripped and tattered. I sure as hell feel like her, except I haven't been laid. This deprivation, so shocking to her until now, seemed a genuine cause for sorrow. She wondered if she weren't becoming completely and irredeemably brazen by imagining herself succumbing to unpermitted sex and thinking of it in terms of sordid, gutter language.

She hoped she hadn't communicated this kind of degeneracy to her father, who had extricated her from this miserable dump and had donated his clean handkerchief as well. She tried desperately to eradicate the image of Linda from her mind, but she felt helpless, as if her mind had been taken over by force like an intruder. Now she knew what Reverend Blue hinted at in his bolder sermons, for Presbyterians everywhere were not supposed to dwell on the dark, unpleasant side of human existence. Nevertheless she saw that hell does reside in unexpected places, and the location of hell lies in those unacceptable feelings that express themselves in unspeakable words.

Chapter Eighteen

Punishments

Although Mr. Nelson fancifully considered pressing criminal charges against all nine of the Hillsdorf clan, he eventually agreed to settle the matter out of court. This compromise meant that he had nine penitents to deal with; the insurance company paid for the car repairs but it was up to him to settle the personal accounts. He finally worked out an arrangement with two sets of parents whereby their offspring would do all the yard work at Locksley Hall, plus take care of the cistern and make minor repairs to the family cars. This arrangement was to last for a period of at least one year. The problem was that the maintenance of Locksley Hall did not require more than one or two healthy young men. There were only so many storm windows to be put on, only so many screens to be carried to the basement. The cars ran efficiently and could stand only a limited amount of oil changes and cleaning and waxing, and the cistern was a self-regulating object that need to be cleaned but once a year.

Nevertheless, every Saturday morning at least seven Hillsdorf boys waited quietly on the lawn of Locksley Hall for the Nelson family to give some kind of sign that they were awake and ready to be served. Joan would hear them before eight o'clock, whispering on the grass beneath her window, hushing up one another while they discussed plans for the morning's work – jobs they had to complete before they were allowed to return to their own farms, where their labor was essential to the plowing, the planting, and – much later – the harvesting. They were always polite to Mr. Nelson; towards Mrs. Nelson they appeared embarrassed, as if she reminded them of some earlier schoolteacher they had never known very well. Joan they ignored; these young men who had formerly blamed Joan for their own irresponsible, drunken criminal actions they now treated as if she were not there. To them she was merely an object that occupied the space they were required to service once a week.

At first this neglect amused Joan, but later it made her angry. How could she possibly have once suggested any kind of importance or threat to them, even in a crazy deluded way, and then be so quickly and unceremoniously dismissed? (Had she looked to her adulterous neighbor for some kind of parallel knowledge she might have learned something, but of course this never occurred to her. Differences in age and circumstances were enough to discourage Joan – and most people, as well – from looking at others who might present clues or explanations to common dilemmas.)

John could provide Joan with insights into country justice, though, and the ways it could be applied. Linda's importance in Joan's ordeal with the sheriff surfaced almost immediately when Joan saw John after graduation night. John considered his relationship strictly his own business, but since he had been seen with her in a less than respectable spot, he felt obliged to clarify his place in her life. 'It's really nobody's business but mine,' he insisted, and then he proceeded to describe the practices of Murray County law enforcement. According to John, the ordinary custom of the police force was to patrol the area only if there were something unusual going on at the time in Clayton, such as the county fair, a well-attended ball game of some kind, or an unusually hot summer evening that would always bring out a large influx of outsiders to town. This meant heavier than usual drinking, and often more complicated sexual alliances. On these evenings the cops would drive through the regular haunts, seeking out newcomers who were not familiar with the accepted conduct of the community. They usually ignored the familiar faces unless someone became belligerent – one very respectable man had once turned his twelve-gauge shotgun on one of the deputies, but it happened to be pheasant season so his weapon was not considered an unusual possession. (He settled with the deputy for fifty dollars and the first pick of the litter from his retriever bitch.)

It was traditional for those who were signaled by the flashing lights of the police car to acknowledge the presence of the law by exchanging currency, but rarely on the spot. Most people preferred paying off with staple items rather than cash, with objects like hams, steaks, cases of whiskey, although folding money was usually the first choice of the police. John claimed that there was a definite relationship between the offense and the kind of payoff: boisterous drunkenness seemed the most serious, and John had known a few men who had contributed large portions of their freezers for this kind of offense. Partial nudity, on the other hand, called for little more than a nod and a smile accompanied by a five-dollar bill, with maybe the promise of a later delivery of two or three freshly killed pullets.

John had been angry that night because he had just finished paying off a debt to one of the deputies and he felt it was less than honorable to be nabbed again before the dust had settled. As far as he knew, this practice had been going on since the war, when it was the custom of the farmers, who had all the gas they could use, as well as meat, butter, and ammunition, to settle their debts with products that were scarce to townspeople. The police department had simply adapted this practice and used it for their patrol. No one objected very much, for it was far preferable to having your name published in the local paper and perhaps even spending time in jail.

John had argued with the sheriff that night because of what he considered an unjust distribution of punishment. He had already persuaded his mother to donate two mallards and an ancient stewing hen, which was her second contribution for the month of May, and he felt that he had since given his share and that the sheriff was picking on him when it was clear there were larger fish to fry.

About Linda he was thoroughly unprotective. 'She's been there with everyone who's parked a car for more than five minutes, and she's probably been there with anyone who's passed through town long enough to buy gas.'

This judgment upset Joan. Although she realized that a large part of John's assertion was exaggeration, she also knew that John would not have selected Linda for his pickup quickies if she were an obstinate female who was defending some hazy principle of chastity or fidelity, for he was simply too lazy to lend himself to strenuous chase. 'How long has it been going on between you and Linda?' Joan asked, knowing the words sounded theatrical but not aware of a better way of stating her question. Besides, the 'it' carried enough weight to imply the sinister occupations being practiced on deserted thoroughfares during dark, country evenings.

'Going on? Hell, it's between her and half the county,' he sneered. 'Jesus, do you think I'm the only one? Do you think I'd be hanging out there if I was? I've got no urge to get a rifle down my neck or my throat sliced upon by that gutless husband of hers some night.'

'How many, then, are – ah – seeing her?'

'How should I know? As many as she'll let them.'

'What about her husband? Doesn't he know?' Joan

could imagine Linda uniquely serving half the county plus every roving salesman who captured her fancy, but she could not imagine Linda enacting the role of community whore with her own husband aware of her activities. It was one thing to deceive one's husband, and quite another to deceive a man who was conscious of deception.

'Of course he knows,' John answered, unable to keep the exasperation out of his reply. 'He knew it before they were married, and nothing has happened since to make him change his mind.'

The original question returned to Joan; why had this man married Linda when he knew the circumstances of her reputation and what looked like her incurable inclination to fool around with anyone wearing pants? If Linda had been rich, powerful, or exciting in any way, Joan could have comprehended a less conventional arrangement, perhaps even a bizarre one, but clearly she was not. An ordinary farm girl, lacking in wit, intelligence, money, beauty – lacking nearly every quality Joan could think of that contributes to a woman's desirability – Linda had nothing to offer a mate other than a growing reputation for sexual notoriety. Joan thought that maybe movie stars could get away with prolonged adulteries, provided that their box-office attractiveness remained secure, but she knew also that they were always getting married and divorced, and that they never seemed to settle down until they were past playing their sweetheart roles. Surely Linda was no Rita Hayworth, so what did she have, then, that allowed her to get by with all those men? And did her husband sit home every night twiddling his thumbs while she was off parking with some indigent or someone well known?

There was something about John's attitude that bothered Joan, too. Although she realized he would not expect fidelity from an easy lay, he was still not the kind of person to willingly share his easy lay with an indeterminate number of men. Joan had always been grateful that John had never made serious passes at her. Part of his reluctance to actively try to deflower her Joan attributed to his generally lazy nature. Whatever energy he possessed, Joan thought, was consumed by his obsessive hatred for his father, which left him little stamina for active pursuit of sex. Joan could see how Linda fitted in with John's inertia. If she were as willing as John had claimed she was, all any man would need was some kind of vehicle and a few dollars' worth of gas. But Joan knew that John shared at least a mild amount of the kind of masculine pride that scorned and ridiculed promiscuous women – she had heard his comments about other girls who were suspected of flexible standards and sexual looseness. She wondered if he were not, after all, secretly pursuing virgins while relieving himself, at the same time, with whores – not such an unusual pursuit except that there were a limited number of community whores available.

Joan was curious but not upset at John's slice of the Linda pie (for so she had come to think of her, as a freshly baked pastry, juicy and bubbling, about to be torn into). She had never thought enough of him to feel hurt or possessive. So much the better for both of us if he can get it from someone else, she thought, but she was distressed at the possibility that Ronald might be another donator to Joe Schultz's collection of cuckold's horns. That collection should by now have filled up his barn, if John's stories were as much as half-true. Even though she was not willing to give in to Ronald, she was not prepared to accept the possibility that someone else was enjoying him. Another foolish thought, she knew, since she had no hold over him and had not even seen him for weeks.

Joan couldn't decide how much information she wanted to absorb out of John's account of Linda's life. It would be easy to get names and dates since he displayed no embarrassment about his part in the affair, yet she wondered what she could do with any more news. Ignorance, at least in some respects, had been blissfully enough for her, and should she now know more there seemed to be no way she could act on her knowledge. She decided to let the matter drop as painlessly as possible. 'I don't want to hear any more about it,' she informed John one evening as they were standing in line for the movies. 'I find the whole thing very unpleasant. I don't understand it at all.'

'That's right. What you don't know can't hurt you.' There was an unmistakable smirk on John's rather flimsy face that his great cow eyes couldn't hide.

'Why should I know more?' Joan responded. 'What possible good would it do me to know more about what goes on at the farm of Linda and Joe Schultz? Besides, it's not my business.'

'You bet it's not your business. And if I ever find out that you've said anything to Joe I'll personally wring your neck.' He gave a twisting motion, delivered with such glee that Joan winced. 'Crack. Just like that. I'll break all those scrawny bones, just like a chicken.'

Threats like this didn't bother Joan, for she knew that John was not willing to sacrifice his life to the electric chair in order to save his own name, and was he really so afraid of the vengeful hand of Joe Schultz or was he protecting something else?

What kind of code of honor did he and his cohorts possess that encouraged them to screw whatever was available while also maintaining friendships that were based on nothing more than land production and crop yields? Joan had heard John discussing machinery and weevils and corn bores with Joe Schultz; in fact, these were the only things they ever seemed to talk about. Were these conversations more precious to them than the affections of Linda Schultz? It would seem so, especially since John was fond of insisting that a woman is a broad no matter where she comes from. 'Turn them upside down and they're still all sisters,' he frequently remarked, echoing a commonly stated assertion among the boys and men in the community.

'Don't worry about telling Joe. I'll never say a word,' Joan promised. 'But how am I every going to look Linda in the face again?'

'That's your problem, Sweetie Pie. I don't have any problem, though, and neither do a hundred guys I know that I can think of. But if you want to make it your problem, go right ahead.'

Joan felt that it had become her problem, even though she could not understand exactly why it had landed on her. She was sorry that she couldn't eradicate it from her mind, but she was glad that Linda lived far enough away to be safe from most chance encounters.

By leaving the problem unsolved Joan's haunting dreams of Linda in her lavender dress continued to dominate her dream life; the dream, itself, evolving and developing at an alarming rate. Now Joan had become an accomplice in the dream; before always visible somewhere upon the periphery of the circle of pastel organdy, Joan had now stepped into the crowd, where she would watch with fascinated eyes the relentless thumping of the indifferent males, identical in appearance, and distinguished only by their faceless shapes as they knelt, pumped, and then zipped.

Chapter Nineteen

Band Concert

Years ago the bandstand in the New Bonn park had been condemned. A child had fallen through its rotten timbers and the town had been threatened with a lawsuit. It was never again used for band concerts, but it remained, either because of people's indifference, or else because of sentimental appeal, but now it was enclosed by a six-foot barbed-wire fence. Occasionally there would be a pair of jockey shorts or a sock draped around one of its barbs, anonymous banners of youthful rebellion, perhaps, which no one noticed very much. The weekly band concerts, held every Wednesday evening, began in May and ended the week before Labor Day. They were held on the lawn of the public school, where the audience usually sat in their cars, although a few people would lounge on the grass if it was terribly hot. Applause consisted of horns honking, a tradition that created a vocabulary among the performing musicians. Pieces were referred to as 'three-honkers', which was the best accolade, and 'two-honkers', a response barely so-so. A single honk indicated the most meager kind of dutiful response.

The regular music teacher was not available for summer work; limited to a nine-month contract, he usually spent the summers in Minneapolis playing in some theater orchestra, but the superintendent of schools, whose job was for the full year, was expected to lead the band during its summer performances. It wasn't important that he had never studied music, for his position was gratuitous, strictly titular, with no real function, for the band actually led itself. Only occasionally did the musicians even glance at the baton of a leader who seemed to be flailing around to sounds completely unrelated to those surrounding his podium. He liked wearing the white uniform though, and he clearly enjoyed stepping onto the podium and clinking his baton for attention. The musicians were paid a dollar fifty each per concert and two dollars if they went to rehearsals. The superintendent told everybody he was conducting for the love of it, but most people knew that he had been skimming the band fund for years and considered this indiscretion his actual pay for services.

After the concert the audience of cars would drift up the street three blocks to the taverns and liquor store, while those with families of small children would have to content themselves with ice cream purchased at the one café that catered exclusively to families. Joan liked the concerts because they seemed like such a good-natured way of getting people together. Little interest was paid to the program itself, but a march like 'The Stars and Stripes Forever' would always produce an enthusiastic reaction – definitely a three-honker, if not a blaster, the highest form of approval. Although she had never become more than competent on the clarinet, she was as good as the two others who occupied first chair. She enjoyed squinting at the music that was clamped to the stand with a clothes pin, her struggle with the arpeggios and glissandos that characterized first-chair music a weekly challenge she confronted with pleasure.

One night a friend let her use her alto sax, an instrument she thought simple-minded compared to the clarinet, and then she coerced an indifferent tenor saxophonist to let her use his instrument. Although there was an oboe player,

Joan couldn't manage the pursing mouth necessary to get more than squawks from that instrument, but she was able, with considerable confidence, to play the saxophone parts of both keys without making conspicuous errors. Sometimes she fancied herself a woodwind virtuoso, but she still felt differently about playing band music from the ways she felt about playing the piano. Band music, she felt, was the perfect background for display; the sounds were not nearly so important as were the rows of obedient musicians sitting in a semicircle, their instruments flashing like precision weapons as they produced amiable sounds to an audience that appeared to admire the same kinds of things.

While it was playing, the band never knew the size of its audience, for the musicians' backs were turned against the cars. They could only guess at its magnitude from the sounds of the horns being honked. Occasionally young people would come from other towns, using the concert as an excuse to cruise around looking for new acquaintances. The summer whites of the band were flattering, for Minnesota summers produce deep tans in people who don't necessarily cultivate them, and under the dim streetlights with the moths fluttering around, the members of the band glowed with health while communicating their musical exuberance.

After the concerts Joan and her friends would collect their money and walk uptown to buy Cokes and potato chips – they had to travel to other towns for their beer. Adults who passed them on the street would nod and smile their appreciation for those few minutes of sounds, organized and arranged with more spirit than talent, but nevertheless minutes that had afforded them pleasures that were, perhaps, only remotely related to the music they had heard. Joan had never before experienced such unqualified endorsement from adults, and in her band whites she felt protected from censure, as if she were wearing a ceremonial garment that granted her precious immunity. She had never felt that way in her choir robe; sometimes, rather, she felt bare and exposed, isolated at the organ with only its keyboards and pedals to draw her attention. Her friends left their instruments at school, but Joan preferred to carry her clarinet. She thought it gave her authority, not that she felt saintly or even faintly righteous, for she knew that the music was mostly a sham, that the audience was without taste or education, but she did feel that what she and her fellow instrumentalists offered was innocent and without taint.

With the summer band concerts she could never feel contempt for philistine tastes the way she frequently felt whenever she finished serious music in church, for she felt that a summer band concert was only indirectly related to the music it offered. One night a low-flying bird had crapped on the white shirt of the second trumpet, and although Joan shared in the band's hilarity at the event, she was also touched by the act, which she saw as a kind of natural applause, a splat of approval.

This sentimental side of Joan's nature was her best-kept secret, and she feared its revelation the way that some people fear the dark. Like bedwetting and masturbation – Joan linked the two as vagaries indicating loss of control – Joan liked to consider herself as someone who had rejected such offenses long ago. (She had never been classified as a bed-wetter – her last offense occurred when she was young enough to still be considered redeemable – and she had quit masturbating when the guilt afterwards became too painful for her to handle.) She tended to classify emotional excesses, such as sentimentality, with vicious habits, like masturbation, until they often overlapped in her mind. Sometimes she would read romances that stimulated definite twinges in her genitals; at the same time she would be weeping tears that she was powerless to thwart. 'Why do you read these books if all they can do is make you cry?' her mother was fond of querying, and Joan thought her mother's question sensible, but off the point. She had never seen her mother cry, although one night, when they were still living in Minneapolis, she thought she had heard her sobbing. The next day she had looked for signs, but her mother showed nothing that would have indicated a previous outburst.

Her father, of course, never cried. Joan had never seen a man weep, and the only adult women who ever seemed to lose control were those she read about in books. These women never seemed much better than pathetic babies who were always falling in love with the wrong man and then getting jilted. Some of them, Joan noticed, would grow up sadder and wiser and end up marrying the right guy, who happened to be hanging around the sidelines waiting for the heroine to wise up, but most of the heroines tended to die after prolonged illnesses that sapped the energies of their families and friends.

Until Joan was about thirteen, her favorite book was *Little Women*, and her favorite part was the death of Beth. She would retreat to her room and spend hours rereading that chapter until she was capable of assuming the role of the dying child, languishing by herself in her horrid little dark room, spitting up blood into hankies that had been newly laundered by the overworked Mrs. March, and weeping for all those whom she was soon to leave behind.

On a Wednesday night in late June, just after the band concert, Joan ran into Ronald at the Korner Kafe. He was just leaving as she and three of her friends walked in. Joan kept her eyes down, clutching her clarinet case until her knuckles turned white, but before she could get all the way in the door Ronald grabbed her arm and turned her aside.

'I want to talk to you!' He looked more fierce than usual, and his voice carried a challenging tone that shook her feelings past their customary gut plunge. What had she done to provoke this confrontation?

'Okay. Right now?' She was prepared to leave, to be dragged by the hair if necessary, but he released her arm and hissed into her ear. 'I'll call you. You stay here. I've got something to do but don't leave.'

Joan followed her friends to a booth and sat down, trying to participate in their conversation while dismissing the strange meeting from her mind, at least for a while. Maryann, her most sympathetic friend, had heard at least a part of the encounter and was curious. 'What was that all about?'

'I wish I knew.' Joan had told no one of the unfortunate episode by the lake although the part about the Goldust Twins would have made a wonderful story. All of her friends adored the Boswell brothers, but indiscriminately. One of them, Carol, had gone out with Brian a few times, which she boasted about to anyone who would listen to her. The brothers had the effect of drawing together into a circle those girls they had recognized as worthy of their attentions.

On this particular night there was a new bartender who took seriously their facetious orders for beer. They had developed a ritual of ordering beer, only to be brought Cokes by the snarling owner whose patience was always being tried by trios, quartets, even ensembles of giggling high school girls requesting beer. Long ago the bartenders and tavern owners had quit arguing about the irrational demands of their underage customers. Instead they silently served them soft drinks, placed with contempt upon the smudgy Formica of the gritty booths. Faced with the unexpected presence of beer, the girls didn't know how to respond. Maryann was the most concerned about parental detection since her mother patrolled the streets whenever her daughter was out, but never at a time predictable enough for her daughter to be safe. The other girls were more bold, perhaps because their parents were not such notorious vigilantes.

Maryann pushed her bottle of beer toward Joan and left the booth to purchase a bottle of harmless soda pop. Carol approved this strategy. 'Good idea. Why don't we get three more and hide the beer bottles so that if anyone comes in…'

'Shit!' Joan was tired of this subterfuge. 'If anyone wants to talk about us they will anyhow, whether we're drinking beer or Seven Up.' She resisted outright mentioning the slander of the Hillsdorf boys on graduation night not so long ago. That subject was still too sensitive to them all and they continued to feel outraged at the ways they had been wronged that night.

Maryann clung to her innocent Coke as if it were some kind of magic potion, which gave Joan the advantage of an extra beer. The others didn't suggest she split it with them, but if they had Joan was ready to tell them to stuff it, for her enigmatic encounter with Ronald was creating a defiance in her that matched her internal turmoil. One minute she thought she was going to heave; her stomach was so queasy that each swallow of beer produced an aftertaste that burned from her throat down to her gut. The thought of waiting all night for a phone call that might not take place made her even more shaky. To divert her mind from her own internal quivers, Joan volunteered to be the guinea pig for the aspirin and Coke experiment that the girls liked to speculate about but had never brought themselves to try.

'Let's once and for all try it tonight. Let's get it over with right now. What's there to lose?' Clearly there wasn't much to lose: the summer lassitude had already appeared, unusually early, Joan thought, since June was not yet over, and there were still July and August to get through, plus a healthy chunk of September before they would be going their separate ways to college.

The combination of aspirin and Coke was supposed to be so lethal that it produced immediate stupor. Why this was the girls didn't know, but they had heard about its terrible effects from a number of people who claimed to have survived the mixture. Joan thought this was as good a way as any to pass the time, and maybe she would even be knocked cold for a while. She took the aspirin and then took two long gulps of Coke. Immediately two undigested bottles of Grain Belt beer, plus several ounces of warm Coke, shot across the booth in an almost perfect arc, landing in an unoccupied spot just inches from the lap of her friend Carol.

'Christ! I didn't know it was supposed to make you sick.'

Joan's face had turned the color of a ripe eggplant and her eyes streamed. One of the girls ran to the bar for a cloth while the others produced Kleenex. None of them looked at Joan until they had finished wiping up. Her color eventually returned to its summer tan but her eyes continued to stream while she dabbed away with her sodden paper napkins. Finally Maryann asked Joan if she was all right. 'Maybe you should go to the bathroom.'

Her suggestion was intended as a joke, since the conditions of the restrooms at the Korner Kafe were almost as notorious as those of the Silver Star in Clayton. No one except outsiders ever used them, and they used them but once. If a girl had to go she either went to another tavern or she waited until she got home. Men, of course, peed in the alley, which itself, at that end of the street, was off-limits to all females.

Joan was able to summon the trace of a smile. 'I'm okay. It just hit me all of a sudden. Did anyone else see?' Being detected was even a greater danger than drinking beer illegally, for there was always the possibility that the place would be declared off-limits to all if only one underage drinker got out of hand.

'No one saw you. You're perfectly safe, but what hit you? I didn't think it was supposed to hit you all of a sudden.'

The combination of aspirin and Coke was alleged to be noxious but slow acting. Some said that it caused the person to eventually pass out, while others maintained that it produced hallucinations that were far more interesting than the ordinary beer whirls or ringing in the ears. No one had heard that it caused immediate vomiting. The girls were disappointed at Joan's mundane reaction, but no one felt like volunteering a second time and no one felt like taking the risk of ordering more beer. They sat there for a few minutes discussing the possible reasons for the experiment's failure until Maryann announced that she had to get home. Joan realized, in a panic, that if she left with her friends she would miss Ronald's promised call, a call that she could neither rely upon nor completely reject. Yet she couldn't stay alone – she had never entered a bar by herself nor had she ever remained in one alone.

'Oh, don't go just yet,' she pleaded. 'It's not really late, and something might happen yet.'

'Why not? There's nothing to do here. God, this town is dead.' Maryann's statement met no resistance from the others, as they got up to leave. The liveliness of ten o'clock, with the few members of the band and a fraction of its audience, had now degenerated to eleven o'clock lethargy. There were only two people left in the tavern, both uninteresting, unappealing middle-aged farmers who were listlessly shaking dice at the bar. In desperation Joan thought of asking one of them to teach her Liar's Dice, but she knew that once the girls left for good she would have to follow. Just as she was beginning to reconcile her disappointment the phone rang and the bartender beckoned to her, an indication that he was not ignorant of the identity of Joan Nelson, and that his selling them beer was not an act of ignorance, either.

'Meet me in five minutes!' There was no introduction to Ronald's summons.

'Okay, but I don't have a car.' Joan's tone was apologetic. She hadn't wanted to mention this lack because she was afraid he would dismiss her completely, but he had to be warned.

'Shit! We'll walk then. Meet me by the lake in five minutes.'

Her friends were waiting for her outside the tavern, clustered about the side of the building like peas in a pod, Joan thought. Once again, she wished she could tell them the whole story of Ronald, the saga beginning with the episode of hysteria by the lake, with the spooky presence of the Goldust Twins haunting the scene. 'Who was that?' they inquired. A lie so uninteresting it would have to be accepted came immediately to mind: 'That was John, of all people. He wanted to come over but I told him it was too late.' It was possible that her friends would believe her, since they knew Ronald never used the telephone to convey whatever messages that he and Joan had once exchanged.

Joan left her friends and headed towards the lake and the direction of her house. Under the dim streetlights their summer band whites seemed to glow. They juggled their instruments under their arms as if they were swords or weapons of aggression rather than devices intended to soothe and please.

Chapter Twenty

Black Hills Gold

Joan found Ronald in almost the same cluster of weeds and rushes that he had left her in the night she had resisted his ardor with her attack of laughter. Lying there and smoking a cigarette he looked like an old-time aristocrat admiring his peasant-made lake. She recognized his gaze as typical of New Bonn residents whenever they considered the lake, this possessiveness which all the natives seemed to feel towards their lake. Simply by refusing to use its name admitted them into a circle of reverent and possessive enjoyers of a unique property. Since there was nothing pretty about the lake – its size actually qualified it as more of a pond than a regular lake – its appeal had to reside in its uniqueness to that part of Minnesota.

In the early spring it often looked little better than a flooded pasture, with its weeds sticking out of the shallow water. Its value for swimming was slight, for during the month of August it was covered by a thick layer of green, scummy algae, a condition known throughout Minnesota as Dog Days. Other Minnesota lakes during Dog Days were green and stinking, but they were also navigable; in New Bonn the smell alone discouraged all but the most insensitive – or drunken – of bathers. Joan was never sure whether the collective sense of pride in New Bonn's lake was admirable or whether it was just another sign of community craziness. Ronald's admiration reflected this community attitude, but she couldn't help but adore the intensity of his gaze as he lay there squinting at non-existent ripples and wavelets.

Joan wondered how she should approach him. Should she quietly sneak up and cover his eyes with her hands and shout 'Boo!' to demonstrate her jocular spirits and light-hearted indifference? Or should she say something slightly suggestive, like 'Been here long?' or 'You seem lost in your depths'? Pondering these possibilities, she misjudged the curbstone and stumbled into a patch of brambles that seemed to be freshly laid out for her arrival, like some tortuous marriage bed. 'Shit!' The word was out before she had a chance to retrieve it.

Ronald looked at her with amusement while she struggled to remove the stickers from her white pants. 'I need a pair of pliers for these things,' she lamented.

Although he didn't offer to help, his look was not totally scornful.

'Do you have a lighter or some matches so that I can get these things out? I can't see a thing.' At least the heavy twill of the band pants had protected her from serious scratches.

'A light wouldn't help you. Just leave them alone and they'll rub off by themselves. Besides, you won't have them on much longer.'

Joan was accustomed to such threats, veiled or both, and now she discounted Ronald's efforts to smooth over the rough spots of an awkward situation. She didn't feel compelled to retort, but she did wonder, as she always did, just how much seriousness was mingled with the outrageous rudeness of his manner. She did think it was all right to call attention to her present disadvantage, though. 'Why didn't you tell me, at least warn me, they were here?' A reproach, she knew, was a bad way to establish the right tone, but her nerves were still jangling and her gut was still rumbling after the experience with the aspirin and Coke.

'I thought you were smart enough to know they were here. And anyhow I have been observing you lately and you seem to be spending enough time here to know the exact layout of the place. In fact, I bet you could draw a map blindfolded.'

Although Joan was flattered to have been under Ronald's surveillance, she knew that he was lying, for the lake was one of the places she had most scrupulously avoided, mostly because of him. 'Who told you that? Whoever did is a liar. I haven't been around here for weeks.'

'I had an interesting conversation with one John Lambert last night,' Ronald responded, as if he hadn't heard anything Joan had said. 'You know the John Lambert you go out with almost every night and who is getting into you regularly.'

'I'm glad you have nothing better to do than have conversations with people you hardly know so that you can both trade lies about people and things that never happened.' Angry as Joan felt about Ronald's lies (or John's?) she was fascinated by the possibility of a conversation between the two. Knights sparring and jousting over their rights to the lady? Or had they discussed her as mutually tormented souls, both struggling to gain her favor while challenged by the formidable powers of her father?

Joan thought her response contained just the proper measure of irony; enough, too, to dispel her own shakiness in anger. She inwardly groaned at what promised to be another episode of thrust and parry, an hour or two, or maybe more, focused upon the same tired argument. What the argument actually boiled down to, even if it was never directly stated, was that she must be screwing with someone, and if she wasn't, why not? Once again she wondered why she allowed herself to be placed in such a position of defense, and why did she allow herself to be so preoccupied with the feelings of this surly cad?

Yet the sight of him, isolated, gazing at the lake as if it were silently communicating to him its secret mysteries shattered whatever resolve she formerly maintained. In his white shirt, with his burnished golden arms and his rumpled hair, she thought he resembled some wondrous Aztec prophet waiting upon a hill for a message from his own personal god, a god that Joan would never see nor hear. Even the moon seemed exclusively his, intelligible perhaps only to the most aggressive members of the male circle. Silently Joan cursed this cold circle of males; knowing that she was to remain a perpetual outsider, never to be granted the position of more than an observer, a kind of passive, silly maiden whose own circle must always be carefully designed by the men who chose her, she could only lament her knowledge without trying to change herself.

Joan wondered what kind of ritual she had fallen into on this summer evening. She imagined a quick defloration, accompanied by a full choir of unseen Catholic boys and men, those same males who confessed with glee to their routine violations of the Sixth Commandment with girls of the Protestant persuasion. As they formed a circle around Ronald, exhorting him to quickly become her lover, they would chant their *Glorias* and *Te Deums* in encouragement. Joan blinked her eyes, hoping to vanquish her imaginary ensemble, and then opened them to meet Ronald's piercing glare. 'Why did you want to see me, anyhow? Just to tell me that I am supposed to be having sex with John Lambert and anyone else passing through town?'

Ronald reached into his shirt pocket, as if he hadn't heard a word she had said, and produced a small white box. For a minute Joan thought he was preparing to hand her a condom. 'I wanted to give you this. For graduation. I didn't have a chance to give it to you before.'

Joan loved the lie; like everything else about him, it

seemed to her appropriately transparent and simple, for he had nothing but time. His college attendance was sporadic, at best, and now that it was summer he had no real pretense at labor other than helping his father with an occasional odd job that proved too much for the old man. Joan knew that Mrs. Boswell adored having her sons sleep till noon, and that she often brought them breakfast in bed when they were too weary or too hung-over to make it to the kitchen on their own. Mrs. Boswell saw nothing scandalous in indulging her men folk, and she was known to scold other mothers for conduct towards their sons that she considered heartless.

Joan, who had never been good at accepting gifts, was even worse when she sensed the significance of Ronald's offering. 'What is it?' This silly question, eternally asked (and often by women whose own sense of importance ranks well below that of the family dog or the current yield of heifers) Ronald chose to ignore, and Joan was grateful for his negligence.

'Go ahead, open it up, it won't bite you.' He looked, for a minute, as if he had forgotten the contents himself, and was as eager as she to see them revealed. Fumbling with the paper, (which she later examined in the light and found to be festooned with horseshoes and Good Luck messages printed in four different languages) she had trouble prying the lid off the tiny box.

'For God's sake, your hands are shaking. Take it easy. Hasn't anyone ever given you a present before?' Ronald's thick fingers, which even Joan could not call aristocratic, managed the box, but his hands were almost as shaky as hers. He returned it to her opened, then obligingly lit a match so she could see more than the two layers of white cotton that formed a nest. Inside the nest was a gold ring designed into the shape of an oak leaf. Around its band miniature hearts looped, entwined by what looked like alfalfa, but which in a better light proved to be tendrils of oats.

'Why, it's beautiful!'

'Black Hills gold. There's three colors.' With the help of another match, Joan could make out a rosy cast and a shade that might have been green. The third, she supposed, was regular gold. 'Aren't you going to try it on?'

In order to avoid the problem of which hand she was to place it on – was it a friendship ring, or should she consider it an engagement ring? – Joan held out both hands.

'You put it on. I'm much too shaky.'

Without hesitating, Ronald placed it on the third finger of her left hand, where it fit snugly but easily.

'It fits perfectly. How did you know what size to get, what my size would be?'

As if he had been waiting all evening for this question, Ronald launched into a long account of his experiences in a jewelry store in Worthington, a narrative that included a surrogate Joan plucked from a crowd of girls who were waiting for a bus on a street corner, a jolly jeweler's wife who had teased him by insisting that he try it on her own plump finger, and two friends who had helped him to choose between an inferior sterling silver heart and the present golden oak, a phony dilemma, he insisted, since he had always wanted the gold ring but his friends had liked the silver heart. More appropriate, they had said, for a girl than some tree, even if the tree was gold. They were almost booted out of the store by the impatient jeweler, who thought they were there just for a lark and were not serious about buying either ring.

Joan was grateful for Ronald's account because it gave her a respite, enough time to rehearse her thank you speech. It also gave her more time to ponder the consequences of the gift. She knew that some strings were attached – they always were – and she knew that she would be expected to figure them out very soon.

'You really like it? You're not just saying that?' Ronald's concern seemed genuine, as if his gift-giving were some sort of test.

'Of course I like it. I love it. I don't know how to thank you.'

The leer that she expected in response to her dumb statement didn't appear. Instead he took her hand, placed it on his mouth, and kissed each fingertip. Joan felt as if she were watching an old-time movie scenario, lifted from some ancient show where the hero kisses the girl's hand as he is departing for war. He kisses her hand instead of her mouth because he's too honorable to disturb the delicate nature of her feelings. She realized that she would have to get her own feelings in order, to establish some kind of perspective, for she couldn't continue to go through life giggling in church, laughing at the wrong times, and asking dumb questions of smart people. Yet how much of the charm of this innocent scene had been already rehearsed, not only by Ronald but by countless other men whose intentions she had yet to question?

She shifted from one foot to another, thereby disturbing the rhythm of Ronald's finger-smooching. Annoyed, but not angry, he dropped her hand and patted her hair. 'You can thank me by not having anything to do with that fucking Lambert anymore.'

The imagined strings were proving much looser than Joan had ever hoped, and she felt she was not betraying anyone when she agreed. 'Of course. He isn't anything to me, anyhow. We're just friends who go to the movies occasionally.'

'I don't know about that. You've been to more than the movies with him. The point is that you're not to anymore. If you want to see a movie talk to me first. You're my girl now.'

Those words that she had so long yearned for, now spoken with confidence and conviction, sounded as contrived and as phony as the 'takes' and 'haves' of other evenings, yet it was clear that they didn't seem phony to him. With tones as measured and controlled as a practiced July fourth orator, he savored the pronouncement, repeating the words, 'You're my girl now, and don't ever forget it.'

So there was to be no further dispute about fidelity. The ring had dissipated his jealousy and had determined her alliance with him. For a minute she was tempted to place a sisterly peck on his cheek in order to sustain the purity that had been established by their exchange, but she decided that he had too efficiently set the scene for her to take liberties with the script. Smiling, she waited for him to make some additional comment about their new commitment, and the smile he returned seemed loaded with newly found joy. His slightly gap-toothed grin expanded into a smile that spread all over his face, enveloping the corners of his mouth until his cheeks looked ready to be sucked into his throat. His rumpled hair appeared to rise and fall with the breeze, and his enormous frame, ordinarily loose and uncoordinated, looked as if it were about to come unglued at the joints. Joan would have liked to have patted him into place, to shape more firmly the rough edges that appeared to be the only materials holding him together. But because he was a good twelve inches taller than she, her physical movements were arrested at his chest level. Tentatively she placed an arm on his hand and requested that he give her a kiss to accompany the gift.

'Happy to oblige if that's all you want,' he replied.

She was thankful that the old note of sparring was recurring, for she knew that if anything could break her down and reduce her to a state of quivering jelly it would be only a few more of his chivalric comments. Accustomed to kindness from men only when accompanied by strong doses of vitriol, Joan was sure she could not sustain one feeling long enough to retain her equanimity. She had never experienced an evening that didn't involve attacks and counterattacks, an evening when she didn't have to spend a certain amount of time planning strategy and defense. Even with John Lambert she felt compelled to struggle against what she spotted as demands against her will, harmless as he was with only his demonic hatred of his father to distinguish him. With Ronald, this tranquillity, this gratuitous peace, were now killing her in much the same way that silence can be deafening to people whose ears are always tuned to noise.

'I'll walk you home now. I have to be up early in the morning. I'm helping my old man paint the pool hall.'

Joan wanted to ask him when the old man had begun to branch out into painting, but she knew that his behavior was a perpetual sore spot for the family. It was enough that he was painting; therefore he was sober enough to work, at least for a few days.

She would have liked to be able to express happiness for the family's spurt of good fortune that she knew Ronald must feel. The pathos of the situation, the strange, orphan-like dependency of father upon sons, made Joan feel guilty about her earlier suspicions of Ronald's conduct. Perhaps she should suggest that he not accompany her home, that he needed his sleep for what was sure to be an awful day's work, yet she wanted him to come home with her. She would have liked the whole town to ring dishpans as they strode down the street. She would have liked flowers strewn in their path so that they would have to trample upon even the most lovely of blossoms, but at this time of night the only indication of life appeared in the lighted porch of the Goldust Twins, a beacon that Joan chose to spit at as they passed by.

When they arrived at Locksley Hall Ronald refused to

come in, which was just as well, since Joan, at this late hour and with so little notice, could not explain to her parents his present significance to her life. Placing his hands on her shoulders, he gave her a quick kiss that, years later, she would describe as avuncular, and he whispered in her ear, 'Don't forget what I told you.'

Then he was gone, striding back on the lake road with his unmistakable rolling gait. Mr. Nelson, peeking out of a bedroom window, commented to his wife that the young man looked like nothing so much as a mule running to catch up with its mother. Mrs. Nelson, perturbed by a judgment she considered inordinately crude, especially when contrasted to their daughter's chaste behavior (for of course they had seen the innocent kiss), told her husband to keep quiet if they didn't want their daughter to hear.

Joan left the ring on its nuptial finger. She would have to construct an explanation for it in the morning, but now she preferred to spend the rest of the evening with her own private thoughts. She wondered if it was too soon to consult Father Sturm about religious instruction.

Chapter Twenty-One

Collapse

Of course there was a hell of a row about Joan's ring. Mrs. Nelson took the position that it was wrong at this time in Joan's life to become serious about any one boy, especially since she was going off to college in the fall, not even two months away. Mr. Nelson attacked Ronald through his father.

'He's no good. No damned good. The whole bunch is all alike. Some days they all sit around the house and no one does anything, not one damned thing.'

Joan wondered where he got his information, but she imagined that her father's assertions were true, except for the good Mrs. Boswell, who could be relied upon to serve iced tea or sandwiches or whatever the men needed while they were all sitting around doing nothing. Joan knew that any defense of Ronald would be futile, for she could hardly cite his distinguished work record or his scholastic brilliance as examples of superiority to the rest of his family. She knew it was unfair of her father to blame Ronald for his own father's character, and she knew he wouldn't do it so much for anyone else. At the same time she wondered how far she would go, if she were in her parents' place, to protect their kid from an unsavory family.

'It's only a token. Like a friendship ring,' she insisted. 'It only means that we're seeing each other a lot. For heaven's sake, it doesn't mean that we're engaged or anything.'

(Didn't it?) 'Lots of the girls have them. At least half of the class were wearing them the night of graduation.'

'At least half the class were pregnant, too,' Joan's father muttered.

Joan decided to ignore this statement. Pregnant girls never finished school, and Joan knew that her father was aware of this fact. From his remark, though, Joan sensed that what Mr. Nelson really thought was that the ring symbolized a public announcement that they were screwing. Most assuredly it was screwing with fidelity, but this tiny circlet of gold must mean the same thing that bloody sheets meant to Mediterranean harpies. Joan could see no way to combat her father's inferences. Short of having him accompany her to the office of the inept Dr. Richardson, who probably didn't know a hymen from a tonsil, there was no way she could prove she was still intact without defending herself as if she were guilty. She couldn't very well say that the ring meant nothing to her, for then they would suggest she return the worthless item, and she was not going to complicate matters by enlisting Ronald to explain his intentions.

She decided to compromise. 'Okay. I won't wear the ring when you're around since it upsets you so.' She removed the ring from her finger and put it in the pocket of her shirtwaist dress. 'See, it's gone. Does that make you feel better?' (I'm still the same person, she would have added, but she knew that she had already gone too far.)

'Oh, wear the damned thing. I don't care.' Her father suddenly looked grim, no longer angry, as if he had already resigned himself to a mixed marriage and a squalling brat every nine months.

Mrs. Nelson looked at her daughter as if she would have preferred to deny any form of kinship, yet she said, 'Oh Joan, how could you?'

How couldn't I, she responded, but only to herself. You

were the ones who brought me to this shitty town, but she didn't say this, nor did she remind them of the nice things she had done, like being salutatorian and organist for a congregation of musical dunces. And being chaste, a condition she resented as well as feared. Instead she kept quiet and let them cool off. She kept the ring in its box on the top of her dresser, and she wore it only at night, when she was going out or when she slept.

Perhaps her parents were encouraged by their daughter's agreement to cherish and not to flaunt the ring, for after several days of completely avoiding the Boswell name Mrs. Nelson suggested to her daughter that Ronald be invited to play bridge with the family 'some night'.

The Nelsons had worked out their own strategy, and one important element consisted in pointing out to their daughter the crudeness of her boyfriend (a term that Mrs. Nelson chose to use). They would do this indirectly, of course, and one easy way to show up a person was to invite him to play a game that all civilized people enjoyed but one that was sure to be unfamiliar to him. The pretense of then teaching him would give them opportunities to demonstrate his lack of refinement.

The Nelsons had failed to consider the education that the New Bonn barbershop endowed to every boy, from the time he was able to walk unassisted to the barber until the year he was old enough to stay after hours on Saturday nights. In addition to blackjack, poker of all kinds, pinochle, and local variations of the basic gambling games, there were always two or three tables of bridge being played at the barbershop. Most people knew – and Mr. Nelson should have realized this – that the really heavy, prolonged gambling took place at the bridge tables. The poker and the other games were strictly small-time, penny ante affairs, but the bridge was played for stakes that would have come close to those played in the private clubs in Minneapolis. No one could explain why this had happened; perhaps because bridge alone is so respectable-looking and not ordinarily associated with sleazy gambling joints. Perhaps the local authorities – if they ever cared – were less inclined to arrest a table of innocent-looking bridge players than a bunch of poker players with colored chips smeared all over the table.

So Ronald did play bridge, and he played it well. He played so well that Mr. Nelson began to enjoy their games, and he demonstrated his enjoyment by offering drinks to everyone, not just beer but genuine mixed drinks concocted from his high-grade bourbon. Joan, who was still learning the game, welcomed the opportunity for Ronald to reveal his gentler nature, as well as his more intelligent one. He rarely criticized her playing; he was always careful to point out that her mistakes were minor, and he was quick to assure her that many times there is no way that a bad hand can be played well. Mrs. Nelson, during their games, was reserved but pleasant. She confined her questioning of Ronald to matters at hand. She never questioned him about college, she was sympathetic about the scarcity of decent summer employment in New Bonn, and whenever he mentioned a member of his family she would change the subject as gracefully as she could.

No one, not even Joan, mentioned his religion.

Joan's success at getting Ronald to come to the house she considered a major triumph. Formerly their courtship had been distinguished by clandestine meetings and chance encounters at taverns or by the lake, but the ring had changed this pattern. For Ronald it seemed like a certificate of respectability, a visible confirmation of a legitimate romance, instead of fervent attempts to seduce a vulnerable Protestant girl. To Joan's surprise, when she had mentioned her parents' request that he participate in a family game, he had consented with alacrity. Now he began to call her at home, setting actual dates and defining destinations.

Nor did she have any problems with John, either. The first time he had called her to suggest a movie she merely mentioned that she'd be busy for the rest of the week. John didn't pursue the topic, and if he was interested in her sudden busyness he failed to mention it. After a couple of weeks he called again. He happened to be in town, he said, and would she like to go for a drive?

'I don't think so. In fact, I don't think I'll want to go out with you anymore, at least not for a while.' She hoped she wasn't being cruel, but it was hard to announce the conclusion of something that had never really gotten off the ground.

'What the hell is the matter with you? Have you gotten someone else to take you around?' At least he was asking questions she could answer.

'As a matter of fact, I have. It's got nothing to do with you, though.'

'It's your old flame, Boswell, isn't it? Congratulations. Be sure and send me an invitation to the wedding. Or a birth announcement. Whichever comes first. And call me some night if you ever get bored, or if he gets too much for you.'

Joan couldn't tell how much of John's sarcasm was genuine bitterness and how much was prefabricated speech, composed, perhaps, in some ancient age for the benefit of all rejected suitors. She felt a little sorry for John, not only because she felt that she had used him (but not as badly as he had used her), mostly because he had to resort to such infantile language to convey his disappointment. Yet she was not about to apologize; she felt their evenings together had been more rewarding for him than for her, and she was sure that he had never before found such a patient ear, such a sympathetic audience for his recital of paternal grievances. 'There's not going to be any wedding, nothing like that. We just have a kind of arrangement where we're not seeing anyone else for a while. At least till I go away to college.'

What was the agreement? So far it was mostly in Joan's mind, and she wished that there were some kind of definite arrangement she could refer to when she was contemplating her future conduct. She and her parents were planning a trip to the Colorado Rockies in two weeks. Was she expected to inform Ronald that he was free to see others during those fourteen days of her absence, or should she promise to write to him every night, letting the letters take the role of betrothed?

College was going to be an even worse problem. Would she go to Oberlin (for that was the current family choice) and wear his ring, remaining in her dorm room every weekend, while writing him letters describing the spectacle of her roommates as they departed for their Saturday night dates?

Her favorite fantasy has Ronald leaving junior college after finally receiving his A.A. degree. He then transfers his C minuses to St. Thomas College in St. Paul, where he is automatically accepted because of his religion. He then pursues a course in civil engineering, or maybe law – he can talk a convincing game when he needs to. She would visit him on weekends, for she has imagined herself enrolling at the secular University of Minnesota. They would stroll through the secluded gardens of his campus, pausing now and then to quietly pay homage to the statues of the saints that line the paths. (Joan would look away while Ronald prayed.) There would be no more talk of sex. He would be busy with his books, and she would study and wait for him.

Joan now called him Ron, a privilege that accompanied the ring.

'No one calls me Ron. Not even my mother. I'm letting you call me that only because you need a different name for me now.' He nuzzled her neck with his chin, a gesture that always sent immediate rays of heat throughout Joan's system.

'What does your mom call you? She can't possibly call all of you by your full names all the time. Brian. Stuart. Leonard. Ronald. Stuart must be "Stu" sometimes. And try to tell me that when you were a little kid she didn't call you Ronnie.'

'Swear to God she didn't. And doesn't. She always calls us by our full names.'

'What does she call your dad, then?' *You old sot*, Joan thought, or maybe, *you long-tooled bastard* after a particularly long idle period. Appropriate epithets but ones she knew would never even occur to the kindly Mrs. Boswell.

'I don't pay any attention to what she calls the old man. Once she called him Sweetheart and nine months later I was born.' He gave a wide, toothy grin, obviously pleased with his interpretation of his parents' sex life. 'We all have the same middle names, though. We're all called Joseph after the most dead-assed saint in the church.'

So Mrs. Boswell had managed to enroll her sons into the community of saints and still preserve the secular Scottish nature of their family name. (Or had it been the old man who had worked out this strategy? Joan was unable to imagine him sober enough to care, even when his sons were babies.) What a marvelous accomplishment, Joan thought, and how stubborn the woman must have been to have held out for her choices and then to have conceded to the Church with those unexceptional names: no favorites there.

Unlike with the old Ronald, with the new Ron their evenings of jabbing and swatting had diminished. If they did take a walk or go for a drive they ended up exchanging a few kisses, and that was that.

Joan decided that with the authenticity of their courtship

Ron would expect a few liberties, and she thought that she might allow him to play with her breasts, so she began to wear dresses with scooped-out necklines to signal her acquiescence. Instead of fondling them, though, he rarely even looked at them. Instead, he would kiss her with tight lips, fiddle with the car radio, and light cigarettes. One evening he groaned and muttered, 'This is enough,' and then started the car and drove her home without another word.

He quit talking about the torture she was inflicting upon him, and since he didn't mention it she wondered if he was no longer bothered. She guessed he might be seeing Linda, or someone like her, on the sly, of course, in order to relieve those heavy feelings he used to say were going to kill him. Joan was relieved, in a sense, for she didn't enjoy having her breasts pushed around, kneaded and mashed like new potatoes, but in another way she was restless. The predictable nature of their now legitimate romance was removing all the fun.

She wondered how two people could become so bland. Before we tussled and fought, she mused, but now all we do is sit around like some ancient married couple who play games with other old people. She knew marriage would have to be a great deal better than this, for at least they could go upstairs after the bridge game and screw till the bed broke down, or till one of them went to sleep.

She had never thought it possible that she would look forward to getting away from Ron's ardor, if that's what you could call it, but now she welcomed the vacation to Colorado, not because she was going to find someone else – she knew she would be true to Ron – but because she could at least escape the smothering neutral existence that seemed to have been foisted on her from the night she accepted his ring.

'We're leaving for Colorado next week,' Joan remarked

one night after her parents had gone upstairs to bed. They had not played bridge that night. Instead her father and Ron had watched a baseball game on TV, a prolonged dreary game that went to extra innings, a game distinguished less by the players' skill than by their perseverance. Joan wandered around the house while her father and admirer were engrossed in the game. Sitting there in the library by the TV, drinking their highballs – Ron was now automatically served the beverage of his choice – they took little notice of her. Their conversation seemed limited to desultory comments about the stance of the batters or the pitcher's knuckleball. Her mother sat in the parlor, reading. At one point she had looked up from her book as her daughter was making her rounds between kitchen, library, and parlor, and had asked, 'Happy, dear?' What had she meant by that? Why the sarcasm at such a boring, tranquil occasion?

'We'll be gone two weeks,' Joan reminded Ron, as if he didn't already know their plans.

'I know you're going. I'm going to miss you, you know.'

Joan melted. Of course he was going to miss her, and she knew she would be miserable without him. She liked the idea of writing to him about her misery, long letters composed after a full day's sightseeing, when she would describe the landscape and the funny people who were always to be found hanging around tourist spots.

Maybe she could get in some horseback riding. She knew there were plenty of ranches where she could hire a horse for the day. She would ride into the mountains, with her bathing suit slung over the saddle. She would find fresh mountain streams, maybe even a waterfall, where she would plunge while the horse munched happily on sweet meadow grass. At night she would eat dinner with her parents in cozy, rustic restaurants that specialized in barbecued steaks and Western hospitality. After dinner they would return to their cabin and light the fire, and the parents and their daughter would read about the geology of the area and talk over the things and the people they had seen that day. Late at night she would write to Ronald; short notes with just enough information to assure him that she was busy and enjoying the beauties of the landscape, with just enough poignancy to show how much she missed him.

'I'll miss you, I know, but it won't be forever. The time will go by fast.' She fingered her ring, which she had slipped on when they left the house, hoping to signal to him her need for some kind of statement from him about his own plans, how he intended to spend his time.

'It's not forever, you know, but it sure is a hell of a long time when you're stuck in this god-forsaken town with not one damn thing to do. I wish I had the money for a vacation whenever I felt like it.'

Joan found it hard to imagine a family never going away, never taking trips, not even going on picnics, but the Boswells did none of these things, and never had that she knew of. She felt sorry for Ron, yet she wondered if he resented her for the things that she assumed every family enjoyed, and she wondered how Mrs. Boswell felt about never going anywhere, always sticking around town while serving her household of males.

'Anyhow,' Ron continued, 'all this is going to change. Big things are happening. Or will be happening, but I can't tell you about them just now. Right now it's all a big secret.'

What was he referring to? What kinds of big things did he have in mind? It never occurred to her that he thought he could do something to make things happen, that he even thought about himself in relation to time. She thought it a good time to bring up her plan to change colleges, thereby relocating both of them to one single spot, removed from the double authority of family and village. 'You know, I'm thinking of changing my mind and going to the university instead. Why don't you transfer your credits and come along? Not to the university, necessarily, but maybe you could go to St. Thomas or something?'

'Change your plans if you want to,' he answered. 'Don't go all the way to Ohio, or wherever the hell that school is. Stick around Minnesota – at least you won't be so far. But I don't want to go to St. Thomas, the University of Minnesota, or any other goddamned college. It'd be more a waste of time for me than it will be for you.'

For a man of few prospects, talking about college as a waste of time seemed unreasonable to Joan. What could be more of a time-waster than the life he was leading in New Bonn, spending half his days piddling around with his father, bailing the old man out of his measly chores, and spending the other half of his time taking classes at a junior college that no one took seriously? Starting classes, dropping them, then starting again on something else. If he really took his lack of money seriously, Joan thought, he'd do something about it instead of dragging around, frittering away his days and half his nights, drinking a little, working even less, and – so far as she knew – not getting laid, either.

'What are you going to do, then?' Joan thought it was sometimes all right to ask this question to a man, especially this man, since he had already mysteriously hinted at a future which he claimed to possess. (When people asked her of her own college intentions, she would reply that she was preparing herself to do something with her music. What that something was she didn't know, but apparently her response was acceptable, for people usually responded – after the predictable jokes about MRS degrees – that she certainly should do 'something' with her music, that hers was a talent she could never lose, that no one could ever take it away from her. As if they'd want it, she would silently add sometimes.)

'I can't tell you what I'm going to do, Toots. Not right now. I've already told you it was a secret for now. But I can tell you that I'm not going to spend the rest of my life in this dump of a town, and neither are you.'

She approved of his linking their futures together, liberating them both from the confines of a community that he, too, must feel was keeping them in bondage. Not that she had ever intended to stay there once she left for college. An occasional weekend visit would be more than enough for both herself and her parents. Yet she thought it gallant of him to offer a mutual escape. Did this mean, then, that he was planning to marry her? And how long would it take her to solve the problems that a marriage to him would entail, most conspicuously that of religion?

Would it break her parents' hearts if she were to marry a Catholic? That's what her favorite aunt told her a few days later during one of their conversations while she was spending a few days in New Bonn. Her aunt had used all the typical arguments: she was too young; she had her whole life ahead of her; she had college to think of. You're only married once, and that's for life. Joan knew her parents were behind this so-called conversation, and realized her aunt had been manipulated into it. 'You didn't finish college and you don't seem exactly heartbroken about it,' she responded after she had heard her aunt's catalogue of reasons against 'getting serious' at a young age.

'Well, I've always regretted I didn't. But Jim did, and that's what's important.'

Jim, her aunt's banker-husband, had taken a long time to graduate from Macalaster, a Presbyterian college well known for its latitude towards offspring of generous parents. 'If it's so important for him, why wasn't it for you?' Joan wasn't really serious – she already knew the answer – but she enjoyed teasing her aunt.

'It's not the same and you know it. It's important for a

man to finish what he starts, and this means more than just in college. He should finish everything he begins that's important to do, even if it's just getting a ditch dug.'

Joan was tempted to ask her aunt how she liked the idea of a ditch digger for a relative. Her aunt had met Ronald only once, and at that time briefly, when he had stopped to pick up Joan for a movie and Mrs. Nelson had insisted that he stay long enough to drink a beer. Joan thought they had gotten along well enough, but it was impossible to tell since her aunt's comments and judgments of people were almost always directed towards how she felt at the time. 'He looked nice to me,' she would say, 'but then I was in a good mood and everyone looked nice.' Joan wondered if her uncle had inspired this kind of self-serving, limited response in his wife, or whether she had cultivated it herself as a kind of protection against serious thinking.

Joan was then warned about the possible disasters that only mixed marriages could produce, disasters that normal marriages among people of the same, or even similar, faiths did not experience. 'Look at Jim. His family was Methodist, but they didn't care what church I belonged to as long as we both joined the same church and attended it regularly.'

Would Jim's family have welcomed their joint membership in the Holy Rollers or the Jehovah's Witnesses, then? Joan giggled at the image of the two of them screaming in the aisles, banging their hymn books on the pews, yelling about being saved; working out their sexual energies in unison until they quietly returned home for a huge Sunday brunch, their appetites finally muted.

'It's not important what church you decided on,' her aunt continued. 'What's important is that you decide together and stick to it.'

'Well then, what, just what would happen if I decided to become a Catholic? Wouldn't that be making the same kind of choice and sticking to it that you say has to happen?'

Her aunt took a deep breath, as if she had been waiting for this moment for a long time. 'That's impossible,' she replied, her voice now tremulous. 'You don't just decide to be a Catholic. You have to be born one.' At Joan's incredulous look she continued, 'Yes, I know, it's possible to change, to convert, but it's never the same thing. People never accept you as one, and you're always treated differently. No one ever takes it seriously. They think it's something you did just so you could get married.'

Was her aunt correct? Were there such obstacles for converts? Did they, perhaps, sit in special pews on Sundays, marked 'converts only'? In isolation from the rest of the worshippers? Joan rather liked the idea of a special place for a definite act.

'Besides,' her aunt continued, 'if you ever decide to become a Catholic – you know that it would break your parents' hearts. You know that, don't you? And if you don't you're a darn fool.'

'I don't think you have to worry about anyone's hearts being broken. I've never heard of anyone dying because somebody changed their mind about religion.'

'I didn't mean that literally,' her aunt replied. 'I meant they'd never be the same. You can change people's lives because of one dumb thing you alone decide to do, and that includes breaking hearts.'

Joan knew there were plenty of ways people's lives changed, and not necessarily for the better, either. For instance, she could have relinquished her precious virginity somewhere around her sophomore year, which would have meant a pregnancy by her junior year, at the latest. Then lives would have really been changed. But how would the Nelsons' lives be altered if she were to become a Catholic? Would they draw the curtains on Locksley Hall, muffle the doorbells, and refuse to answer the telephone?

'Look,' she said to her aunt, knowing full well her response would be immediately conveyed to her parents, 'I think it's strictly my business about what man I marry, so let's drop the topic for now. If it makes you any happier, let me tell you that I have no intentions of getting married for a long time. I haven't even been to college yet.'

An admirably firm statement, Joan thought, by no means apologetic, yet there was just enough to reassure all of them that she was not being driven out of her mind by both sex and religion.

'Okay, I'll tell your folks. They've been going half out of their minds with worry, that you'll do something rash.'

Rash! Was playing bridge with one's parents and repressed boyfriend rash? Or did her parents actually feel that she hopped into the back seat with Ronald as soon as they had left the house – in her father's car, no less? Did they feel that she was so sex-hungry that she spent every minute away from the house either screwing or else thinking about it? 'What do you mean by rash? What do they mean?'

'They're scared to death you'll elope. That you'll drive to Iowa some night and get married, and that you'll come home and announce that you're now Mrs. Boswell.' Her aunt looked at Joan as if she were contemplating impounding her driver's license, and then sighed. 'Just remember one thing. If you change religions you can't have a nice wedding.'

Joan was not sure later how she had come out of the discussion, how well she had communicated her own position. She was pretty sure that her aunt would inform her parents that Joan was safe for a while, that there were no immediate marriage plans, but she also knew that her aunt was not totally convinced of her sincerity. They all probably were afraid that it was just a matter of time before the predictable occurred: a fumbling lay or two to consolidate the couple's serious intentions, six easy lessons in catechism, and a quickie wedding at the priest's house, family and friends excluded.

The night before the Nelsons were to leave for Estes Park, Joan brought up the question of correspondence. Aside from the practical question of logistics, how did he think they should handle the letter writing? As they were sitting on the downstairs porch sharing a beer, Joan asked about his plans, if he had anything in mind to do while she was gone.

'I don't know. Screw around, maybe play a little baseball. Fish some. Don't worry, I've got plans. The time will go fast.' Not what she wanted to hear! Why couldn't he say he'd pine away and count every minute? She wished he would tell her about the plans he so mysteriously alluded to, but he clammed up so severely while looking so pleased with himself that she felt scared bringing up the subject. She suspected that whatever plans he actually had, if they were any good or very real, she would know sooner or later about them. 'Do you, that is, should I – do you want me to write?' Why did she have such trouble asking simple questions?

'Sure! Write if you want to, but don't expect me to answer back. I'm not one for writing letters. I never even wrote to my mother when I was in the army.'

Joan visualized Mrs. Boswell, faithfully checking the post office every day, hoping to hear from her delinquent son and fearing he had been sent to some remote post with inadequate laundry facilities and no Catholic chaplain: never hearing from him that her fears were unfounded, waiting and worrying until he returned home shed of uniform and dismissed from further military experience.

'I used to call home once in a while, though. No one in the family writes. Or wrote. My brothers didn't write, I didn't write, and I don't intend to start now. Besides, where would I reach you?'

A good question; where would he reach her? General

delivery was always a possibility, but their itinerary was never airtight because her father liked to deviate from his plans whenever he felt like it. They might even spend their whole vacation at a place that spontaneously appealed to him, forgetting the other points that he had so carefully circled on the map.

'I guess it's more trouble than it's worth. I don't really know where you'd reach me, and besides since you don't write there's no point, is there?' She wanted him to object to this assertion a little, to suggest that there was always a way if there was a will. What kind of suitor was he that he couldn't outguess a vacationing family and at least take a chance on a P.O. box? 'I'll send you a card now and then, just to let you know where we are.'

Without replying, he grabbed her wrist and pushed it into his groin. Her departure must be doing something to his glands, she thought, for he had never before taken such a chance in her house. Her parents were awake. She knew that they were packing quietly in their room, folding shirts, inserting cosmetics and shaving equipment into the side pouches of suitcases. They did their packing harmoniously and silently; long accustomed to vacations together, they prided themselves on their efficiency, and it was a well-founded pride – they never forgot an item, and sometimes they even remembered to bring things for Joan that she had not bothered to consider.

'This is my letter. All I need is your envelope.' He rubbed his hand around the general area of his zipper, and although she felt a slight bulge she could detect no pain on his face. She was sorry she had brought up the writing issue, but maybe bad jokes were what she deserved for thinking seriously about it.

'Okay. Lay off! This is no time for fun and games, and besides, everyone in the house can hear you.'

'Let 'em!' His clasp on her hand tightened as he forced

her hand harder into his groin. Joan was afraid that he would start to moan. She was convinced that he was becoming excited simply because the conditions for any kind of sex were impossible. Then she felt his tongue in her ear, and he began to make slurping noises like a kid sucking on a Popsicle.

'For God's sake, cut it out!' She pushed his hand away as hard as she could. For a second it waved in mid-air, and then it landed full force on the coffee table, knocking over all the magazines and their two glasses of beer.

'Shit! Now you've done it!' He held up a forefinger that was spurting blood.

Joan, who felt she hadn't done a damned thing, was appalled at his bleeding finger. The broken glass could be swept up in no time, but now her parents were alerted. Within minutes they came downstairs, her mother by the front stairs, her father clumping down the back stairs. Joining somewhere near the library, they arrived together. 'What happened?'

Although the evidence on the floor was self-explanatory, Ronald felt compelled to launch into an explanation that would get him off the hook. 'You daughter, here, is so clumsy that she thought the table was the floor.'

Had they really been listening to him they would have questioned how their daughter's clumsiness had managed to wound his hand, but they were paying more attention to his blood than to his words. Mrs. Nelson, whose specialty as a doctor's daughter included all domestic injuries, major or minor, took his hand and examined it, while checking at the same time for vital signs.

'Your pulse seems normal. Your color is a little off – pale – but otherwise you look all right. And the bleeding seems to have stopped, or at least slowed down. Let me get you a Band Aid.' Instead, Ronald stuck his finger in his mouth. Joan thought her mother would be horrified at such a childish gesture, but she smiled at him as if she approved. 'You'd better have someone look at it tomorrow. It might need a stitch or two, but I don't think so.'

Ronald stood up, a man of more than six feet, sucking his finger like a helpless infant. 'I've gotta be going anyhow. It's getting late and you'll be wanting an early start tomorrow.'

Joan thought his courtesy touching. Despite his vulnerable, injured-kid look, he had managed to recover his dignity and to sound as if he really cared about their hours and plans. She even forgave him for blaming her for his own dumb accident, for she knew that it would be impossible to explain his actions any other way. 'Do you want a ride home?' She knew that her offer might start off another scene of tussling and groping, but this was her last chance to see him before she left. And she was also half-ready to listen to his pleas; he had done so much that she had wanted and he had behaved himself, by and large, that she wondered if he wasn't, at last, deserving something better. It would be her last chance, too, to twist the hair that curled behind his ears, to admire his gap-toothed grin and his slightly slumped posture that always reminded her of cowboys or men on ships. She was willing to stake a lot tonight for all this, and the idea of it made her shiver a little.

'No thanks. I need the exercise.' He spoke to her, yet looked at her father, as if this announcement would somehow create an immediate solidarity.

'I'll see you to the door, then.' Poor man, she couldn't even say she'd walk him to his car, so bereft he was of standard, material conveniences.

The two left the Nelson adults standing in the library, Mrs. Nelson still holding the proffered Band Aid, Mr. Nelson next to his favorite armchair, an ancient brown monstrosity that looked as if it had been upholstered with rags. He called out after them, 'Take care of that hand now.

See a doctor if you have to, but don't neglect it, take care of it right away.'

Joan liked the way her father had elevated Ronald's injury. From finger to hand must mean that her father was coming around, that he could concede some worth to her dangerous suitor. She smiled at the promise of a more amiable domestic atmosphere, and Ronald must have caught some of her optimism because he smiled benevolently in return. As she opened the door for him he passed a hand down her back, once again creating the tremors that she had felt months ago whenever she said his name to herself. She raised her head for him to kiss, but instead of kissing her he put his arm around her waist, gave her a quick squeeze, and whispered in her ear, 'Have a good time. Hurry back. But don't bother to write.'

*

Three days later Mr. Nelson's heart broke for good.

They had been traveling through South Dakota and Nebraska. One night they had stopped at a small town in South Dakota where Mr. Nelson owned an interest in an enormous cattle ranch. He had spent part of the day looking at the ranch, talking to tenants and inspecting the crops, while Joan and her mother stayed in town, reading magazines at the motel and attempting to swim in its dinky pool. The next day they had detoured to Mount Rushmore, where they had fought the crowds to gaze at the outlines of four presidents whose significance was minor, Joan thought, compared to the gargantuan, dusty labors of immortalizing them. They had seen a number of bears, too, which had thrilled Joan, especially the sight of a mama bear and her twin cubs huddled by the roadside.

On the third day they had finally crossed into Colorado and were nearing the town of Grand Junction when Mr.

Nelson suggested they call it a day. Although it was earlier than they usually liked to stop – it was just three o'clock – they did agree that they were tired and hot, and that a drink and a rest were better than driving on to Denver. Joan, who was driving, thought her father looked a bit gray and tight-lipped, but she imagined they all did, for it was hot, and the car, with its two passengers and driver, was considerably hotter than the outside desert air.

They found a motel without trouble – another good reason to stop early – where they took adjoining rooms. Joan was in the habit of plopping down her suitcase on the nearest bed wherever they stopped, barely pausing long enough to extract her bathing suit, but she had also assumed the responsibility of getting the ice and mix for the three of them. She was just returning from the motel office with the ice cubes and oversized bottle of charged water when she saw her mother standing outside the door of her room. 'Come quick!' she yelled and vanished back into her room.

Joan ran to the door and looked inside. The blinds had been pulled against the western sun, but in the shadows she could make out the outline of her father lying on the bed, his face the color of wet clay. She ran over to the bed, forgetting that her arms were full of mix and ice. When she stopped to dump them on a table she saw her mother leaning over the bed, attempting to loosen her father's shirt. She couldn't tell if he was breathing; his mouth was slightly open but his body seemed absolutely still, his eyes tightly shut. Her mother looked at her briefly, with an expression so grief-stricken that Joan knew that whatever she was going to say would be useless. Her right hand encircled his wrist, but Joan could see she was not counting pulse beats. Her left hand lay on his forehead, as motionless and without force as his body.

'Get someone to call a doctor.'

Joan raced to the motel office, where the officious caretaker, after realizing she was not being asked to pursue another mere tourist request, selected the name of a doctor from a ledger bearing names to be used in case of emergency.

By the time Joan had returned to the motel room the bedspread had been pulled over her father's face. Joan and her mother waited for the doctor without saying anything. It would all be said later, Joan knew, and just this once she wanted to preserve the silence.

Chapter Twenty-Two

Rebounds

The aftermath was terrible. For days it seemed as if the nightmare would never end. There were so many extra complications just because Joan's father had died away from home. Someone was always on the phone, and for two more days Joan and her mother were stuck in the motel until they could complete all the funeral arrangements.

Joan's mother insisted on having the funeral in Minneapolis, and she refused to consider returning to New Bonn until everything was over. Joan didn't care where the funeral was held. She thought that a New Bonn cemetery plot was probably as good as one in Minneapolis, yet she was grateful to her mother for sparing them, at least for a time, that first sad visit to a changed house.

The Minneapolis funeral was more elaborate than either Joan or her mother had wanted, for arrangements had to be made to fit in Reverend Blue. Somehow he had convinced the Minneapolis Congregational minister that his Presbyterian services had been as important to the life of the deceased as were the past ceremonies of the Congregational church.

On the day before the funeral both ministers suggested to Joan and her mother that this ritual should not differ from other familiar Christian rituals, that a death was actually an occasion to rejoice – uniquely so, they claimed – and that the music should reflect a joyous spirit. At her mother's request, Joan had selected the music, and her choice included the songs she knew her father liked best. Not very good musically, she knew, but her father's musical judgment was based on favorite tunes that dated from his own early years. Reverend Blue had not rejected the selections – 'Abide With Me' and 'The Strife Is Over', but he had suggested they include another as a kind of emotional boost. 'How about "Onward Christian Soldiers"?'

'Too military.' Joan considered this hymn an obnoxious example of evangelical rabble-rousing. She thought it Lutheran in spirit and message, yet she could see that she was about to get sucked into a hopeless argument with two diverse members of the clergy who seemed to be inextricably allied on this one issue. Her mother, after an hour's private conversation with both men, had retired into the master bedroom of her uncle's house after instructing Joan to take care of the musical arrangements. Joan turned to the two clergymen who seemed to be concerned with sound; ten minutes, at most, of combined noises on a relative harmonic scale that made, in the long run, no real difference to anyone, dead or alive. 'Let the soloist decide. That's what he's paid for.'

The high-priced soloist, who also doubled in light opera on the side, did have better taste than Joan had credited him with, so that the third selection had just enough optimistic Christian sentiment without cloying the palates of the more sensitive listeners, which left the funeral goers musically soothed. After the services Joan had heard a number of people comment on the wonderful music, so restrained, they said, so appropriate.

Just what the hell was inappropriate, then? Joan thought that anything must go in this most subdued and genteel of Protestant worlds, so long as it's decided by a person who makes a living off the ceremonies of the dead and not picked by some upstart who happens to have learned a lot about the musical tastes of Protestant congregations, small-town or otherwise. Joan wondered what a blast of sober Bach would do to their musical appetites. Too mechanical, they would undoubtedly judge. Too contrived, like mathematics, totally unsuitable (inappropriate!) for the occasion of death.

Three days after the funeral, after the last relative had departed and after the third night of Seconal-induced sleep had left Joan and her mother in a state of drugged indifference, Joan and her mother left for New Bonn. Joan was not sure why they needed to go, yet New Bonn was where she and her mother lived, or had been living, before her father's death. Fortified by a fifth of Old Grandad that Joan's uncle had thoughtfully deposited in the back seat, next to a pillow for Mrs. Nelson, they arrived at Locksley Hall in the early evening.

'I hope the electricity is still on.'

Joan knew what her mother meant. No one would have turned off the electricity, just as no one would have let the furnace die in the winter had their loss occurred then. Joan knew that her mother was expressing some kind of plea that everything be natural, but not painfully so. From Joan's knowledge of the ways of the town, she was not worried that they would go without food or company. She felt that the scene they had just played in Minneapolis was about to be repeated in New Bonn. The main difference was that the Minneapolis mourners had included relatives in their numbers whereas those in New Bonn would consist entirely of neighbors and friends. She imagined more women bearing casseroles covered with dishcloths to preserve their warmth; women bringing homemade breads and pies, their husbands driving them to Locksley Hall and then returning for them after a decent amount of time had passed. There was bound to be the obligatory visit from

Reverend Blue, this time on his home soil and not intimidated by the rank and class of the big-city minister, who had taken over at the funeral and had made the small-town clergyman look like a hopeful apprentice trying out for a job.

The only person Joan looked forward to seeing was Ronald, and she was bound to see him soon. She hadn't heard from him while they were in Minneapolis; he could have sent flowers, or at least a sympathy card – these things required no handwritten messages – and she meant to scold him for his thoughtlessness. But she knew she would quickly forgive him.

Her need for his attention was too great to be ruined by her indignation at his ill-mannered negligence. She was waiting to crumple into his arms and cry. During the past week her tears had been frequent and copious, but they had passed, for the most part, unsoothed. He didn't have to say anything to her, just hold her and occasionally pat her back.

Their arrival at Locksley Hall was evidently observed by the most efficient of newscasters, for within an hour there were telephone calls and at least six people at the house who brought food. Mrs. Nelson, whose voice was hoarse from a week-long binge of talking, greeted each guest the same way she had admitted her Minneapolis visitors. She expressed gratitude for condolences offered; agreed that a sudden death was preferable to the futility of a prolonged, painful illness, and then launched into an outline of their plans, their intentions for the rest of the summer. Frequently the details of the plans changed, but their essential information was the same: they were to sell Locksley Hall as soon as her husband's affairs could be put in order; Joan would be in college in another month or two, but not Oberlin, since it was too far away and would be too hard on her at this time. Mrs. Nelson intended to take a smaller house somewhere in Minneapolis where she could be nearer her daughter. The variations of this master plan lay mostly in the amount of time it would take to settle affairs and what mother and daughter would do during this time.

Sometimes Mrs. Nelson mentioned a short trip where they could mourn apart from familiar names and faces. Other times she suggested a more extensive journey, perhaps to New York or Washington, D.C. Always a believer that travel is broadening, she now felt that it had to be therapeutic. After one of these confidences Joan wondered if the next step would be a Caribbean cruise, but then she felt guilty for associating her mother with such selfish and graceless motives.

A day went by after their arrival at Locksley Hall, then another, and still Joan hadn't heard a word from Ronald. Her mother was beginning to pick up on Joan's anxiety, and finally she couldn't refrain from attacking the young man as rude and ungrateful.

'Ungrateful for what?'

'All those times he's been to the house, acting as if he was family, and now he hasn't the manners to at least call you or come to see me.'

Joan knew this was true, yet she didn't like to think of him in terms of gratitude. She would have liked to call him, but the danger of his mother or brothers – even his lush of a father – discouraged her from trying. Any one of them could just as easily answer the phone as Ronald could. She knew there could never be a legitimate explanation for his behavior, but she was ready to accept an apology. She couldn't explain this to her mother, though, whose exasperation, she was sure, would turn to resentment and finally to rage if he didn't come around soon to cool her off.

Joan decided to enlist her friend Maryann in getting hold of Ronald. After a few phone calls, Maryann reported that the family was in town, as usual, but Ronald hadn't been seen for some time. Not that this was unusual, since he could keep himself scarce if there was a good enough reason for temporary anonymity. She promised to find out as much as she could about him, which wouldn't be hard since she was getting ready to pay a visit to her distant relative, Lorraine, who, as a telephone operator, provided the best detailed information available.

Later that evening Maryann dropped by to see Joan. It was a strange encounter, for neither girl quite knew how to manage the visit. They couldn't greet each other with an embrace, as Mrs. Nelson's women friends now greeted her, and yet they couldn't just carry on as usual, with Maryann saying a few words to Joan's mother before both girls departed to Joan's bedroom to smoke and talk privately. Joan thought it would be far simpler to just drape everything in black and stare numbly at people until it was time for them to go instead of carrying on with this poisonous mixture of grief and business-as-usual. The problems of mourning behavior were complicated ones, and Joan was getting no help on how to handle them. She noticed that people would often tell her not to cry, but then when she attempted a smile they would look disappointed, even outraged.

After more than an hour of polite exchanges with Mrs. Nelson, exchanges that involved Maryann's college plans (Macalaster), and a few desultory comments about the health of Maryann's parents, Joan's friend got up to leave.

'You don't have to go yet. Come and stay a while. Have another cigarette.' Joan knew that this was a good way to leave for her room, for her mother didn't like to see her smoking publicly now. Once they had reached Joan's room and Joan had slammed the door, she turned to her friend, 'What did you find out?'

Her friend looked frightened. Her face was red and she kept sweeping her blonde hair away from her face. 'I don't know how to tell you this, but—'

'Good God! Is he married?'

Maryann giggled nervously and shot Joan a quizzical look that suggested Joan's complicity in the sexual act, an act that had evidently taken place in a number of imaginations. 'He's not married, but he's gone. He's gone to Texas or Oklahoma, or some such place.'

'For God's sake, why?' The finality of the South, even if it wasn't the genuine, magnolia-landscaped Deep South, stunned Joan. She knew of no one who had gone South other than those who had been drafted into the army, where they claimed serving out their terms in the stinking, dusty heat was worse than being sent to Korea, and the possibilities of combat.

'I don't know exactly why. I got this fourth-hand, remember. It seems Old Man Boswell was gabbing as usual one night in the liquor store and told everyone how one son, at least, was finally going to make something of himself. Incidentally, this was some time before – at least two weeks before – your, that is, before you left for Colorado. But I don't think anyone made much of it at the time, just Old Len talking in his cups, you know. Then Lorraine had to put in some long-distance calls – that's how she explains it – and I gather that Ronald had gotten accepted into some kind of training school where you learn how to repair TVs and work on refrigerators.'

'Do you know when he left?' Was it before her father died, or after?

'I'm not sure. Like I told you, I got most of this way down on the grapevine, but I gather he left a day or two after you went to – went on your vacation.'

This would explain his neglect at writing to her. Also it would account for his boasts about the future, his claims that he had an escape route planned out of New Bonn. It would also explain why she hadn't heard from him now, that what looked like his indifference was really a matter of genuine ignorance, for how could he get any news if no one in that family wrote letters?

Joan must have looked stricken, for her friend said, in compassionate tones, 'Don't feel too bad, Joan. I've heard it's a good deal. There's a bundle of money to be made in TV repairs. Maybe that's what he's trying to do, getting himself ready for Easy Street.'

But why Texas, or Oklahoma, or whatever weird place he'd chosen?

Maryann couldn't explain Ronald's peculiar choice, but she was sure it had something to do with the GI bill. 'Not all of those schools are approved, you know. There are a lot of fly-by-night operations going, and maybe he had to be careful about getting one that was okay, and that's why he had to go so far.'

Joan imagined Ronald walking the streets of some gritty panhandle town, weary after a day's explanations of the intricacies of TV sets and small appliances, exhausted from straining his eyes looking at tiny colored wires and wiggling images on faulty screens. She imagined him as a lonely figure idly sitting on a bank next to a dried-up, silty creek, longing for the clear blue waters of Minnesota's ten thousand lakes, while prying chiggers out of his navel.

'It seems a long way to go to some school, but I guess he knows what he's doing.' If he were so confident about his future, why hadn't he said more to her before he left? Yet in a sense she was relieved, for had it been California or Florida that he had chosen, or even New York, she would never see him again, for he would have gone to those places with something more in mind, something grander and less practical than a course in vocational training.

'The course only lasts eight weeks, I heard. At least that's what his mother said when someone asked her how he was doing.'

'You mean his mother knows how he's doing? He writes to her, then?'

'No, she writes. He doesn't, but she sends him the paper. She was complaining the other day in the post office that she had gotten only one letter from him since he left, and it was only a card, not a letter. But she said, "What do you expect from a family that never writes?" At least she sends him the paper and writes to him once a week, promptly, or so she said.'

It was conceivable that Mrs. Boswell might have overlooked writing to her son of the death of Mr. Nelson, but it was impossible for Ronald to have missed reading about it in the paper, a weekly publication that had carried the death of Bert Nelson on the front page in addition to the long obituary in its midsection. Now it was obvious that he was not ignorant of Joan's loss.

In his quest of the sure meal ticket out of New Bonn, he had completely ignored Joan's grief and loss.

Maryann left, an uncertain, puzzled look still on her face. Had she done the right thing by playing messenger with all this bad news? But how could she have spared her friend? She had to know about it some time, and it's certainly better to hear it from a friend than from some malicious gossip like Lorraine, who would like nothing better than to play on Joan's naïveté and throw her the bombshell of her boyfriend's departure. She had spared her friend almost nothing, only the one detail that she would conceal under threat of death, and that detail involved Ronald's departure for Oklahoma City the day after Mr. Nelson's death had been made known. She knew this for sure because she saw him herself, saw him wave goodbye to his mother at the bus stop in Worthington.

Maryann had eyed him there, actually at a restaurant that offered its customers bus service. Travelers who were setting out on complicated bus trips that involved switching vehicles and stopping at every hamlet on the map until the passengers could finally catch up with the main line – these were the travelers who waited in this restaurant. She had seen Mrs. Boswell give her son a final, satisfied peck on his cheek before she saw him climb aboard the smelly vehicle, carrying a bulging leather suitcase that looked as if it had barely survived the Depression and two major wars. He had settled back in his seat and had opened the window to make some final comment to his mother, who by now was looking less proud than distressed. Maryann hadn't heard what he'd said, but she thought it was something like, 'Don't cry, Mom, it won't be for long,' for she figured that's what all sons said to their mothers when they left home. She knew that Joan would be heartbroken, and she would have liked to have intervened and to have pleaded with him to at least explain his departure to her friend – to postpone it never occurred to her.

Yet in a way she was glad he was leaving so abruptly and so cruelly, for perhaps this is what was needed to bring Joan to her senses. Still, why did he have to be so heartless about it? She wondered about the course of their romance, if that's what you could ever have called it. At first she had thought he was in it strictly for the material fortune, that he could stand to gain a hell of a lot if he were only patient and waited around long enough. Now she was not so sure. Men who are after money alone simply don't leave home when they discover the source is available practically for the asking, as Mr. Nelson's unexpected death would assure him quick rewards. And they don't take courses in TV repair.

That evening Joan's tears fell in isolation. Now she cried for herself, and not for her father and the things she had wanted to say to him but had never managed as she had been weeping for days. At one point, when she thought she might never stop, she heard a pause outside her door –

undoubtedly her mother – but instead of knocking or even entering without permission, she had walked away. Perhaps, then, she already knew about Ronald and had nothing to say, for once. If she doesn't know she'll know soon, Joan thought, and with a new burst of sobs she wrenched the ring off her finger and tossed it into the wastebasket. She knew it did no good to wish she were dead, yet the choices of life were as miserable as an untimely death or a dreary illness. She knew that she would never be the same, and she wasn't.

Mrs. Nelson must have heard about Ronald's leaving at the same time Maryann told Joan, for she quit hounding her daughter about him. Her attacks on his character stopped altogether, a display of delicacy that Joan appreciated. She encouraged her daughter to get out of the house – to get a little sun, even to go swimming. She stopped talking about taking trips and going on vacations, and she seemed to be spending a lot of time talking to lawyers and insurance men about her husband's estate.

One morning at breakfast Mrs. Nelson looked at the haggard face of her daughter – 'pinched and white' was the way she later described it to a friend – and packed Joan into the car for a trip to the doctor. Not the inept Dr. Richardson but a new, young doctor who practiced in a clinic in Worthington. Yet the new doctor's examination differed little from one that the incompetent New Bonn man would have given her, Joan was sure, and she was not surprised when he told mother and daughter that there was nothing the matter with her.

'She's basically healthy. Right now maybe run down, but basically she's fit as a fiddle. I don't suppose she's been eating enough lately.'

Joan, whose diet for the past few weeks had consisted mostly of Cokes and cigarettes, could only nod.

'What you have to do is get out, try to enjoy yourself.

Forget about yourself for a while. You can't live on tears forever, you know.'

Joan would have loved to get outside of herself, to forget about herself for at least two minutes. But how could she find anything when everything was clouded over with tears? The doctor wrote a prescription (which she later learned was for Phenobarbital) and told her to take one or two four times a day, especially when she was feeling blue.

What happens when I feel green, or pink, or yellow, like now? But of course she couldn't ask him questions he wouldn't like, which sounded too much like sarcasm.

'Let me know how they work; how you feel – in two or three weeks, let's say. Maybe we'll have to try something else if they don't work, but I think they will. Get some exercise, and stop thinking about yourself, young lady.'

The look he gave Mrs. Nelson was so sympathetic, so profound in its communication of shared understanding, that Joan felt like socking him with his stethoscope, flailing him with its hard rubber until he screamed in pain for mercy. He's treating me like a difficult child, she thought, and so is my mother; she's in on this. I'm only here because she can't do anything for me and she thinks she can force something on me from him.

What that something was Joan didn't know.

On the way home from Worthington Joan cried quietly all the way while her mother drove, grim and silent. As soon as they arrived at Locksley Hall Joan went upstairs and flushed all the pills down the toilet. 'So much for your quack cures,' she muttered. 'I don't need pills. I don't need someone else to tell me that I'm thinking about myself too much. I don't need someone to tell me to get outside myself, that I'm a pain in the ass. I know this. I want to know *how* to do it, and I know that these pills aren't going to tell me anything.'

Mrs. Nelson, like Joan, was going through a bad time.

Her husband's affairs were in a worse mess than anyone had anticipated. Like most businessmen who take enormous pride in straightening out the complicated holdings of others, Mr. Nelson had possessed little regard for the nature of his own mortality, which meant that Mrs. Nelson, with the help of her lawyer and an old banking friend of her husband's, had to spend hours untangling the mysterious financial web that her husband had woven for more than thirty years.

She discovered deeds that had not been recorded lying in a pile in a corner of his office safe; some of them had been there for years waiting for a messenger to deliver them to the office of the county clerk. She found second mortgages for lands that she never knew he owned, and she discovered shares in companies that neither she nor her advisers had ever heard of.

Somehow Reverend Blue had gotten to him, too, for among the papers was a pledge of five thousand dollars designated for the church building fund. (Her lawyer insisted it was perfectly legal, which meant that she was obliged to pay it.)

Everyone knew that Mr. Nelson had left a will. It was something one accepted without liking to discuss it, for, like religion and politics, wills were expected of businessmen. But wills were also expected to be decorous documents, without ostentation, allowing the traditional widow's portion and the corresponding shares to all survivors. Mr. Nelson's will was unexceptional but for a recent, bothersome codicil, an item of fewer than four lines which expressed feelings that distressed his survivors, close as well as distant.

The codicil was disarmingly simple: it merely stated that if his daughter were to marry a certain Ronald J. Boswell, aged twenty-two (how had he determined the correct age and middle initial?) she was to receive nothing from the estate until she reached the age of twenty-five or had been married at least five years, whichever occurred first. This restriction did not pertain to the insurance annuity of twenty thousand dollars that was to come to her on her twenty-first birthday, for there was no way he could have attached his personal strings to a neutral insurance document. He had added the codicil just two weeks before Joan's graduation from high school, during the time when Joan was not seeing Ronald at all.

When Joan learned about this financial edict she wondered what her father had really known about herself and Ronald. Had he guessed her feelings and then decided that they were dangerous, or had he actually known something about Ronald that no one else did, something sinister enough to make him pass judgment on her future? And if he knew something really awful, why hadn't he told her mother, who was just as much in the dark about the will as she had been?

'I wouldn't worry about it too much. I don't think it's very legal,' her mother had advised her.

How could something be very legal? As opposed to rather legal? Or sort of legal? It made no practical difference to either Joan or her mother, since the terms of her father's will, with or without codicil, had hardly made Joan an instant heiress, but it certainly made an emotional difference. Joan couldn't help feeling queasy about the things her father hadn't said during those months she was so wrapped up in her own feelings about Ronald. And although her grief for her father was still in its first stages of gut-shaking, heart-choking loss, she couldn't help feeling that what he had done amounted to a hell of a way to tell her that he disapproved of her boyfriend.

Several days after their visit to the young doctor Linda called. After telling Joan how sorry she was at the loss of her father, she went quickly to the point. 'Look, I know you don't feel like doing much of anything, but can you come over soon for supper? I don't bet you're eating much these days, but maybe a change of scene will perk you up.'

Joan doubted that her appetite would be restored by a meal in different surroundings, but she liked Linda's directness; she also thought it remarkable of her to guess so accurately about her feelings and her stomach. 'Sure. Okay. Why not? When should I come?'

'C'mon over tonight. That is, if you're not doing anything. We'll eat about six.'

Joan remembered Linda's pathetic efforts at gaiety last time she was entertained at her house, and she hoped that she wouldn't now attempt to force high spirits out of the muck of her sorrow. 'Don't do anything special for me. I mean, don't go all out. I mean, sure I'd like to come but I don't want it to be any trouble to you.' Joan's manners were leading her into the shoals – everything she said seemed to turn itself around into an insult or a threat or some ghastly kind of rejection. She couldn't very well tell Linda not to have a party, for she knew that a party was not the purpose of the invitation, and she could hardly tell her not to fuss with the food when she knew that Linda liked to decorate cakes and fool around with recipes. 'Thanks a lot for the invite, but don't go into hock over it.'

Joan knew how much pride Linda took in her husband's prosperous farm, a pride that was reflected in her abundant spreads. There was also something about Linda that fascinated Joan. Her reputation as an inspired cook was almost as notorious as her reputation as an easy lay. The difference between the two kinds of reputations lay mostly in the people who voiced the legends. Among the less fortunate farm women, Linda was a wicked spendthrift who would send her husband to the poorhouse if she didn't stop showing off at the table. Among the men of the community the sentiment also seemed to favor poor Joe Schultz, who would either die of heart failure from screwing his wife too much, or else die of heart failure from having learned that his wife screwed too much. Joan, herself, knew that Linda was a Blue Ribbon, A-Number-One cook, and that she probably screwed anything and everything that wore pants, but she thought that a visit to Linda committed her to nothing, for she certainly wasn't expected to either screw or cook on the spot. She was also curious to see how Linda managed a farm in such a way as to make resentful old biddies talk about the Waldorf Astoria.

On the way to the Schultz farm, Joan mused about her feelings concerning farmers. She was glad that her original supercilious attitude had modified and she regretted now how much she had lost in feeling so high-minded about an entire group of people.

Such attitudes, she now realized, kept people apart and deprived them of knowledge and understanding that everyone could use. It didn't help that her position was merely a reflection of the community, that she was different from other villagers. She should have known better than to get sucked into a whole way of thinking simply because it belonged to a majority. Her father didn't think that way, Joan realized, too late.

Why hadn't she caught on that her father's ability to get along with all kinds of people made everyone like him? The funeral eulogies emphasized this, at least the ones that Joan could stand to listen to without breaking down. Such pleasure he took at people's company and friendship! And how had Joan missed this? How sad, she thought, and now too late.

Linda was not the choice Mrs. Nelson would have made for the restoration of her daughter's appetite, but she was better than nothing, and the way Joan was carrying on, it was nothing these days. She had worked for days going over the accounts, and she was weary of domestic problems, so she was more than glad at her daughter's plans for the evening, a welcome change from the silent dinners where no one ate much and there was not any conversation to relieve the sadness. Mrs. Nelson's preoccupation with her own anxieties was based on the loopholes they kept discovering in the estate, compounded by the embarrassing codicil to the will. Most of her concern, though, was directed at the difficulties of selling Locksley Hall. The house that she had named and loved had now turned into a realtor's nightmare.

'People just don't buy houses like these any more, Carrie,' her lawyer had told her, and the banker had nodded his silent assent. 'It's too big, too damned big. In fact, I don't see how you managed all these years with just the hired country help.'

'This house isn't any good for a big family, either,' the banker had added. 'Can't you just see what a pack of kids would do to those stained-glass windows and parquet floors?' He made a slicing noise with an imaginary knife, grimacing as if he, too, were about to be cut and mauled.

Being unable to sell Locksley Hall for a while meant that Mrs. Nelson would have to hang on longer in New Bonn, delaying the purchase of her house in Minneapolis. It also meant that Joan would probably have to delay college for at least a semester, for she knew that her daughter would never leave her in New Bonn while she was still occupying their house, distasteful as staying on in Locksley Hall might be to both of them. These worries, which she didn't want to discuss with her daughter, made her more gracious about Linda than she usually was about her daughter's simple invitations. Linda's modest country supper now took on the dimensions of a Roman banquet. 'It's lovely, simply lovely that you're going. I know you'll have a good time, and be sure to give her my love,' she had gurgled, almost unaware of how forced her message sounded.

No rules and no real demands. With Ronald out of the way, Joan really had nothing for her mother to fret about anymore. Joan's feelings about him had gone from hope to rage, alternating back and forth between the two states until she had finally reached the despairing conclusion that he had ditched her forever, for reasons she would never know. When she tried to put him out of her mind, he crept in through the side door of her dreams, for she dreamed about him every night. Terrible frightening dreams where he was all mixed up with her father, when their faces would change and their bodies merge into one amorphous shape, which would then split up and dissolve into shadows before she could overtake either of them.

She had retrieved his ring out of the wastebasket and she kept it in a tiny heirloom dish on her dresser. She knew she wouldn't wear it again, but she didn't want to throw it away either. She couldn't figure out what use it had finally served, but she promised herself that if she ever figured it out she would dump the damned thing – enough of his mystery would then have been solved to allow her to carry on without the usual pain at his traces. Only one thing she knew for sure, and that was that the will couldn't have been responsible for his leaving, for he was already settled into his new vocation before the seal on the will's envelope had been broken.

By the time Joan arrived at the Schultz farm it was after six, an ordinary lapse that was permitted everywhere but on farms, where regular meals and hours are essential to the complicated management of the fields. Joan shook Ronald out of her head and walked up to the front porch, which she noticed had been remodeled recently. There was now a larger enclosed area, screened off from mosquitoes and other pests, and in addition to the customary rocker and wicker chairs there was now a cobbler's bench hewn from the blondest oak Joan had ever seen. Next to it was a coffee table of maple so red that Joan was immediately reminded of barns.

Linda's greeting took in Joan's recognition of the changes. 'Like it? Joe made it. In his spare time.' Linda gave her husband a fond pat on the shoulder, at the same time tugging him gently by the sleeve so that he reached out and formally shook hands with Joan.

'I was sorry to hear about your father,' he said. 'We'll all miss him.'

A genuine statement, its honesty unimpeachable, and Joan succumbed to its sincerity with a fresh flood of tears. Linda and her husband seemed to expect it of her, for they waited quietly while she wiped her face and blew her nose. They did not look directly at her, yet they didn't gaze into distant fields, either, not failing to meet her eye when she was finished, as so many others had done.

'Let's not go in and eat for a minute. Let's sit here for a sec. I've got some beer for us.' Linda waved them to chairs on the porch and retreated into the kitchen. Joe sat down on the rocker and put his feet on the coffee table, stretched out his arms until they extended over his head, and sighed deeply.

'Ahhh. Sure am thirsty.' He looked so satisfied and without need that Joan wondered how this contented man could possibly down so much as one ounce of beer, yet when Linda brought the bottles and glasses he took a long pull, straight from the bottle, that reduced its contents by at least half. Linda looked about the same as she had the night of her party. She wore her hair piled on top of her head with a mass of curls arranged in a fringe above her forehead, an elaborate hairdo that Joan was sure took hours to arrange. Instead of the red silky party dress, tonight she wore a simpler pink dress with pastel flowers splashed all over the skirt. A cheerful dress, Joan thought, but obviously not washable.

'That's a pretty dress,' Joan commented. 'I like the flowers. Are they nasturtiums, or what?'

'I haven't the slightest. I saw the material in Sioux Falls and I bought it before I had time to think about the price. Sure beats feed sacks.' Linda smiled at her husband in a kind of silent tribute to his talents as a provider, and then she said to Joan, 'God, you look like hell. You look like you haven't eaten in a month. I betcha you don't sleep much, either. Do you?'

True to both questions, but Linda didn't listen for an answer. 'Let's eat now, and then, if you feel like it maybe we can play some cards. All right with you?'

Joan found that she had more appetite for Linda's food than she had felt for weeks. Maybe it's all those starchy casseroles, maybe a diet of fruit and nuts would get me over the worst, she thought, yet Linda's food, though not exactly without starch, had little resemblance to those endless covered dishes. The table was heaped with platters of ham and mounds of mashed potatoes, and there were huge ears of steaming sweetcorn with butter running down the sides of each ear, looking like rain pouring from the eaves of a house during a thunder shower, Joan imagined. I'm getting poetic, she observed. This must be a good sign, getting inspired from a bowl full of food normally associated with pigs.

They ate quickly and without conversation, farm-style, interrupting themselves only to ask for salt, more butter, or extra gravy. When Joan had eaten so much she was sure she was going to burst, Linda reminded her to save some room. 'There's pie on the way.'

'Let's wait a minute,' Joan suggested. 'Or you go ahead. I'm so full I can't hold another bite. I'd like some pie later, though,' she added.

'Sure, we'll all wait. I guess we made pigs out of ourselves, as usual. Oink oink oink. Maybe we'd better sit around for a while and see if it's going to stay down. Just kidding. Why don't we go outside? I can bring coffee and pie out there.'

Joe Schultz walked out of the door without a word, but Joan thought she should stay and at least offer to help with the dishes.

'Heck no,' Linda responded. 'I let the dishes stand. I just pile them in the sink and leave them to stand for days. Until we don't have clean ones. Then I do the whole mess. That way I only have to do them once.'

Joan remembered her mother's objections to Linda, her horror at her slovenliness, and she thought this a juicy detail but she knew she would never mention it to her mother. Any time-saving device to spare a person from the tedium of the kitchen routine Joan approved of, even if it did mean the kind of unsightliness her mother loathed, although Joan did put the lid on squalor.

'C'mon, let's go out on the porch.' Linda walked out of the kitchen just as car lights began to shine down the driveway. Joan stayed in the kitchen until the bright haze of the one high-powered beam separated into two distinct lamps, and then she joined the Schultzes on the porch. She knew there was nothing unusual about unexpected visitors on the farm. People were always popping in and out, and often they were unexpected relatives from North Dakota or someplace who would spend two weeks or more, but more often they were merely neighbors from adjoining farms needing to borrow a tool or to arrange for some help with crops the next day. Sometimes a whole family would pile into a pickup at nine o'clock at night and drive ten miles just to return a tool. The kids would be lined up in the back, shuffling around and poking one another with straws while the grownups stood around the yard and chatted.

There was nothing unusual about this car heading down the driveway, except that neither Linda nor her husband bothered to speculate about the identity of the driver. Neither of them said, 'Now who could that be?' or 'Wonder who wants us now?' Joan sensed that she had been set up, but she knew, also, that it was too late to do anything about it. The only way she could leave now would be to jump into her own car and drive headlong into the approaching one – a spectacular exit but not a very safe one. By the time the vehicle had drawn to within thirty feet of the farmyard, Joan recognized it as belonging to John. She wondered who had staged this one.

When John emerged from his pickup Joan had already composed the little speech she was going to deliver to him: 'How've you been, John? Good to see you. Got to be going now. See you again sometime.' It never occurred to her that he also might have been composing something, too, so that when he did speak it was to her first.

'Hi. I'm sorry to surprise you like this, but we had to work it this way. Otherwise you never woulda come.'

He looked about the same, but then it had only been about three months, if not less, since she had last seen him. His hair was still arranged so that the little curl spun around his forehead. His clothes were fresh and soapy smelling, and his eyes still looked like fawn's eyes – large, liquid, and round. He looked strong and clean, standing on the farm porch, smiling at her, yet also looking scared that she might be offended at their strategy.

What the hell? she thought. At least he's reliable, and he cared enough about seeing me to make elaborate arrangements so that he could at least hear what I had to say to him in person.

Three months later, in late November, Joan became Mrs. John Lambert.

Chapter Twenty-Three

Bride

A month before they were married John gave Joan a diamond ring, and Joan decided that the ring-giving was as good a time as any to get rid of her virginity. John didn't have to be coaxed. Although he had talked about virginity as being important to a bride, he also admitted that he held little stock in it. Yet he had never tried to force sex on Joan – it was something that she'd have to decide, he told her, because once you tried it you could never return.

Their first session was worse than Joan had expected. She tried to work up some passion but all she really felt was a tight, painful prodding at her crotch, then a series of painful squeezes, followed by a lot of foamy stuff running down her legs. John liked it, though. While he was pushing he kept groaning, and when it was over he clasped her hand and wiped her forehead and kissed her several times. For a few days afterward Joan felt panicky about getting pregnant until John assured her that from then on they would use a rubber, and that she should use a diaphragm when they were married. But they only got around to doing it twice more before their wedding day. Both times were about the same for Joan, although it was not quite so painful when he rubbed her crotch before he entered her. Most evenings they were content to talk about their plans after marriage, which left them little time to get all worked up over sex.

Joan's friends were unhappy about her plans for her

wedding, although they realized that the obligatory mourning period dictated only the most modest celebrations, including weddings. There was to be no reception – only cake and punch in the church basement for the immediate family – and the customary bridal dinner was eliminated too. Mrs. Nelson was adamant about the details: no showers, no bridesmaids, no festivities of any kind, and Joan was glad to follow her rules, for she had no heart for celebrations that would call attention to herself. She wasn't sure just why, but she was satisfied that her condition of newly fallen virgin was not as important as she had once thought it would have been. She knew that her sudden modesty, or shyness, or whatever it was she was feeling, had something to do with her father, but she couldn't figure out what would have been all right with him and what would have met with his disapproval. He had never liked John, and his opinions of the Lambert family in general had never changed, but it was for Ron that he had saved his great disapproval. Since she wasn't marrying Ron, Joan felt that her father might have approved of John, at least a little in contrast.

'I think he would have come around,' Joan stated to her mother one morning, a few days before the wedding was to take place. Would he? Why this cheery optimism all of a sudden? Why was she seeking answers from her mother?

'Of course he would have come around. The problems would have been cured in time, especially with the first baby. Then you wouldn't have been able to keep him away. He would have moved in on you permanently.' Mrs. Nelson looked so wistful that Joan wondered if she was already buying layettes on the side. 'I don't think you have to worry about his feelings right now,' her mother continued. 'Just remember that he wanted you to be happy.' She looked at her daughter as if she were about to reveal some early confidence of her husband's, perhaps something to do with the Lambert family or sex. Whatever she was trying to say seemed difficult for her, so difficult that Joan decided she didn't need to know any of her father's private thoughts, at least not right now.

If Mrs. Nelson was disappointed that her daughter had abandoned her college plans in favor of marriage, she didn't reveal it to Joan. All she had said when Joan informed her of her intentions was, 'Perhaps this is better, after all. There's not much future in music, especially for a girl. Not that you're not talented. It's just that there are so many with as much, if not more, than you. You'll always keep up with your music, I know,' and as a kind of assurance, she had ordered a Baldwin spinet to be delivered to the marital abode as soon as it was ready.

'By the way, Maryann called her mother from St. Paul and asked if there was some way she could give you a little party,' Mrs. Nelson informed her daughter that evening. 'Nothing big, just some little gesture. She seems to feel that you aren't properly married unless you have some kind of celebration beforehand. Anna Handslip called me this morning and asked me. She said she knew how we felt about no parties, but she wanted to know if we could make an exception in just this one case since Maryann wants to have a little dinner for you. Maybe this weekend, since if it's all right with you Maryann can come home for it.'

Joan wondered how much of this intended party was Maryann's idea and how much was her mother's. Maryann, although certainly her best and most loyal friend, did not strike Joan as being smitten with the necessity of a party for every occasion. Maybe she was hurt at being denied the position of maid of honor – then she could have worn her gorgeous graduation dress another time. Joan imagined it now lying unused on a top shelf in her dorm closet at Macalaster, nestled in tissue paper, abandoned in favor of the Puritan gray skirts and matching sweaters that Joan thought all Macalaster girls wore. Also, it wasn't like Mrs. Handslip to take anything other than a morbid interest in Joan's affairs, so her sudden alliance with her daughter's interests seemed strange to Joan. 'I don't know. What do you think?'

'I guess it wouldn't do any harm,' her mother replied. 'It's not as if we were entertaining, and since Maryann is your oldest friend here, well, a small dinner party wouldn't be too amiss.'

Dinner party? Had Mrs. Nelson substituted dinner for supper or was Maryann going through a quick change now that she was away from New Bonn? 'Okay. Tell her it's fine with me, but to keep it small. That's all I ask – just a few of the girls, if they're around. Maybe Carol can make it home, too, and whoever else is around.'

'I knew you'd feel that way. I was pretty sure you'd agree. I think you're doing the right thing. It was nice that Anna and Maryann wanted to wish you well this way.' Mrs. Nelson appeared genuinely pleased. Her smile seemed to erase some of the tension that usually creased the corners of her mouth.

I'm not going into a convent, I'm getting married, Joan thought, yet maybe to her mother it now looked as if she were packing herself off to a nunnery. But it had been her mother's idea to keep the wedding simple after she'd been informed of her daughter's intentions, so why was she acting now as if they were getting ready for another funeral and not a wedding? 'Wasn't all this your idea? I mean basically. Wasn't it your idea that we shouldn't have a big wedding and make a fuss over anything right now?' The words sounded like an accusation, yet it was true that her mother had made all the arrangements and stated the rules.

Mrs. Nelson sighed. 'Yes, I know it was my idea to keep everything in good taste, but I didn't realize that it would be so gloomy. As if it isn't a wedding at all.' Mrs. Nelson's voice choked on 'wedding', as if she, too, were thinking of funerals. 'Why don't we just spend the money on a trip, maybe go to California and see the orange groves or go to Europe and listen to some operas?'

Joan had never heard such an extravagant proposal from her mother, and for a minute she was inclined to take her up on it, but she knew her mother would regret her flamboyance as soon as she had spoken. From her, it was a slip of the tongue, the sooner forgotten the better.

'I'm joking, naturally. But I don't want you to worry about expenses. If you want something please ask for it. So far this hasn't cost anything, and there's certainly more than enough if you want to spend a little more.'

Joan knew that it would be easy to extract whatever she wanted but she couldn't think of anything that appealed to her. Aside from the money for the new house – the bridal cottage by the stream, as her mother put it – she could think of nothing to spend money on right now. 'Thanks. I'll let you know, but right now I'm satisfied. I'm picking out furniture and stocking the kitchen.' Joan pointed to her head. 'It's all up here, so far, but I'm getting a lot of good ideas from the magazines you gave me.' She gestured toward the stack of magazines on the coffee table: *Good Housekeeping*, *Better Homes and Gardens*, *Bride*, *Ladies' Home Journal*. They were full of hints and advice on what kinds of chintz to buy when the bride selects maple furniture, and what to choose for meat when your mate is tired of casseroles. Linda should contribute to the home decorator's columns, Joan had thought when she first began to pore through the stack. She could also tell everyone a thing or two about how to get it up when he's tired from the work in the field.

Joan became absorbed, despite her early skepticism, in the multitude of ways to order, reorder, or disguise one's dingy walls, and she ended up totally hooked on the advice

– especially the kitchen hints. She reached the stage where she would cut out whole columns and paste them into a scrapbook – she preferred the columns with a lot of colored illustrations. She thought it rather like playing with paper dolls, except that the houses were real and real people supposedly occupied them – real people who made a difference to the lives of others living in those houses.

Maryann managed to locate three of their friends who could make it to her party for Joan. 'Not exactly a bridal party, but a little whoop-te-do in honor of the occasion,' is how she described her intentions. 'Dress casual. I mean, don't wear your wedding dress or anything. It's just us, and I've gotten Mother to promise that she and Dad will be gone that night. So we can talk.' Maryann chuckled, already anticipating an extended conversation about sex, undoubtedly concluding with the bride-to-be solemnly promising to reveal all her first-night secrets.

Joan was not aware that her friends had discussed her plight among themselves so much that they had finally declared a halt to further discussion, so angry and rancorous had their feelings been after their last discussions. They hated Ronald Boswell with a passion. They felt he had ditched their friend for no reason at all, that he had cut his own throat in doing it, but that it was more than likely that he would never feel any loss since it was Joan who was doing all the suffering. They assumed he had deflowered her – probably when she was drunk, Maryann hopefully suggested – and he had then proceeded to use her disgrace as his weapon until he tired of such a sure conquest.

'Poor girl, she really took it for a long time. She's well out of it, even if she did get dumped,' was Carol's summation of Boswell's fling, as they privately called it. About John they felt less anger. It was obvious that he was after her money, they asserted. His perception of Joan was based on the insurance money and the many frozen assets she promised, which bothered the girls, but at least, they claimed, his greed was more or less out in the open, which made it far more preferable to the underhanded trickery of Boswell. John was rather simple, they felt, even boring. His tirades and complaints against his father were not enough to make him interesting, yet they conceded that he must be what Joan needed – or seemed to need, for it was all the same – and at least he was a man whose actions were for the most part understandable.

'She's probably marrying him because he's the first guy who's said anything nice to her since her dad died,' Maryann offered as explanation. 'How do you know what you'd do in her place? You'd probably marry the first thing in pants that looked twice at you if you'd been through what she had.' Despite a sense of queasiness, the girls felt the truth of Maryann's conjectures. Which of them wouldn't feel desperate, wouldn't jump into bed with the first decent-looking man who spoke to them without snarling?

Joan felt compelled to play the blushing bride and wear a dress to the party. Jeans were out, and would be from here on in. Never again would she be permitted to look as if she had just returned from the stables. (Her horse, long ago sold, continued to haunt her. One of the attractions of living on the Lambert acres – for this is how she imagined herself situated – was John's promise to her that she could have another horse as soon as they could find a good one. She intended to spend a lot of time shopping around; this one would have to be tamer and easier to handle. She would never make the mistake of getting another one-owner horse, for hers had been almost impossible to sell. His habit of shying with strange riders had almost taken him off the market.) In her Kelly green jersey dress, Joan thought she looked appropriately matronly, serious if not a little severe. The other girls were also wearing decent clothes – skirts and sweaters with beads and an occasional charm bracelet – which Joan appreciated, for their efforts to elevate the gathering into something more than just another hen party assured Joan of their understanding.

Mrs. Handslip greeted Joan cordially. She was wearing a black dress and no apron, and Mr. Handslip had left on his coat and tie. As soon as Joan had given Maryann her coat the two parents walked to the door. Mrs. Handslip took one of Joan's hands and commented on her dress while her husband stood by the door. 'My, how pretty you look. You'd never know it to look at you that you'll be a blushing bride in just a few days. I'm so glad you wanted to come. I know you girls can't wait till we oldsters leave so you can let down your hair and have fun. Supper's all ready. All Sissy has to do is take it out of the oven. And you aren't to help her, you hear. You're not to lift so much as one finger.'

Mrs. Handslip pinched Joan's cheek, a light painless nip. Joan realized that this was the first time that any of her friends' mothers had ever touched her. Not that they should have, but she still thought it odd. 'Remember now, not a finger! You'll have your fill of that soon.'

Mrs. Handslip's admonition seemed so good-natured and easily stated that for a minute Joan wondered who she was talking to. How could this woman, who had always been considered the enemy, now present such an outpouring of geniality? What had she done to merit such approval?

As soon as her parents left, Maryann dug out a bottle of whiskey that she had hidden in her closet. 'Risky,' she said, 'but you're worth it. And what's a party without champagne? In this case, though, it's quicker, the whiskey I mean. And I knew that you wouldn't come to a party without booze.'

Joan had never considered herself the town lush, but she knew what her friend meant, and she didn't resent being the excuse for their indulgence. No one seemed especially eager to eat, and the girls, after a few awkward first minutes when they talked about their various colleges and the courses they were taking, seemed more than happy to settle in for an evening of drinking and reminiscing.

'Just like old times,' Carol said, from her position on the couch where she was thumbing through an old copy of *Women's Home Companion*.

'Well, sort of,' Marjorie corrected her, 'except that we're here for new times.' Joan thought this pronouncement unusually clever for Marjorie, who tended to merely echo the statements of others, but sometimes not very accurately if she'd had more than two drinks.

Carol announced that she had a bottle of Southern Comfort in the car, purchased for this special night by her Macalaster boyfriend. The girls were grateful to Carol although they knew that their gratitude would be tested by having to listen to an account of him. As if to postpone the narrative, Maryann offered to see to supper, suggesting that if they wanted to dispense with the candlelight and table-cloth they could eat buffet-style where they were. Joan liked the idea of properly sitting down and not having to struggle with slippery lettuce and noodles spurting off the plate as soon as the fork got stuck, but she saw that her friends were more relaxed and convivial with Maryann's plan. Marjorie sprawled out flat on the floor until her toes touched the TV stand at the edge of the room. 'This is better,' she sighed. 'This way we can talk without having to get up and move dishes around.'

Maryann set the whiskey bottle on the coffee table. 'Here. Help yourselves. From now on you're going to have to get your own mix, though. And we've got to clean everything up before twelve. No traces, either, so don't forget.' Looking at Joan, she quickly added, 'But not you, Joan. You're the guest of honor.'

Joan was touched at her friend's desire to make her feel important. She felt as if she should give a speech, or perform something to make their efforts worthwhile. For a change she felt shy in their company, as if she were already miles and miles apart. She wondered if they felt that way, too, or if they were somehow feeling sorry for her. She stared at her plate, a little surprised at the soupy mass that was gathering in the center. Too much cottage cheese and mayonnaise, she noticed, mixed into the spaghetti sauce until the whole thing runs together and turns into this sticky stuff that looks like bloody semen. The image made her wonder if she weren't blushing, and she peered more closely at her plate to hide her face. Maybe it's the booze, Joan thought; otherwise I wouldn't be thinking such outrageous things, especially with my special friends.

Maryann, as if she were reading Joan's mind, jabbed Joan's elbow and said, 'Hey! You haven't been listening to me. Didn't you hear my question?'

Joan looked at her vacantly and smiled. 'I guess not. I'm sorry. I must be a million miles away. What did you say?'

'I said, did you get your diaphragm yet?'

Joan was astonished. Why would anyone care about her arrangement for contraception? Did they think she was getting married just for sex? 'Yes, as a matter of fact I got it last week. It's packed away, though.'

'What was it like? The doctor's exam, I mean?' Carol looked genuinely worried; her face was knit into a frown and she was tugging on a strand of hair between her fingers as if she were preparing to yank it out of her head. Perhaps she's thinking of getting one herself; Joan wondered how much of their questioning was motivated out of self-interest. Were they all contemplating having sex now that they were safely at college and had access to health services and other anonymous-sounding resources?

'It was sort of awful,' Joan answered. 'Not painful, though, but awful enough.'

'What does he do? Exactly?'

Joan decided to let them have it, to answer their questions without sparing any details, to let them know that sex is something you have to work at if you don't want to get caught. 'Well, he sticks his finger in you, and that hurts, and then he pushes around so he can see what size you are. He also tells you stuff about using the goo that goes with it and how to know if you've got it in right. Otherwise it could slip around and not do any good.'

Joan noticed horror on Maryann's usually placid face. 'He can't tell if you're a virgin or not, at least I don't think so since he didn't say anything to me.' Was that detail enough to inform them of her lost virginity? Or had they all lost it and wanted reassurance now that no one could detect it for sure? 'He gives you the thing and then he told me that I should practice putting it in and taking it out for at least two weeks before I get married.'

This was a flight of fancy that occurred to Joan when she looked at the fascinated gazes of her friends. 'Anyhow, why do you want to know all this crap? There's more to marriage than just sex, you know.'

'Is there?' To Joan her friends now looked like a single face, one composite girl who all of a sudden was demanding her personal code of marital ethics. 'Why are you getting married if it's not for sex?' Did Marjorie ask her this, or did they all?

Joan took a deep breath. The room tipped, twirled once, and then settled back into place. 'I'm getting married because, if you must know, I—' What the hell was the answer? And would they ever understand if she did have the words to tell them? Could she ever admit that her world had come to an end when her father died, that she knew then that the reigning princess of Locksley Hall could never become queen of anything? (Had she been able to explain that in marrying John she was trying to prove that the princess can kiss the frog and still not expect anything more than no warts, her friends might have wondered at her example but not at her wisdom. Yet her pride would not permit her such gross explanations.)

Instead, she said, 'I guess it's because he's here, he likes me, and I know what he's going to do tomorrow and the next day and a year from now. Isn't that enough?' She knew, as soon as the words were out, that it wasn't.

★

Joan's wedding was small but nice. There were only Mrs. Nelson and the Lamberts in attendance; John's old grandmother stayed home, reluctant to be pushed around in her wheelchair, even for the wedding of her only grandchild. To compensate she sent one of her English plum puddings, an entirely inappropriate contribution to their austere, Presbyterian rites. Joan wore a yellow silk dress, an autumnal shade that made her look washed-out and frail, but it was cut so that she could wear it again if she needed to.

Three days after the wedding Mrs. Nelson sold Locksley Hall to the very convent of nuns who had once persecuted Joan for her irreverence. Now it seemed they needed more room for the fresh-faced young lasses who arrived every spring straight from Ireland, and who spent their days trying to teach English and history and mathematics to resentful kids, while their nights, Joan supposed, were spent in prayer and clandestine whispering. Mrs. Nelson was able then to find a charming house in a good Minneapolis neighborhood, one that contained smaller houses as well as stately manors.

She confided in her lawyer that she hoped she had done the right thing by encouraging Joan to marry instead of attending college. 'I don't see how she could have gotten anything out of college in the state she was in. Everything was so disrupted. She was at loose ends so much that I even had to remind her to eat. Getting married should settle her down, much more than college ever would.'

The lawyer privately thought that his client had pushed the marriage because she couldn't figure out what to do with her daughter and couldn't stand the prospect of living with her. The three of them, mother, father and daughter, had gotten along because Mr. Nelson was able to mediate and balance the conflicts of the two, but mother and daughter together would be lethal, and the lawyer gave her credit for realizing this, even if the knowledge came on an unconscious level.

Chapter Twenty-Four

Pastorale

Mrs. Nelson still maintained that Joan's choice of marriage instead of college was a sensible one. Their lives had been so disrupted, she insisted, that concentration would be impossible. Money would be wasted on a futile experiment, which is what she now considered college for her daughter.

She did finance a cottage for her daughter and her new husband, constructed on a site near the creek on the Lambert farm, a lovely and genuine body of water that ran the full length of the pasture. If they needed more money, they could always borrow from the insurance policy that Joan was sure to collect, and there was also a healthy return on some acreage that Mr. Nelson had bought for Joan over ten years ago: eighty acres of unimproved land in another county, over one hundred miles from New Bonn. It promised a substantial return each year, especially if the tenant handled the land responsibly.

Mrs. Nelson had engaged an architect for the cottage – actually a contractor with grandiose ideas who fancied the title of architect; since his price was negotiable, no one complained much about his fraudulent pretensions. The couple moved in once the rites were pronounced to their darling little cottage, which caused Joan to feel as if she were living in an enchanted forest by a tiny dell in something like an elves' hut. Right out of Snow White she observed, except she felt she was the only one in the landscape to bear any resemblance to the fairy-tale characters.

Her mother's whimsy, combined with the contractor's desire to please all his clients, no matter how eccentric, created a five room, one-story building, fabricated out of Pipestone granite, but designed to look like Irish moss. There were low ceilings with exposed beams that ran the length of each room. There was an open fireplace that displayed, instead of the usual mantel and figurines, a recess, which allowed Joan to hang up the copper pots and pans that thoughtful people, who had seen the house plans, sent her for wedding presents. Two tiny bedrooms were set off to the side of the cottage, scarcely bigger than cubby holes, which held the bedroom furniture she had inherited from Locksley Hall. In the cottage the maple and mahogany looked out of place, but she intended to replace them with rough-hewn woods of some kind. Crude but simple was what she wanted, but these kinds of objects were hard to find.

She had thought that her greatest adjustment to marriage would be the continuous presence of her father-in-law, that foul fiend who continued to haunt the existence of her husband. She was wrong, though, for Mr. Lambert proved amazingly docile. Although he never allowed himself to become jolly in her presence, at least he was never sarcastic or denigrating to her the way his son claimed he treated him. Shortly before they were married, John had said to her, 'I don't understand it. You've managed to charm the old man. What'd you do?'

So far Joan had done nothing except refuse to be terrified of him. 'I don't know. I don't think he's so bad, at least not as bad as I thought he was going to be.' A hurt look from John made her modify her statement: 'But then I didn't have to live with him for some twenty-odd years. Maybe that's the trick, not living with him. That way you can see more what he's like without having to watch yourself every minute, scared shitless that he'll catch you in some dumb mistake.'

'You got it, Baby! Not living with him, that's the trick all right.' John flicked a thumb across her blouse, tweaking a nipple so emphatically that she flinched.

Mrs. Lambert was never any trouble, either. Other than an amiable curiosity about the kinds of nourishment her new daughter-in-law was providing her son, she left the newlyweds on their own. Now and then she would wheel her mother to the cottage for an afternoon visit, and Joan liked her for always knocking on the door first, not barging in the way less thoughtful people might have entered.

It was John's grandmother who appeared most forsaken by the marriage. She would concoct imaginary errands for him to run for her, just so she could see him every day. She started knitting him sweaters and socks, a pastime she had abandoned years ago because of her arthritic hands. Now she began to besiege him with garments, and some of them were quite nice. The sweaters always fit – they had to since she was constantly measuring an arm or shoulder – and her eye for colors was astute; everything she made for him complemented his eyes or brought out the highlights in his chestnut hair.

She didn't actually refuse to knit for Joan, either; she just concentrated on John, but she did cook up little delicacies for them both – jams, jellies, meat pies, and her renowned English specialty, trifle. She took to visiting them more and more. Millie Lambert would bring her to the cottage for afternoon tea and would return for her at suppertime, only to be told that Johnnie hadn't come in from the fields, which meant she couldn't leave until his return. Since it was winter, with the fields lying fallow and covered by a good six feet of snow, what she really meant was that she was waiting for John to return from town, from one of the taverns where he spent most afternoons, drinking a little beer and talking crops with the other winter-bound farmers.

At first Joan tried to entertain the old lady during those long winter afternoons when John was away, but she seemed more content playing solitaire and reading magazines, activities that she had been pursuing for many years at the Lambert home. When Joan realized that her husband's grandmother really didn't want to be entertained, she began to play the piano more, simply to while away the time, for there wasn't much to do after the morning dishes had been washed and the housecleaning finished. Unlike the occupants of the main house, the cottage dwellers possessed no animals, neither stock nor pets, although John had promised Joan a dog in the spring. 'Too muddy now,' he explained. 'You don't want muddy paws all over the place, do you?' Joan knew she was expected to agree, although she wouldn't have minded a dog, or even a kitten, for company.

Instead of the Steinway baby grand that had been at Locksley Hall, Joan was now playing on a Baldwin spinet, another gift from her mother, who felt it was a perfect match with the rustic décor of the cottage.

John's grandmother – he called her 'Gram' or 'Grammie' but Joan could never call her anything other than Mrs. Edwards without feeling foolish – was not a music lover, but she didn't seem to resent Joan's playing, and at times she would nod her head and smile with great cheer while Joan was playing a particularly demanding or noisy piece. One night, when John had failed to return from town before ten o'clock, her usual bedtime, she suggested that she spend the night rather than troubling her grandson to take her home. 'He'll be tired, poor lamb, and having to lug me up the hill through all the snow will make him even more tired.'

Tired from lifting his elbow, Joan thought; the exercise should do him good, but she didn't protest. Thus the pattern was established, and it wasn't long before Joan realized that a visit from John's grandmother also meant an overnight stay. Then the duration of the stays gradually expanded from one night to three or four. Certain articles of clothing began to appear when they were tucked away into the dresser of the spare bedroom: nighties of flannel, a hairbrush, changes of underwear, and finally a cosmetic kit that contained her toothbrush and medications.

One day, as Joan was hanging the old lady's dresses in the closet, she wondered how many she owned. Was the major part of her wardrobe now hanging there? And just where the hell was she living, anyhow? Yet no one remarked on her gradual relocation; technically she still resided with her daughter and son-in-law; it was just that she spent most of her time with her grandson and his new wife. Joan began to spend more time in bed, sleeping late when the old woman was there so that she would be spared that first early-morning jolt that she invariably felt whenever she saw more than one person at the breakfast table. John didn't mind, though; in fact, he told her that he preferred his grandmother's breakfasts to Joan's, a comment that Joan thought sensible but heartless, but she knew that his feelings would be injured were she to complain about the old lady's perpetual presence.

Sometimes Joan thought she had missed something by not at least starting college, but she had no strong regrets. This life seemed pretty tranquil and uncomplicated, and she would make new friends later, she knew, as soon as she had settled down a little and acquired a better domestic vocabulary.

Whenever Mrs. Edwards stayed with them they would refrain from sex, for it was far too noisy. (They had also refrained from drinking a lot and swearing, but Joan had expected to do this once she was married.) Neither Joan nor her husband liked disturbing the old lady's rest, for they both knew what it cost her to get to sleep at night. Some nights she didn't settle down until after midnight, so intense was the pain from her useless legs and her inflamed arthritic joints. Not that she and John were ever very passionate; their lovemaking tended to be controlled, almost silent, with the exception of a yelp from John whenever he ejaculated. Joan didn't mind the abstinence; sex was something she was sure she could do without quite easily. Sometimes she wondered if it would have been any different – any better – with Ronald, but she decided that it probably would have been pretty much the same, since all men had cocks and they seemed to be the main point of the act.

Mrs. Nelson wrote often. She seemed pleased with the life she had adopted in Minneapolis. Not exactly a continuous round of parties and bridge games, it seemed a pleasantly low-keyed social life where she was often the odd number but never condemned as one. Since her husband's death, Joan's mother had developed a keen eye for business and had invested some capital in real estate. Joan was a little envious of her mother's new independence, but she felt that it would be a handicap to her if she were to spend much time with her, so she refused her mother's frequent invitations to spend weekends or full weeks at a time when they could attend concerts and do some shopping. John refused, too, claiming lack of time, which was hard to believe since there was nothing to do on the farm in the winter that couldn't be accomplished by someone else, and just as well, in less than an hour. But Joan didn't really care. The longer the winter nights became, the more she slept. She didn't bother to accompany John on his squire's rounds of beer joints, either. Now that she was married she knew that she would never be refused beer or booze, so her age was no drawback, but she preferred staying in her cottage, even with the old woman there, for it seemed to protect her from whatever chances she might have to take if she were to venture outside her domain.

For some reason Joan could never count herself as a real member of the circle of farmers. She could not accept the fact that living on a farm made one a farmer; participating in farm life, sharing the qualities of farming that kept the land thriving were, to her, beside the point of being considered a farmer. She thought that she and John more closely resembled the country squire and his lady, dabblers in the soil but not dependent on it. Besides, she had never met farmers who lived in stone houses, had wives who played classical music, and relatives who drank tea. She didn't miss her old New Bonn friends as much as she had thought she would. Maryann and Carol had established themselves at Macalaster, but Marjorie had surprised everyone by eloping with a sailor she had met at an amusement park at Lake Okoboji, and she was now sending postcards from her new home in San Diego. Joan thought Marjorie's accomplishment quite grand.

In early March there was a spring thaw, one of those regular Minnesota occasions that seem so weird to outsiders. Overnight there was instant spring: the snow melted and the grass was so visibly green that its lushness appeared to contain an energy of its own. Birds appeared which were still supposed to be in their southern migratory territories, chirping and tootling like an army of pipers. Cows, which normally stood in the snow huddling together in lumps to keep warm, now boldly separated themselves from their herds and swished their tails as if they were anticipating August flies.

The sun woke Joan one morning. Instead of the old lady's muted affections to her grandson, instead of the sounds of her husband clumping his boots across the stone floor, this morning the sun's rays beamed directly upon Joan sleeping. She drowsily looked up and wondered if she were in some other world.

No one was at home that morning. John had left for whatever errand or duty call he thought he needed to perform this day – he had said something the night before about replacing a part for a pump located in the barn – and his grandmother had returned to the Lambert-proper farmhouse the night before. Joan felt as if she had no time to waste, that she needed to get out in the sun. Yet she needed an excuse, for it would be considered irresponsible to go somewhere without a goal in mind. John, of course, needed an errand or chore to fulfill before he could allow himself time in the taverns, and he was no different from others. She looked out of the window and saw that her red Buick was gone but that the pickup was parked in its regular place. She decided to take the pickup and drive to Sioux Falls, which was less than a hundred miles away and provided shopping that couldn't be so efficiently done in a town like Clayton.

The day was gorgeous. The people she encountered seemed to duplicate her feelings, for everyone appeared to be smiling and laughing and celebrating the good fortune of a balmy spring day. For a change there appeared to be no remorse; no one commented that such fineness couldn't last, that early spring days only meant longer winter nights. Joan bought herself a pair of jeans, a concession towards her new status as gentlewoman-farmer, she thought, perhaps even a gesture of homage. She browsed around in a couple of furniture stores and toyed with the prospect of ordering a bedroom set of starkly blond oak – a nice contrast to their rustic décor, but probably too severe. She ate a tuna sandwich in the coffee shop of the city's best hotel, glancing at a magazine while she ate and idly twirling her wedding ring to discourage the salesmen and other lechers whom she knew were always hanging around hotels.

On the way home she sang boisterously to herself. She usually hated to drive the pickup – old, with most of its springs missing, it bumped worse than a tractor – but today she enjoyed the rhythm of its plunges and dips, and she enjoyed being free from the demands of a car radio. She had left a note to John informing him of her destination, telling him that she would probably be back after supper-time (she still had trouble with his word), and she had suggested that he grab a bite with his folks. She knew that they wouldn't mind; genuine farmers maintained informal eating arrangements where entire trashing crews were often accepted as easily as one extra guest.

She was surprised to see her car parked next to the cottage when she pulled into the yard, for it was not yet six o'clock, still too early for him to get home if he had eaten with his parents. She was afraid that something was wrong, that perhaps he was angry at her for her spontaneous trip, innocent as it was.

She entered the house. There were no lights burning and the fireplace was cold. Evidently John had not been home long enough to attend to the furnace, either, for the air was chilly and damp, and there was a musty, dank smell that she had never noticed before, a smell that reminded her of barns and mice and cow manure. For a second she cursed the contractor's naïveté, his stupidity at designing a country dwelling more appropriate to an English village than to a Minnesota farm. She tossed her packages on the piano bench and flicked on the light switch. John was sitting at the kitchen table, a large bottle of whiskey in front of him.

He was wearing her wedding dress, and he had stuffed napkins in the front to create breasts. The yellow silk shone the way it had during the brief time she had worn it, but there were now little flecks of soot stuck to the neckline and on the bodice, and on one sleeve there was a damp stain that could only have been whiskey. He must have tried to start a fire in the dress, which explained the soot, but how could he, a man of six feet and no less than one hundred and eighty pounds, have managed to stuff himself into a size eight dress?

Joan quickly glanced for signs of rips and tears, but saw none. Then she noticed that he was actually wearing only half of the dress, the front part, for the back was unzipped, revealing a gap of at least a foot where his back stood out, bare, without a T-shirt. As far as she could see, he wasn't wearing boxer shorts, either. Twirled around his forehead was a bandanna of clover and sour-smelling grass, an ugly circlet without color, and his feet were bare. For the first time Joan noticed the length of his toenails; like claws, they were ivory-colored and looked more like hooves than human growths.

'Hiya, Honeybunch!' he slurred. 'How come you took off and left me all by my lonesome?' He wasn't angry, just drunk, fatuously, hopelessly drunk, swaying in his feminine garb with little trickles of spit running down his chin, his great brown eyes teary with booze and self-pity.

'Just what the hell are you doing in that?'

'Thought I'd surprise you. Whassa matter, can't you take a joke?' He lurched up from the table, pushing his arms against its edge as if he were tackling a steer. 'Whassa matter?' he repeated. 'Iss only a joke. Gotta have some fun once in a while. We never have any fun.'

Joan looked at this parody of a man, a person whom she had promised, less than four months ago, to love, honor, and obey, and she decided that the joke was on him. She walked into the bedroom, then thought better of it and walked, instead, to the front door. Without looking back at the man whose head was now slumped onto his arms, she left the cottage, got into her car, and drove away. By the time he had slept off the effects of the booze, she was in Minneapolis, once again at the home of her mother.

Epilogue

Mrs. Nelson was less angry with her daughter than Joan had expected. Of course Joan exaggerated the circumstances, knowing that the slightest hint of any kind of sexual behavior that was even remotely abnormal would provoke both disgust and outrage from her mother – and her support.

Mrs. Nelson tried to get an annulment for her daughter, but she was out of luck. The Lambert family's terms were too high, and no lawyer that Joan saw felt that her transvestite story would hold up in court. Joan ended up divorced at nineteen. Too young for a bride among most high-minded people, a divorced teenager was considered a freak. John ended up the legal owner of their stone cottage – it was, after all, built on Lambert property – but Joan did manage to salvage her piano out of the settlement. By the time she was twenty-one the insurance money was consumed. Much of it had gone towards the purchase of that ill-fated brookside dwelling, and the remainder was used to send her to college – Macalaster, after all – where she surprised herself by winning music scholarships and laudable grades.

As a divorced woman – no longer a girl – she was exempt from ordinary college life. Her mother lamented this nun-like existence, and sometimes she would sigh as if longing for the good old days. Yet Joan was not too disappointed; she had never expected much from a bunch of Presbyterians. She had expected John to remain at the cottage with his beloved old gran to see him through, at least to keep house for him until he could find a suitable wife. Surprisingly, the old lady refused to return to the cottage, claiming the ride was too brutal for her old bones and that the kitchen was too inconvenient for her handicaps.

Mr. Lambert died of hypothermia two years later. A gruesome death, where he had driven his pickup into a snowbank less than a mile from home. Instead of walking the rest of the way, he had remained in the truck, probably expecting John to come along and rescue him. When he was found the gas tank was empty and the battery was dead. The heater had failed to keep him warm enough to survive the night, and evidently the flashing lights had failed to attract anyone's attention. An unusual occurrence, some might say suspicious, since the road of his final night was quite well traveled, by no means an isolated country lane.

Mrs. Lambert promptly sold the farm and moved to a retirement compound in San Diego; John and the old lady went with her. Joan heard about him through Marjorie, another Minnesota transplant to southern California, but a questionable source since she often preferred fabrication to dull facts. He was said to have taken up photography as a kind of semi-vocation, but he spent most of his time doing volunteer work with troubled boys. He had even been named Bog Brother of the year for southern California, Marjorie had mentioned. Maybe being a brother has cured him of his father, Joan thought. He certainly was one lousy husband, for which there was no organization to help him.

Timmy Getzel, the valedictorian, traveled through seminary without pause and became a parish priest in a town in Wisconsin almost identical to New Bonn in size and ethnic proportions. He was popular with his parishioners, maybe because he continued to oblige them with German-language Masses long after it was expected of the clergy to communicate bilingually. Eventually he was elevated to monsignor and given another parish where there were fewer old-timers but larger social problems. He seemed to thrive there too, for occasionally Joan would see his name mentioned in the Minneapolis paper, usually in connection with some community concern. Joan was sorry that he had become a priest because she considered his talents far too vast for the confines of such a rigid authority, but she was happy that he had been so well received. She felt that he deserved to be a bishop, at least, but she knew that he probably didn't care.

Joan never saw Ronald again. She never forgot him, though, and she never could decide whether his vocational choice and abrupt departure from New Bonn were the results of some mysterious change of heart toward her, or if he had left because he had been tipped off. Some corrupt county clerk could have spirited him a copy of her father's will. But who? And why? As time went by Joan's hurt diminished until she was able to look upon that one detail of their arrested affair as something Dickensian, a comic device that should never have happened in real life. She heard that he married a Catholic farm girl, no doubt a virgin. 'One of his kind,' as her mother would say. He became successful in the TV repair business, ending up with a good-sized business in a medium-sized Iowa town. True to form, his wife produced a baby every year.

Linda is the success, though, out of all the unlikely candidates for something better than mediocrity. Linda brought off what no one else dared to dream of accomplishing, for she became rich and famous in a way so natural that it's remarkable more young females don't imitate her ascent. Linda was barren, much to her sorrow, but she did like to sew and make things for her multitude of nieces and nephews. The object that all the kids liked best was her teddy bear, for she made teddy bears as no one else had ever done. Not exactly cute or whimsical, they were tough-looking creatures with just enough charm to make them harmless and just enough strength to make them look real. Women would admire them, and after a while a few women asked Linda to make some for them. Always practical, Linda agreed, but she insisted that she be paid for materials, plus cost of labor. Although the women were offended by what they considered Linda's venality – friends and acquaintances shouldn't be expected to pay, they felt – they couldn't very well refuse such a direct request, especially if they wanted the teddy bears.

Within a few months Linda was making teddy bears on consignment for a few local stores, and soon one of her productions caught the eye of a New York merchant who happened to be visiting his Minnesota relatives. Within five years Linda had opened factories in New York, St. Paul, and Atlanta, had endowed her bears with a US trademark, and had made enough money to send her parents to Florida for winter vacations and on summer trips to genuine fishing lakes. Other relatives tried to take advantage of her generosity, but she drew the line at second cousins. And at Disneyland. 'Let them go there on their own; too commercialized,' she often remarked. Joe Schultz died just when Linda was making her biggest splash. People said he died in her arms, ignorant till the end of her myriad infidelities, and praising the ingenuity of his uniquely wonderful wife. This may not be true, though, since even the mild-mannered Joe knew how to put two and two together. What is true, however, is that Linda never remarried. She kept the farm and hired someone to work it in shares, and she kept the house open for occasional visits, no more than two or three days at a time. She would arrive at the farm, notify her parents and whatever close kin she happened to like at the time, and invite them over for a gigantic feast. Then, just as unexpectedly, she would leave.

Joan's mother didn't remarry, either, although for a time there were a lot of suitors. During the period that she had spent settling her husband's estate, she developed what she called a sixth sense for business, so she was not easily deceived by the show of admirers her husband's death brought to her. They amused her, though, and she rarely turned down an opportunity for a dinner engagement at a good restaurant, or theater tickets and symphony concerts. Her forays into real estate were lucrative – a good joke on those men who had thought they were supplying her with minor tips in order to gain possession of her widow's holdings. She was distressed by her daughter's failed marriage, but she had acquired enough wisdom from her own attempts at controlling devious men to not attempt to push her back into marriage. The most she would say in reproach was, 'You made an awfully cute couple, you two. He so dark, and you so fair. You would have produced beautiful children.'

The idea of children by John was always so horrifying to Joan that her mother's comment never failed to bring tears. 'My God! What on earth would they have done for a father?' she would wail to her mother in protest. 'And for a mother, for that matter. We were just stupid kids playing house until it got too much for us. For *me*, then,' she would add at an incredulous look from her mother.

Yet it was sad, and Joan, herself, would occasionally think of the nice-looking kids they could have produced: perhaps flaxen-haired girls with liquid brown eyes, or dark-haired boys with deep blue, Scandinavian eyes, like her father's.

In time Joan met a man who possessed neither bovine eyes nor disturbing patricidal complexes. He was a musician who had been educated by Jesuits – nuns, too, along the way – a woodwind player who made her early attempts with the clarinet seem dilettantish and self-serving. Yet his initial attraction for Joan lay not in his musicianship – that talent would be revered later – but in his distinction at having been excommunicated from the Catholic Church. Had he been served formal notice, written on illuminated parchment and delivered by a papal messenger brilliantly gowned in scarlet?

'No, but I expect one any day, riding in on a Papal Bull.' His own sense of the Church's subordination to his life, his amusing perspective concerning his own small part in the total scheme of religious policy, immediately endeared him to Joan. They were married after what seemed to Mrs. Nelson an indecently long courtship. In a sense he was her first love, for until he came into her life her few other sexual episodes had been as blighted and as enervating as those married episodes with John.

Joan now has two children and the same husband. None of them has ever seen New Bonn, nor has she ever suggested that they take a day's drive to visit her rural home of almost five years. Although she was never a real native of New Bonn – she was a resident there for only a short period of anyone's life – she still thinks of herself as one of its products, especially when she's depressed. She sometimes thinks of the unmarked graves that George Eliot talks about in *Middlemarch* and wonders if that common fate that was so much in evidence in New Bonn might not be so bad, after all. An unattended grave in a tiny, provincial village isn't the worst thing a person can say about a life.

Yet she knows that these musings are idly romantic, less than sensible, just as she knows that her reactions to one chunk of her life should add up to no more than a calm, reasoned judgment upon a series of episodes. A totality: some good, some horrible, none really unique. Yet she still has trouble incorporating them into a long-range view.

She's trying, though, and she still has hidden her ring of Black Hills gold.